REMEMBERING *for* tomorrow

A History of the Canadian Conference of Catholic Bishops, 1943-1993

Bernard M. Daly

Canadian Conference of Catholic Bishops

Cover:

Photos: 1) Portrait by Jean-Luc Pinxit. Reproduced with permission of the Archdiocese of Montreal; 3) © Giordani, Foto Attualita; 5) Moderne Enr.

Published by:

Publications Service
Canadian Conference of Catholic Bishops
90 Parent Avenue
Ottawa, Ontario
K1N 7B1

Printed in Canada by:

Tri-Graphic Printing

Available also in French under the title *Se Souvenir pour demain*.

Legal Deposit:

National Library of Canada, Ottawa
ISBN English version: 0-88997-340-7
ISBN French version: 0-88997-339-3

Canadian Cataloguing in Publication Data

Daly, Bernard M. (Bernard Michael), 1925-

Remembering for tomorrow: a history of the Canadian Conference of Catholic Bishops, 1943-1993

Includes bibliographical references and index.

ISBN 0-88997-340-7

1. Catholic Church – Canadian Conference of Catholic Bishops – History. I. Catholic Church. Canadian Conference of Catholic Bishops. II. Title.

~~BX1905.D35 1995~~ 262'.12 C95-900883-7

Table of Contents

Foreword

Remembering for Tomorrow outlines the story of the Canadian Conference of Catholic Bishops (CCCB) over its first fifty years. In addition to pointing out key moments in the Conference's history, the book helps the reader to understand the sequence of events as well as the more general context of the Catholic Church in Canada over half a century.

The work is neither an official history nor a comprehensive study, but a well-informed view by a journalist and sociologist who worked at the CCCB for thirty-three years.

The memories that Bernard Daly presents will certainly be of interest to Canadian Catholics. Indeed, as the author reminds us, the Church's history is the seed for its renewal and future.

The national Conference of Bishops is but one structure in the Church. Nevertheless, it is a unique forum for coordination and planning on the national level. Pastors who are members of the Conference find it an important vantage point for discussing apostolic initiatives and supporting one another in serving the People of God. The history of the CCCB accordingly provides a special perspective on all the Church in Canada, which is why this work by Bernard Daly is not only an important but invaluable resource.

The Canadian Conference of Catholic Bishops was founded in 1943. During the course of the 1960s, the Second Vatican Council was a determining influence on the direction and activities of the Conference. By emphasizing episcopal collegiality, Vatican II inspired and stimulated the CCCB in the areas of ecumenism, international development, liturgy, missions, religious education and social justice. As a consequence, the bishops discovered new approaches for collaborating with families, laity, religious and the other ordained ministers.

One of the greatest challenges facing any Conference of Bishops is finding how best to work with communities, organizations and groups within and beyond the Church, as well as with individuals in the Church and in society. Bernard Daly reminds us of this challenge by describing several events which might be considered controversial. Such experiences are to be found in any organization or group, and when lived in the light of the Gospel, they can become stepping stones to further goals and new courses of action.

The Conference of Bishops is not the national headquarters of the Catholic Church in Canada. It is an expression of episcopal collegiality and solidarity; a service to the Christian community, and an opportunity for the bishops to work together in their ministry. Its importance is especially evident when so many key ethical issues face the nation and the world.

Since its beginnings, hundreds of persons have contributed to the growth and work of the CCCB. *Remembering for Tomorrow* names a number of these; however, it has not been possible to mention all. The Conference and the Church in Canada owe a debt of gratitude both to those named and to the anonymous. On behalf of the bishops, I thank everyone who in whatever way has assisted the Conference.

It is hoped that this history by Bernard Daly will encourage other researchers in various disciplines to reflect on the actions and accomplishments of the CCCB over the years. May this story from the Canadian Church's past encourage us all – not only as individuals or as members of various communities and organizations, but as the People of God – as together we help determine today's and tomorrow's story.

† Jean-Guy Hamelin
Bishop of Rouyn-Noranda
President of the Canadian
Conference of CatholicBishops

August 28, 1995
Feast of Saint Augustine,
bishop and doctor of the Church

Acknowledgements

When I turn to thanksgiving, I start with the executive committee of the Canadian Conference of Catholic Bishops (CCCB). It was the members of the executive that first thought of this book in view of the CCCB's 50th anniversary in 1993, and of me as its author. At the time the project began, the 1991-1993 executive comprised Archbishop Marcel Gervais, president; Bishop Jean-Guy Hamelin, vice president; Archbishop Francis J. Spence and Bishop Jean-Louis Plouffe, treasurers; with general secretaries, Rev. Alexandre Taché, OMI, and Monsignor James Weisgerber. The history recounted is up to and including 1993, but the writing and editing process was completed under a new executive: Bishop Hamelin, president; Archbishop Spence, vice president; Cardinal Jean-Claude Turcotte and Archbishop Austin E. Burke, treasurers; with Msgr. Weisgerber and Rev. Émilius Goulet, PSS, as general secretaries.

Special thanks also go to the former presidents and general secretaries who made themselves available for taped interviews during the summer of 1992.

Thanks, too, to all other CCCB members who replied to a questionnaire sent to them in June-July 1992. Directly or indirectly, all CCCB office directors and other professionals came generously to my aid: Aubert April, Jacques Binet, Paul Boily, Lucien Casterman, Tony Clarke, André Desrochers, Claire Dubé, Bernard Dufresne, Donna Geernaert, Dennis Gruending, John Hibbard, Bede Hubbard, Lucien Labelle, Jennifer Leddy, Marcel Lefebvre, Claude Lortie, Jacques Paquette, Bernadette Tourangeau. For archivist Monique Hudon I must add praise to my thanks.

The same is true for Pierrette Warwick, who led me through the workings of word processing; and for Ron Tourangeau, who handled the book's design and production. For being available when needed throughout my research work, thanks to Annette Arbique, Lise Bergeron, Anita Bissonnette, Yvonne Dufresne, Thérèse Dupuis, Adèle Gauvreau, Huguette Lépine, Louise Mainville, Patricia McKale, Dorothy Riopelle, Micheline Roussel, Céline Vermette. All these former colleagues also will understand how hard it is to say how much I owe to former French assistant general secretary Roland Denis, who died while I was doing my research.

Once I had words on pages, Marjorie and Terry Phalen of Ottawa generously spent hours of their holiday in Grenada reading and commenting helpfully. Rev. Bill Ryan reviewed the entire first draft to help decrease its bulk and sharpen its focus. The careful editing done by Art Babych, Anne Louise Mahoney and Jim Davidson was helpful. I also gratefully acknowledge the work of Gaëtan Landreville, who prepared the French translation; Marianne Fournier, who rechecked the bibliography, references and notes; and Gisèle Goudreault, who prepared the index. As well, without Mae Daly's advice, backing, confidence, determination and much more, I would not have started, or kept going, or finished the book. It is dedicated to her.

Introduction

This essay has the advantages and disadvantages of being the first extensive study of the life and work of the Canadian Conference of Catholic Bishops (CCCB). An advantage is that the field is wide open; one could head off in any direction without bumping into someone else's work. A disadvantage is the temptation to try to explore every corner the first time around, and so take on far too much.

My closeness to the subject is both a help and a handicap. I write as an outsider about the first fifteen years of the conference, from 1943 to 1958. After that I was involved, in varying capacities, as editor of the English information service (1958-1966), director of the Family Life Bureau (1967-1974), member of the pastoral team (1974-1982), assistant co-ordinator for the papal visits (1983-1984 and 1987) and English assistant general secretary (1984-1991).

Nobody will fail to notice, then, that I tell this story as a believer – in the Roman Catholic Church, in the Second Vatican Council, in the Canadian bishops and also in their conference, where I was respected, challenged, supported and stretched during thirty-three years of professional service. A different account might be written by a sceptic, an agnostic, an opponent. Canadian theologian Bernard Lonergan has argued that authentic subjectivity is authentic objectivity.[1] This essay aims at authentic objectivity in that fashion, presenting what I believe to be salient points in the life of the CCCB. The story's limitations are my limitations, then, and I confess in advance to having many.

My formal training is in journalism and sociology. The methods of research and analysis that I use – participant observation, interviewing, content analysis and storytelling – are those of sociology. Historians using other research tools and analytical methods someday will add information as well as important new insights and reflections. My commission was to write a popular book of modest length by an early deadline, as part of the CCCB's observance of the fiftieth anniversary of its foundation.

I had to limit my research to the archives of the CCCB which, while extensive, have some gaps and dead ends. Later researchers may find additional material in the archives of Canadian dioceses led by bishops who played prominent parts in CCCB activities over the years. Some parts of the story may be amplified and perhaps refined by material from the files of the Apostolic Nunciature in Ottawa and various offices of the Holy See in Rome. This was obviously the case for CCCB-Vatican relations, including dealings with the papal representative in Canada and several specific pastoral questions that involved protracted discussions between the CCCB and Rome. I try to indicate in the text where I came up against the limits of the material I could explore. Future researchers may find omissions of which I am not aware.

* * *

This is a history of an institution. It is also an account of the lives and work of a group of Canadians – bishops and their co-workers, women and men – whose richness and diversity as human beings are always present, even though this essay pays more attention to formal activities. There are bishops who play classics on the piano, polkas on the accordion, jigs and reels on the fiddle. There isn't room to mention everything, but I was told I had to mention the cartoons of Bishop Robert Lebel, drawn even in the solemn surroundings of a meeting of the Synod of Bishops in Rome. I was also told I had to tell about the time Bishop Norman Gallagher, of celebrated quick wit, visited the Apostolic Delegate in the company of Archbishop Philip Pocock and Bishops William Power and Alexander and Emmett Carter. As they prepared to leave, Archbishop Emanuele Clarizio held Gallagher back. The other four waited in the car outside, Power in the driver's seat and Pocock and the two Carters in the back. They speculated that Clarizio was asking Gallagher to move to one of the dioceses then without a bishop. When he joined them a few minutes later, he was immediately bombarded from the back seat with pleas to share the secret. Their teasing gave way to gales of laughter when Gallagher quietly said: "He asked me what I thought of Bishop Carter. I asked, 'Which one?' He replied, 'The nice one.' I said, 'Oh, I didn't know there were three.'"

* * *

The first chapter of this book tries to present the concept of collegiality – the idea that the "college" that is made up of all bishops shares with the Pope in the leadership of the Catholic Church. This could have been developed more fully as a sociology of knowledge, a study of how an idea comes to public awareness and takes on social reality. The discussion is deliberately kept very brief here. As a theological concept, collegiality was brought to the attention of modern minds by the Second Vatican Council (Vatican II). The idea of collegiality divides the CCCB's fifty years into two parts: twenty before the Council and thirty after it. Out of collegiality grow two other concepts that are central to this story: co-responsibility and communion.

The second chapter sketches the life of the conference and its activities prior to Vatican II. Chapter Three is a very brief reminder of the participation of Canadian conference members in the Council. To keep this essay to the agreed upon size, even a survey of the contents of Canadian interventions at Vatican II had to be left for some future work.

The fourth and fifth chapters review the CCCB's years after Vatican II. Chapter Four tries to show the continuity with the activities of the first twenty years described in Chapter Two, and to indicate the innovations resulting from implementation of the teachings of Vatican II in Canada. Chapter Five holds up for more detailed examination what the conference did about a number of tough issues. These deal with the application of traditional moral teachings in the social context of changing civil laws. Chapter Six gives some examples of Vatican-CCCB relations. Chapter Seven is a rapid review of two special events: the Synod of Bishops that Pope Paul VI founded in 1965, in which the CCCB has participated perhaps more seriously and more collegially than any other bishops' conference; and Pope John Paul II's 1984 and 1987 visits to Canada.

The conclusion is a personal assessment for which I alone am responsible, even where I cite the words of others.

CHAPTER ONE

From Concept to Reality

One of the first requests that the Vatican sent to Canada after the bishops' conference had been organized was for aid for war victims. It was the fall of 1945. The carnage of World War II had just ended, but its horrors persisted. The request was answered in a way that set a distinctive style that would mark many exchanges during the next half century. The reply was generous and loyal, reaching out directly to the Pope, but with a touch of originality that might surprise some people. After all, what other bishops' conference sent Pope Pius XII 75,000 bushels of Number 2 Northern wheat?

At their September plenary meeting, called mainly to sort out details of their first constitution, the members of the Canadian bishops' conference had been told by Cardinal Jean-Marie-Rodrigue Villeneuve, their president, how much money had been raised in this country for Pontifical Aid to War Victims. The Holy See was willing, the Cardinal had added, to accept wheat of equal value. By November 30, the wheat was on its way to Italy aboard the S.S. Highland Park out of Montreal.[2]

One can only imagine the headaches this caused for Monsignor Giovanni Battista Montini, the future Paul VI, and other Vatican officials as the train bearing this two-million-kilogram Canadian reply rolled into the Vatican from the Italian seaport of Castellamare. However, Montini's letter to the general secretary of the Canadian Catholic Conference (CCC)* spoke only of "how much His Holiness was touched by this filial gift, which will enable him to respond to so much suffering, made still worse by the approach of winter."[3]

* * *

Examine anything in the Roman Catholic Church and some part of what you touch is at least 2,000 years old. This is true for the Canadian bishops' conference, although it was set up only in 1943, and received the approval of the Consistorial Congregation for its first constitution in June 1948. Like every Church institution, the conference is evolving and may become something different from what it is today.

The story of the CCCB is, in part, an account of how several Vatican II concepts came into being and of the continuing efforts to make them a social reality. It is a story about theology, canon law and Church politics, and about changes in the modern world and among God's pilgrim people. The end of the story cannot be told, however, because the CCCB continues to evolve.

Most people know in a general way that the Catholic Church is headed at the world level by the Pope and in each diocese by a bishop. Popes and bishops are 2,000-year-old institutions. Across twenty centuries of change, as dioceses spread around the globe, the need for both unity and diversity have been met. A shared faith calls for unity. The insertion of that faith in various cultures calls for diversity. In general, unity is assured by the Pope and diversity by the bishops.

In every century, the chief way to plan a common action or to handle a dispute has been to call a meeting. Depending on the historical period or the kind of agenda, popes and bishops have given their meetings such names as synods or councils. Around 1850, the name "conference" begins to appear. To respond to the rapid and far-reaching changes of the nineteenth century, bishops in various countries felt the need to meet to take stock, compare experiences and plan common actions. Church (canon) law provided for synods or regional councils, which could pass

* Note: The name Canadian Catholic Conference (CCC) was used until January 1, 1977, when it became the Canadian Conference of Catholic Bishops (CCCB) to emphasize it was the association of bishops. Throughout this book, CCC is used for events prior to 1977 and CCCB for subsequent events.

new and binding decrees. However, it was too cumbersome and time-consuming to convoke a synod or council only to discuss and perhaps agree on some program that each bishop might launch for his own diocese rather than to pass new legislation. A "conference" emerged as a new kind of meeting of bishops.

The bishops of the various nations were not alone in seeing the value of meeting as a conference. The Pope and Vatican officials also realized the importance and convenience of being able to communicate and plan concerted pastoral actions with groups of bishops. Rome began to approve constitutions for conferences in the 1800s. With support from Pope Benedict XV, the bishops of the United States began to meet during World War I and formally founded their conference in 1919. Similarly, especially in messages through the Apostolic Delegate to Canada, Pope Pius XII made it known that he looked favourably upon the formation of a Canadian conference.[4]

The Canadian conference began in the fall of 1943 as the terrible final battles of World War II were taking shape and grave post-war pastoral problems were discernible. In Canada, as elsewhere, the pre-Vatican II conference was a voluntary association. The 1917 Code of Canon Law presented particular councils, to which conferences were related, as deriving from the Church's highest authority in virtue of Church law, and as exercising their authority through delegated papal power. As seen at that time, a conference did not exist in virtue of ecclesiastical law, and had no power of its own. A bishop was not required to belong. A conference meeting was unofficial. Its decisions were not binding, although each bishop could decide to implement in his own diocese some program or policy on which a conference meeting had agreed. Many CCC decisions were implemented in this way, shaping the Church in this country from 1943 until Vatican II (1962-1965).

* * *

For a relatively new Church institution like the fifty-year-old Canadian Conference of Catholic Bishops, Vatican II stands as a great divide. The story that follows, about the CCCB's development and activities from 1943 to 1993, will be told as an account of the difference the Second Vatican Council has made.

Soon after Vatican II opened, a long and difficult debate began about the idea of "collegiality." From it emerged the teaching that, just as Peter and the other apostles formed a college so, too, all the bishops are collectively a stable body or college. With the Pope, and never without him, the college of bishops shares in the leadership of the entire Catholic Church. Ordination as a bishop gives each bishop full status in the college in his own right. His place in the college is not arrived at by delegation or as a concession.

The collegiality debate dealt in part with bishops' conferences. The college of all the bishops shares with the Pope in Church leadership, but what status has a national conference, which includes only some of the bishops? The college exists by divine law, but does a conference? Does a conference share in the responsibilities and powers of the college? Questions like these were debated during the Council, during the 1969 and 1985 Synods of Bishops and during the preparation of the 1983 Code of Canon Law. These questions have not been fully resolved; theologians and canonists continue to debate them. Some major points have been agreed upon, however. These are crucial for the CCCB and other conferences.

The Vatican II *Decree on the Bishops' Pastoral Office in the Church* ("*Christus Dominus*") defined a conference as "a form of assembly in which the bishops of a certain country or region exercise their pastoral office jointly in order to enhance the Church's beneficial influence on all men, especially by devising forms of the apostolate and apostolic methods suitably adapted to the circumstances of the times" (paragraph 38). This definition, it should be noted, is placed in the decree's chapter "concerning the co-operation of bishops for the common good of many churches," and not in the chapter on "the bishops in their relation to the universal church."

Similarly, the 1983 Code of Canon Law deals with conferences in its section on "Particular Churches and their Groupings" and not in the section on "The Supreme Authority of the Church." "Particular churches" refers mainly to dioceses. Canon 447 specifies that "The episcopal conference, a permanent institution, is the assembly of the bishops of a country or of a certain territory, exercising together certain pastoral offices for Christ's faithful in the territory."

This teaching and law about conferences highlight the need to understand more about dioceses. In November 1985, an extraordinary Synod convened by Pope John Paul II met "to celebrate, verify and promote Vatican II in the life of the Church." As an official delegate, the CCCB's president, Bishop Bernard Hubert, drew attention to dioceses in his report on the Synod. He noted:

> In its reflection on the episcopacy, Vatican II provided us with the theology of the local Church. This concept is still new to many Catholics. The Church is seen first in its universal dimension. The diocese is perceived as a division of a whole which depends on the Pope. The bishops' authority appears to be more the fruit of Roman delegation than Christ's mission to the Apostles. The complete "reception" of the Council implies that we are trying to discover and assimilate what the Church is to the faithful. This is important not only for understanding exactly the bonds which unite bishops to the Pope, but also for perceiving correctly the differences manifested by neighbouring local Churches which, while in communion, exercise their autonomy differently, faithful to their history and in conformity with their pastoral needs. We have to find ways to include the theology of the local Church in the conscience and practice of Christians.

What follows can be read, then, as a progress report on how this awareness and practice developed in some aspects of the Church's life in Canada during the thirty years after Vatican II.

CHAPTER TWO

In the Beginning

I. FIRST BISHOP

Bishop Laval arrived in Quebec in 1659. From then on, the Church in New France was never just mission territory, subject to the bishop of a diocese in France. Quebec was a diocese in its own right, relating directly to the Holy See.

The original Quebec diocese reached across the continent and as far south as Mexico. Today's Catholics, in their pews across the country, may not think about it, but Canada's bishops are aware that their ministry has a certain unity because the territory of every Canadian diocese was once part of the diocese of Quebec. Canada's second archdiocese, Halifax, was not set up until 1852. The other archdioceses that existed when the conference began in 1943 were Toronto (1870), St. Boniface (1871), Montreal and Ottawa (1886), Kingston (1889), St. John's, Newfoundland (1904), Vancouver (1908), Edmonton (1912), Regina and Winnipeg (1915) and Moncton (1936).[5]

As new dioceses eventually were formed, the bishops began to meet for various common purposes. From 1850, formal councils were held at

Quebec to fix Church laws to meet particular problems of the vast area. Later, Quebec also played host to annual meetings of all the archbishops – thirteen of these meetings were held by 1936. In addition, starting in 1928 and every five years thereafter, the archbishops were joined by all the bishops for a plenary meeting in Quebec. The 1943 meeting in this series was being planned when the archbishops held their annual meeting in Quebec in October 1942. One idea on the agenda of the archbishops was the proposal that a permanent organization of the Canadian episcopate be established. This suggestion, to be taken up by the Inter-Episcopal Relations committee at the 1943 meeting of all the bishops, resulted in formation of the Canadian Catholic Conference (CCC).

II. EARLY MEETINGS

On the face of it, nothing about 1943 made it the ideal year to start a new structure for annual meetings of all Canada's Catholic bishops. The country was at war, and divisive political passions stirred by the plebiscite on conscription had not entirely cooled. As they made their long journey by train from their dioceses to Quebec City, the ten archbishops, thirty-four bishops and one abbot probably thought about such secular problems. They also carried documents listing seventy-five items for the agenda of a two-day meeting. The items had been grouped under eleven headings: Inter-Episcopal Relations; Politico-Religious and Politico-Social Questions; War and Post-War Problems; Catholic Action; Christian Education; Hospitals; Propagation of the Faith; Marriage and Divorce; Clerical Discipline; Pastoral Discipline; and Liturgical Discipline.

Because of what they decided on the first item, the Canadian bishops' conference formally dates from 1943.[6] The first committee, on Inter-Episcopal Relations, was headed by Archbishop James C. McGuigan of Toronto, with Bishops Louis Rhéaume of Timmins, J.-Arthur Papineau of Joliette and Gerald C. Murray of Saskatoon as members. They had before them twelve suggestions from bishops that they should unite in a permanent body of some kind. These suggestions had been noted by the 1942 meeting of the archbishops alone, and referred to the 1943 gathering of all the bishops. There, things moved quickly. The plenary assembly approved the committee's recommendation for "the establishment of a permanent organization of the Canadian Episcopate."

It would have six commissions of bishops. Their six areas of responsibility were defined as political-religious and political-social questions; war and post-war problems; Catholic action and Christian education; missionary problems – home and foreign; hospitals and works of charity; and moral and liturgical discipline. Each commission would have French and English sections, the two to meet together when questions of common interest required it. The six commission heads and all the other archbishops not elected to chair commissions would make up the national board. It would meet every year in Quebec City. The board would prepare the agenda of the plenary, to be held every five years. There would be an executive committee composed of the Archbishop of Quebec, *ex officio*, and two French and two English members of the national board, "chosen for five years by their respective groups" at the plenary. The executive would "have a clear mandate to act in the name of the whole hierarchy when deemed necessary or convenient," the minutes noted. The executive was also to set up a permanent secretariat.[7] One of the first assignments given to the newly-named general secretaries was to study the constitution of the United States' conference as a model for the Canadian conference.

It all seemed clear enough. However, when the board held its first meeting in January 1945, it was noted that differences between the French and English reports of the 1943 plenary had given rise to some difficulties. The board accepted Regina Archbishop Peter J. Monahan's suggestion that the unresolved questions be submitted to a plenary. That plenary was called for the fall of 1945 in Quebec. The board also decided that the dioceses should be assessed on a per capita basis for expenses of the planned secretariat. The sum of $22,325 was fixed as the budget requirement for the first year.

The special 1945 plenary meeting was largely devoted to questions about the new organization. It would be called the Canadian Catholic Conference (CCC) and would meet annually, not every five years as proposed in 1943. As Cardinal Villeneuve summed up, it would be only "an organism of vigilance, of consultation and of co-ordination which would assure the Church in Canada a stronger influence and an increase of prestige." It was agreed to have one Administrative Council replace the National Board and Executive Committee that had been set up in 1943. Its members would include its *ex officio* chairman, the Archbishop of Quebec, and six other bishops, three French and three English, elected by secret ballot by the plenary. Elected at that meeting were Archbishops McGuigan, John Hugh MacDonald, Alexandre Vachon, Joseph Charbonneau and Murray (now coadjutor archbishop of Winnipeg), and Bishop Philippe Desranleau of Sherbrooke.

III. CATHOLIC HOSPITALS

As the bishops travelled to Quebec for the 1943 meeting that launched the CCC, health care insurance was the political question most worrisome to many of them. The previous year, Prime Minister Mackenzie King had set up a committee to study a national health insurance plan. Catholic stakes in the question were high. In 1942, religious sisters were responsible for thirty-four per cent of hospital beds and forty-two per cent of nursing schools in Canada. The Prime Minister's plan would be shelved in 1946 for lack of provincial support, but in the fall of 1943 his proposal was a source of concern for the nuns in every province and for the bishops in whose dioceses Catholic hospitals were located.

The future welfare of Catholic hospitals was not a new question. From 1916 on, religious orders that operated Catholic hospitals in Canada had sought strength in unity by joining the Catholic Hospital Association of the United States and Canada (CHAUSC). Membership in the U.S. body served the Canadian institutions well for a time, but during the 1930s the Canadian hospital representatives began to organize what is now the Catholic Health Association of Canada. It was their new body, at the time called the Catholic Hospital Council of Canada (CHCC), that set up its health insurance committee in the fall of 1942 and began to prepare for the expected public debate in Canada.

When the bishops met in Quebec in October 1943, Archbishop Monahan of Regina reported that his committee had studied a report by Rev. Émile Bouvier, SJ, on the proposed federal health insurance plan. Bouvier warned the bishops against the socialization of medicine. He saw in the government's plan a certain measure of control over the internal affairs of Catholic hospitals, perhaps handicapping private initiatives or even making them impossible. The bishops' study committee found the question too important for an immediate decision and referred it to the permanent commission on health and works of charity, which was set up later at the meeting. Archbishop Monahan and Coadjutor Archbishop Georges Cabana of St. Boniface were named to chair its English and French sections. Bishops Rosaire Brodeur of Alexandria and Joseph-Eugène Limoges of Mont-Laurier were named secretaries.

The CCC's position on the insurance plan was outlined in a statement of principles issued the following January by the two sections of the bishops' commission "to guide" the CHCC. It said, in part: "State Medicine, which implies ownership and operation of all Hospitals, is condemned. State Health Insurance, while not approved, is tolerated, because of the proximity of its introduction by the present Government, and because of the impracticability of opposing it at this stage...."[8]

As the Catholic hospital organization continued to develop, the bishops' conference, through its commission on health, played creative and supportive roles. At first, the bishops were directly responsible for naming the priest who filled the hospital association's top executive office. The history of the association, published in 1990,[9] shows that in 1952, the bishops recommended a broader definition of a Catholic hospital, to include lay-directed Catholic hospitals: "Predating Vatican II by some ten years, this initiative indicated that the Canadian bishops were attuned very early on to the slow but very real current of change at work within Catholicism," the history notes (p. 70). Later, in the steps leading to federal incorporation of the Catholic Health Association of Canada (CHAC) in February 1965, "the Canadian episcopate was eager for the CHAC to get in step with the profound changes sweeping society in general and Christianity in particular" (p. 126).

The changes in Canadian society and in health care have affected the evolution and development of the CHAC. Although less directly involved in the association's affairs than they once were, the bishops continue to name one of their members to its board.

IV. IMMIGRATION

At the 1943 meeting that launched the CCC, "Missions to the New Canadians" was an agenda item. It referred especially to Asian men who were entering Canada despite high landing taxes. "There is need of greater zeal for the conversion of these New Canadians," the minutes note. "Two difficulties stand in the way, the difference of language, and the fact that so many Chinese are married and their wives still live in China.... The new Canadians who were married in their own country should be allowed to bring their wives to this country," the bishops said.[10]

Five years later, the bishops took up the immigration issue again. Canada by then was one of the major receiving countries for post-war European displaced persons and refugees. Winnipeg was the headquarters of the Catholic Immigrant Aid Society, which was founded in 1928. Archbishop Murray of Winnipeg brought details of the situation to the CCC meeting. Displaced persons were helped by the International

Refugee Organization. However, East Germans were excluded. The Canadian Christian Council for the Re-establishment of Refugees (CCCRR) was set up to help such refugees. A Catholic representative was needed overseas for most of this work. The services of a Winnipeg Oblate priest, Rev. Noah Warnke, were available. Several other bishops affirmed the need outlined by Archbishop Murray. Bishop Arthur Douville of St. Hyacinthe asked whether it was time to set up a CCC department of social action. Cardinal McGuigan, seconded by Douville, moved that the department be established. It was agreed to grant Warnke $1,000 a year for immigration work, and the same amount to Monsignor Jean-Charles Leclaire of St. Hyacinthe and Rev. F.A. Marrocco of Peterborough as the first French and English heads of the CCC social action department.

The immigration workload of the social action department grew rapidly. The task was to create Catholic channels to help Catholic refugees get out of Europe and into Canada. The CCC's immigration staff soon included two priests, two lay persons designated to handle Dutch immigrants and war orphans, and Warnke, who went to Germany for the CCCRR on behalf of German Catholic refugees. The two priests in Ottawa were Marrocco and Rev. Georges-Édouard Brosseau of St. Hyacinthe; two months after offering Leclaire's services for both social action and immigration, Douville had proposed that Brosseau come to Ottawa for immigration work, leaving Leclaire to concentrate on social action.

Something of the purpose and spirit of CCC immigration work at the time is indicated in the 1950 activities report. "Contact was maintained," it said, "with government and other agencies working in the field of immigration, thus making it possible to continue safeguarding Catholic interests in day-to-day developments. Very good examples of the fruitfulness of this work are the blocking of Christian Reform Church efforts to gain control of the $2,500,000 Dutch fund, the widening of regulations in favour of Germans, and the clearing of many cases with the International Refugee Organization." Thirty years later, the Dutch Reform Church, "successfully blocked" in the early 1950s, would be among the closest partners with CCCB representatives in the Inter-Church Committee for Refugees (ICCR).

A 1951 change in Canadian government immigration policy created a new situation for the Churches. German nationals became admissible as ordinary immigrants. Warnke wrote to Marrocco that his work overseas was ended and that the new needs were in Canada. One of his last overseas activities was to attend meetings in Geneva early in 1952. The Provisional Intergovernmental Committee for the Movement of Migrants from Europe (PICMME) had been set up. From intergovernmental (largely United States) funds at its disposal, PICMME, through the Vatican-directed International Catholic Migration Commission (ICMC) in Geneva, offered the CCC a grant of $100,000 for a travel loan fund to help needy Catholics to enter Canada.

How would the CCC respond? There were two Catholic bodies in Canada with mandates for immigration work. One was Winnipeg's Catholic Immigrant Aid Society (CIAS). The other was the Rural Settlement Society of Canada (RSSC) in Montreal, which had been set up to deal with the fact that the post-war population of Quebec was moving from farm to city. This urbanization was resisted by many Church leaders. The RSSC had been founded in 1946 to co-ordinate various groups and plans to promote settlement in rural areas. The society never enjoyed great success in resettling farm families in Quebec. However, it served as a high-profile existing structure when the CCC began in 1952 to consider how to respond to the Vatican's refugee travel loan plan. After several months of study, it was decided that the RSSC would be entrusted with the responsibility.[11] The CIAS and its federal charter remained in existence, however, and resumed an active role six years later.

As one result of its new mandate, the RSSC took up Canada's seat in the ICMC's general council in Geneva. In October 1954, the CCC broadened the RSSC mandate. Early in 1955, it was given the additional responsibility of handling CCC grants to designated dioceses with immigration centres to help immigrants resettle. Also, the federal government recognized the RSSC as one of four religious organizations officially engaged in Canadian immigration operations (the others being the Canadian Christian Council for the Re-establishment of Refugees, the Canadian Council of Churches and the Jewish Immigrant Aid Society). In the fall of 1956, RSSC was also one of the organizations called on by the federal government to help in resettling the 37,000 Hungarian refugees who came to Canada between November 1956 and September 1958.

In November 1957, the RSSC recommended a rearrangement of immigration responsibilities. The Catholic Immigrant Aid Society of Western Canada (CIAS) was reorganized under the name Catholic Immigrant Services/Services pour Immigrants catholiques (CIS/SIC) and centred in Montreal. It was to take over the RSSC mandate. This merger was "not a happy one," the CCC was soon informed.[12] Immigrants had indeed been helped. From 1952 to 1960, assisted by the revolving fund, just over 20,000 people had been moved; another 11,000 had been helped through other programs. However, the costs were high. The CCC had advanced $400,000 to the revolving loan fund. While, in theory, these were recoverable funds, the annual costs of administration were not. From a staff of one in 1952, at a cost of $1,800, the CIS operation had increased to a staff of forty by 1960, costing more than $232,000. "Unless the Canadian Hierarchy is willing to continue annual increases and practically write a blank cheque, some changes must be made," Bishops Alexander Carter and Paul-Émile Charbonneau said in a 1961 report. They recommended that the CCC cease annual grants to the travel loan fund. Complete control of the administration of finances, they said, should be taken from the secretary general of CIS and given to a reorganized board.

Changes followed quickly. Early in 1962, the CCC's two representatives on the new CIS board reported that the head of CIS operations had been replaced. Other staff had been reduced from forty-two in May 1961 to twenty-eight some eight months later. Monsignor J.A. Malouin of Montreal and Rev. Claude J. Mulvihill of Toronto also reported that they had asked for a committee to recommend further reductions in staff and expenses, to establish a non-deficit future for CIS.[13]

What Malouin and Mulvihill could not foresee in 1962 was that the CCC would still be wrangling with CIS more than fifteen years later. After ceasing to make further grants in 1962, the April 1967 plenary meeting called for the return of the nearly $400,000 loan at the rate of $50,000 a year. At the beginning of 1974, CIS asked for an administrative grant. The CCC authorized CIS to use part of the $200,000 still owing. Then, at its January 1977 meeting, the CCCB administrative board decided that CIS would no longer be considered a financial responsibility of the CCCB, that its work did not come within the current priorities of CCCB funding, and that "the $95,000 which CIS still retains in its possession be still considered as a loan, with the appropriate consequences should CIS cease operations."

As will be seen, the fate of CIS fits a pattern. In general, conference bodies designed in Canada to respond to local needs have fared better than those that are conceived in Rome and set up in this country at least partly as expressions of loyalty with the hope they might be adapted suitably to the Canadian situation.

Collections for the Vatican

All the time that the bishops' conference was negotiating with RSSC-CIS about funds for immigration, it was involved with Vatican officials in a separate round of discussions about the same money.

When the CCC began in 1943, one of the administrative tasks it assumed was management of collections taken up in the dioceses and shared between projects in Canada and the Vatican. One was a missions collection, which will be discussed later. Another was an "Anti-Slavery" collection at Epiphany, the proceeds from which were sent to Rome for direct support of African missions.

At its 1953 plenary meeting, the CCC responded to "directions of the Holy See to have an Immigration Sunday, and a special collection to be sent to Rome for this work." The bishops decided to write to Montini, Vatican pro-Secretary of State, "suggesting that in Canada the only practical method would be to designate the Feast of the Epiphany and to send the collection heretofore taken up for African Missions to the Sacred Consistorial Congregation for immigration purposes."[14] The Consistorial Congregation was pleased, but the Congregation for the Propagation of the Faith was shocked when it learned it was getting nothing in 1954 from Canada for African missions. As intermediary, the Apostolic Delegate in Canada suggested that perhaps both ends could be served "by announcing that the (1955) Epiphany collection will be for immigration and other missionary aid projects of the Holy See, and that the results of the collection be shared between the two congregations as the CCC members see fit to decide."[15]

During 1965, the Canadian bishops began to ask questions about the arrangement. By then they were sending CIS about $170,000 a year from their Fund for the Works of the Bishops. They had learned through CIS that Canada seemed to be the only country in the world to send the entire returns of its annual immigration collection to the Vatican. In reply to an inquiry, the Apostolic Delegate in Canada reported that three-quarters of each year's collection went to Consistorial and one-quarter to Propagation and that the totals ranged from about $200,000 to nearly $250,000.[16] In June 1966, all the bishops were reminded that at their December 1965 meeting in Rome, the board had asked CCC president Louis Lévesque "to negotiate for new arrangements in order that all or a large part of these funds be used here in Canada."[17]

The matter was discussed at the October 1966 plenary. At year end, diocesan treasurers were informed that they should send all the funds raised by the joint collection for immigration and African missions directly to the CCC secretariat and not to the Apostolic Delegate, as they had done formerly. At its January 1967 meeting, the board agreed that one-quarter of that collection would be sent henceforth to Rome for African missions and three-quarters kept in Canada for immigration work. Rome got even worse news two months later. The executive committee agreed to write to the Apostolic Delegate "to point out that this year, because of particular circumstances caused by financial commitments made to the Fraternité Sacerdotale[18] and to the Christian Pavilion (at Montreal's Expo '67), the CCC intends to keep all of these collections for one year or part of them over a two-year period."[19]

The Vatican's reply came in the form of a request from Cardinal Carlo Confalonieri, prefect of the Congregation for Bishops, that the CCC's decision "become operative only over a period of ten years and even then that twenty per cent of the collection be sent directly to the Holy See." The CCC board responded by deciding to send the twenty per cent immediately. When the CCC plenary met in April 1968, it was informed of yet another suggestion from Rome. The bishops voted to send the Vatican one more share, but to discontinue the annual national collection and cease all grants to dioceses for immigration work. Individual bishops were left the option of taking an immigration collection or not, and sending something to Rome if they wished. The June board meeting then voted to send $100,000 for 1968 and $75,000 for 1969 for the Vatican's immigration work. In November 1968, the board also voted to enact immediately the April plenary's decision that the CCC would no longer be concerned with the immigration collection.

V. SOCIAL ACTION

Canadian bishops were involved in the country's social institutions and activities before they themselves were organized as a national body. The agenda of the 1943 meeting at which the CCC was launched took up a number of social concerns that had been dealt with before. In particular, the bishops tried to end a decade-old controversy about whether Catholics could support the Co-operative Commonwealth Federation (CCF) political party. During 1933-34, individual bishops or small groups of them had issued pastoral letters warning against socialism in terms that left no doubt that they were referring to the CCF, although they did not name it. Coadjutor Archbishop Georges Gauthier of Montreal, however, did name the party in a 1934 letter. At their 1943 meeting, the bishops made two points. Condemnation of any federal political party, it was agreed, "should not be made by any one bishop, but only by a general declaration of the whole episcopate." Then, in their first joint statement as a conference, the bishops declared "that the faithful are free to support any political party, which maintains the fundamental Christian principles, which are traditional in Canada, and which favours, in the economic and social order, the necessary reforms demanded with insistence in pontifical documents." Again, the CCF was not named, but unofficial interpretations made the connection.[20]

* * *

Even if some bishops were nervous about new movements like the CCF, there were acceptable Catholic models for social change to promote. This was the purpose of the "study days" held in Toronto on February 4-7, 1944. These days were planned to give a boost to Catholics in English dioceses in the task of "the Christian reconstruction of Canadian society" or "building a Catholic-inspired Canadian social system," in the words of one of the leading Quebec priests who helped organize the event.[21] Two topics were discussed: Industrial Relations and the Rural Problem. The main organizers were Abbé J.C. Leclaire of St. Hyacinthe, Quebec, and Henry Somerville, editor of Toronto's *Catholic Register* and a man deeply steeped in Catholic social teachings through earlier involvement in Catholic Workers' Schools in his native England.

The fifty delegates from Quebec were drawn mainly from the Canadian Confederation of Catholic Unions (CTCC) and the Catholic Union of Quebec Farmers (UCC). Their presence reflected the fact that Quebec was entering the post-war era with a vast array of Catholic bodies organized for all aspects of social life. English-speaking delegates, such as Somerville and Rev. Moses Coady from Antigonish, Nova Scotia, shared with Quebec participants the theories about society that shaped the social encyclicals of Popes Leo XIII and Pius XI. They hoped that through labour schools and other forms of adult education, Catholics in English areas of Canada could build counterparts or adaptations of Quebec's Catholic social bodies.

The study days were not built around social theories alone. So-called neutral unions based in the United States and grouped under the Congress of Industrial Organizations (CIO) and the American Federation of Labor (AFL) were poised to challenge Quebec's Catholic unions. Unofficial representatives of these "neutral" unions, which already dominated the lives of organized workers in English areas, were among the English delegates and special guests. There was some tension and a certain distrust as the discussion of industrial relations opened, Leclaire later recalled. Nevertheless, under English and French co-chairs, and with Jesuit Father Jean-D'Auteuil Richard of Montreal translating summaries in French or English, the delegates shared their differing views about the role of the state in labour questions, owner-worker collaboration, relations among unions, collective agreement benefits, the possibility of reducing strikes and "the corporative organization of society." The latter topic dealt with the Catholic view that, ideally, social affairs should be directed and social harmony guaranteed by three-way collaboration of the state, associations of industrialists and strong, responsible unions of workers.

About a thousand people came to Toronto's Columbus Hall for a Sunday evening public lecture during the study days. The Catholic social vision was described by the main speaker, Bishop F.J. Haas of Grand Rapids, Michigan. A Christian's first aim, he said, is to accept and spread the idea that God is father of all humans, who are brothers in Christ, who is King of the World. From this followed the second aim: to assure everyone all that is needed for life and human welfare. This implied full production and full employment. For this, industrial councils were required, in which representatives of industry and unions would share equally, to work in three-way co-operation with government to set production goals, hours of work, prices and wages. Every effort should therefore be put into organizing labour unions, the bishop argued, because their numerical weakness was the main obstacle impeding the social vision he had sketched. Bishop Haas was thanked by Paul Martin, parliamentary secretary of the federal Minister of Labour. Martin remarked that "for the first time in the history of Canada, representatives of the three big unions had met for discussion without a lot of pomp and ceremony, which fact alone would justify the decision by the bishops' committee to hold this meeting."

After the tensions of the opening discussions about industrial relations, the closing sessions about rural life were a complete success, Leclaire believed. There was no question of union rivalry. Delegates from English and French dioceses agreed easily about such issues as the need for clergy collaboration, the adaptation of schools to rural populations, adult education requirements, the urgency of a higher economic standard for rural families and the benefits of co-operation.

At the close of the meeting, Leclaire spoke on behalf of Bishop Douville of St. Hyacinthe, "who so much wanted to be here." He paid special tribute to Somerville for having found the formula by which the meeting could fully respect Canadian bilingualism. True, no definite conclusions had been reached, but that should have surprised no one. Now that a start had been made, it would be easier to build a Catholic-inspired Canadian social structure. The idea of joint meetings of all Canadian Catholics was something to retain. It was a way to share varying conceptions of papal social teachings and the directives of the bishops. "It is with joy," Leclaire concluded, "that we will meet again with our English-speaking brothers, here or elsewhere, to work together at the Christian reconstruction of Canadian society, for the good of the Church and of our country, Canada!"[22]

* * *

When Leclaire was named the first French social action director in 1948, he could devote one-third of his time to the CCC, the rest going to his duties as vicar general of the St. Hyacinthe diocese. Leclaire got right to work on his social teaching duties for the bishops, preparing a brief on immigration and overseeing the publication of two works: 7,000 copies of a thirty-five-page brochure on professional organizations in Quebec, and 3,000 copies of a one-hundred-page book on workers' participation in the life of a business enterprise. Leclaire also worked with a group of priests on a press release about municipal and school corporations and their employees. He got involved in many discussions about the bitter asbestos strike of 1949-50 in Quebec.[23] He gave courses in St. Hyacinthe to initiate priests to union work. He also continued to head the organization for priests' social study days, the Commission sacerdotale d'études sociales (CSES). The Quebec bishops would later draw attention to duplication of work by the study days and the CCC social affairs department, and recommend that the study days be integrated into the Conseil national d'action sociale, organized by the CCC department in the mid-1960s.[24]

Like Leclaire, Rev. Francis Marrocco of Peterborough took up his appointment as English social action director with a primary interest in teaching the Church's social message. He worked hard on immigration cases, but they were not his first love. His main goal, he would recall later, "was to live up to my belief, and help others to do so, that it is at least as Christian to remove the causes of hunger, thirst, poverty, exploitation and persecution, as it is to bring people a hand-out of some kind.... My concept of true social action was far removed from adhesive tape medication of the socially disadvantaged. It was rather an effort to broadcast the causes and initiate programs to remove the causes of social disadvantage."[25] As a major instrument for his social teaching, he established the Institute of Social Action at St. Patrick's College in Ottawa in collaboration with the Oblate Fathers. There he honed and promoted his ideas about the formation of socially conscious and active Catholics through his lectures to young people. The Institute became the centre for an eighteen-lesson "Course for Workers." An institute research study led to the creation of study materials for groups across Canada. Through it, thirty-two co-op housing study groups were created in Ontario alone. A youth leadership course was also started, to use and adapt to other parts of the country the youth club materials coming from the diocese of Calgary.

Thus, while Leclaire's work reflected a Catholic Action approach, and Marrocco's, the Antigonish adult education model, their efforts were inspired by a common Catholic social vision that could be found in papal teaching. Leclaire and his immediate successors as CCC French social action directors – Charles Mathieu, Jean-Guy Hamelin and Charles Saint-Onge – worked from the perspective of priest-chaplains who were present to and inspired all levels of Quebec society. Marrocco, Francis Smyth and Peter Nearing were three disciples of the Antigonish adult education approach. With some cultural differences, English and French, these priests who directed the CCC's early social programs shared the corporative vision that social peace and justice lay in the direction of the three-way collaboration of owners, workers and the state as an expression of Catholic social values.

In the early 1950s, the CCC gave a positive response to the Vatican's urging that Quebec's annual Semaines Sociales should be adapted for English dioceses.[26] In 1953, therefore, the thirtieth Semaine Sociale at Edmundston, New Brunswick, and the first Social Life Conference at Antigonish, Nova Scotia, had the same theme: "The Parish: Basic Cell of Social Life." In Antigonish, there was keen awareness that something new and important had begun. About 500 people travelled from various parts of Canada for the August 2-4 sessions. Resolutions at the end urged that the proceedings be printed and another gathering on a new theme be organized for 1954. They also called for training in teaching Christian social living for both religious and lay teachers. A special session of clergy, in turn, felt "impelled to beg...the hierarchy to consider ways of introducing a study of social matters to our Canadian seminaries, so that in these critical times there may issue forth to our parishes priests versed in social matters and in the techniques of creating and leading the lay apostolate."[27] In this way, a Quebec social education plan quietly entered the life of English Catholics in Canada and grew in importance until it was overtaken by events flowing from Vatican II.[28]

VI. EDUCATION

One of the early undertakings of the CCC was to assist in the organization of a national body to promote the interests of Catholic education. The efforts to set up the Canadian Catholic Education Council (CCEC) paralleled those for national bodies to serve Catholic hospitals, charity agencies and others. Looking back on a long career with the bishops' conference, Cardinal Emmett Carter recalled in a 1992 interview that his first contact with the conference began when, as Canon Carter of Montreal, he was mandated to establish the CCEC.[29]

The CCEC was set up according to what came to be known as the Canadian Catholic Conference model. It had English and French sections, each with its own board and executive, and both responsible to the CCC's episcopal commission for education. It achieved complete structural parallelism, each sector having representation from all ten provinces, as well as from Ukrainian Catholics.

Because the Canadian constitution assigned responsibility for education to each province, the CCEC had modest national aims. It sought to promote the cause of Catholic education on a national basis, and to further the co-ordination of Catholic organizations in that field. Although the 1964 evaluation of the CCC recommended, "as need arises, the setting up of an 'Education Office' for the French sector,"[30] only an English-sector office was established. From 1966 until it was phased out after the CCC's 1972 evaluation of operations, it was directed by Rev. Edmund J. Roche of Prince Edward Island.

As executive secretary for the CCEC's English section, Roche's work was defined at the outset by the CCEC's aims. One of the major undertakings of the office was a study of Canada's Catholic universities and colleges, for which Dr. Edward Monahan worked with Roche.

The office mandate was extended, however, after it was decided that the 1971 Synod of Bishops would study the priesthood and social justice. For the priesthood study, the CCC's French sector could call on its Office national de clergé in Montreal, which was directed by Abbé Yvan

Desrochers. For the English sector, Roche was mandated to work with Desrochers and the bishops who were preparing for Canada's participation in the Synod's study of the priesthood. After the Synod, Roche returned to his home diocese of Charlottetown. His responsibilities for anglophone clergy questions were taken over by Rev. Bernard DeMargerie of Saskatoon from the fall of 1971 until the spring of 1972, when DeMargerie returned to Saskatoon. Soon afterwards, the work of the clergy offices for both the French and English sectors was taken over by a member of the CCC Pastoral Team, which was organized after the 1972 evaluation of CCC operations.

VII. CHARITIES

The CCC was involved for thirty years in attempts to form a national organization of Catholic social workers and diocesan welfare agencies. The difficulties of this effort illustrate the clash of two ways of building up Church structures. Some were working from the bottom up, trying to start a national organization that would help Catholic social workers. Others worked to form a Canadian organization that would be the national correspondent of Caritas Internationalis, which had been set up by the Vatican.

Each of these efforts resulted in a structure that had partial claim to recognition by the bishops as Canada's national organization for Catholic charities. By the time various study committees sorted out a suitable way to bring them together under one constitution, the time of Catholic charities had passed. Social welfare had become a department of each provincial government and private Church-run agencies ceased to be major actors. Therefore, the CCC's social welfare department was phased out not long after it was finally organized.

The first recorded effort to form a national charities body is a November 1944 meeting of seven Canadian priest-social workers, in Brooklyn, New York, during sessions of the United States National Conference of Catholic Charities. Three of the priests were from Montreal, two from Toronto and one each from Ottawa and London, Ontario. The CCC was thirteen months old, the priests were aware of it, and their aim was to have a division of social welfare established within the CCC secretariat in Ottawa.[31] Early the next year, a larger group of priest-social workers from English and French dioceses met in Toronto.[32] They submitted a plan for a national organization to the bishops, and were encouraged to present a more developed plan to the bishops' commission for social questions.[33]

The idea resurfaced when a group of Quebec priests proposed in November 1949 that the Assembly of Quebec Bishops should authorize a provincial conference for charity and social service agencies. Then the Holy See organized a gathering of national representatives for the purpose of setting up an international Catholic charity organization. Abbé Louis-Philippe Latulippe of Montreal represented Canada. He reported to Cardinal Paul-Émile Léger, who informed the 1950 October CCC plenary meeting about the new international body and the "need to have a national organization for Catholic charities agencies." The CCC commission accepted the principle of such a body, but suggested that existing agencies should study it more fully.[34] Early in 1951, interested Quebec priests worked on a draft constitution for a "Canadian Catholic Welfare Conference," to which the Quebec bishops agreed in August. During the October plenary meeting of all Canadian bishops, approval in principle was given "to the organization of a Canadian Catholic Welfare Conference with two autonomous sections, English and French." For the protection of Catholic interests, the bishops added, representatives of the new body should take part in the Canadian Catholic Welfare Conference – the national non-confessional body. It would seem best, the CCC also said, to organize the new Catholic body on a provincial basis.[35]

Interested priests in Quebec began at once to organize both a French-sector Canadian body, as suggested by the CCC, and a Canadian link with the international body being promoted from Rome. In May 1952, a group led by Latulippe met at the CCC offices in Ottawa with ten priests from English dioceses. On the grounds that they had not been officially mandated by their bishops, the anglophone priests proposed that a decision on a Canadian body be deferred until another meeting in Quebec City in June. On the basis of agreement there, plans went ahead for an official launching of the French sector of the Canadian body. At the same time, Cardinal Léger, who was also CCC president, initiated a diocesan branch, calling on all Catholic social workers "to assure the success of this new initiative of the Holy See."[36]

When the CCC members met for their October 1952 plenary, they hesitated to make a full commitment to the new international body, but agreed that Latulippe should be the Canadian representative at the International Conference of Catholic Charities.[37] The next February in Montreal, the French section of the Canadian Catholic Welfare Conference was inaugurated. A little over a year later, in May 1954, came the next step, one that the Canadian bishops had not foreseen or authorized. The

Montreal group changed its name to Caritas-Canada, with a constitution that provided for formal links to the Vatican body, including a substantial membership fee.

Caritas-Canada lacked both a revenue base and a detailed program. Even as it began granting the new organization $5,000 a year, the CCC began studying "the question of different ways to support Caritas-Canada and the manner it should participate in social works and welfare organizations."[38] Its constitution provided for an English section, but English Catholic social workers disliked the European conception of Caritas-Canada.[39] In October 1961, an English "Catholic Charities Council of Canada" was formed, and a committee was appointed "to facilitate co-ordination at the top level" between it and Caritas-Canada.[40] The adjustment of the two sectors continued to go slowly. In a 1963 report, Bishop Valérien Bélanger recorded official regret that the CCC's 1952 call for provincial sections had not been followed up and that Caritas-Canada, meanwhile, had developed outside the framework of the CCC recommendation.[41]

Early in 1966, ten years and fifteen meetings after the Caritas-Canada study began, the matter was resolved by transforming the Caritas-Canada secretariat into the new French-sector office of the CCC's social welfare department.[42] Parallelism was achieved, with an English office in Ottawa and a French office in Montreal.[43] Success at last, but not for long! The Montreal office was one of those phased out in the restructuring of the CCC after the 1972 evaluation of its expanding operations. The Ottawa office, in turn, closed after the National Catholic Council of Social Services decided to dissolve at the end of 1973.[44]

VIII. CCCB OFFICES

In hindsight, remarked Archbishop Gilles Ouellet in a 1992 interview, he could see that the CCCB should have built its own office building. The former CCCB president had just returned from a stroll along Ottawa's Clegg Street, past one site where such a building might have been built. The conference would have saved a lot of rent money, he said, although he conceded that earlier options had not been based on economic considerations alone.[45]

The choice of Ottawa as the locale for a conference office was influenced by the fact that the apostolic delegation was in the national capital. No other city was seriously considered, it seems. The original plan was to construct or buy a building that would provide office space, apartments for the English and French general secretaries and a meeting room.[46] To begin with, however, office space was rented. Just before Christmas 1943, Paul-Émile Meunier of Ottawa, the CCC's first lay employee, began to organize a small office near the front door of the University Seminary on Ottawa's Main Street. Two adjacent offices were occupied early in 1944 by the two general secretaries: first Monsignor Paul Bernier for the French sector, and then Monsignor Basil Markle for the English sector.[47] The general secretaries also lived at the seminary. Meunier served both of them until François Granger took up the task in May 1948, starting his twenty-year career with the CCC.[48]

The seminary was never seen as a permanent home. The search for a property to purchase began at once. The first executive meeting at the Ottawa office, on April 27, 1944, "decided to postpone the purchase of the Kirkpatrick property" at 539 Island Park Drive in Ottawa's west end.[49] Less than eighteen months later, at their 1945 plenary meeting, the bishops had their eye on another Ottawa property. Bernier was asked to describe "the Gleeson property and to explain the present cost of administration and the probable cost and utility of the proposed purchase." The decision to buy, on a motion by Bishop J. Gerald Berry of Peterborough, seconded by Archbishop William Mark Duke of Vancouver, was taken Thursday night, but was amended Friday morning. "Returning to the question of a suitable arrangement to house the secretariat, Archbishop O'Sullivan of Kingston proposed that in the motion adopted yesterday the words 'to buy the (Gleeson) property' be replaced by the words 'to buy or to rent a suitable property.'" This time, Berry was the seconder. It would be more than twenty-five years before the CCC again came that close to buying a home of its own.[50]

The seminary arrangement ended in the fall of 1948. The Oblate Fathers needed the space occupied by the CCC. Ottawa's Archbishop Alexandre Vachon offered the bishops the use of an archdiocesan building at 447 Sussex Drive. A motion by Archbishops John Hugh MacDonald of Edmonton and Joseph Charbonneau of Montreal began a rental arrangement with the Archdiocese of Ottawa that continues to this day.[51] The space at 447 Sussex Drive served until the spring of 1958, when the move was made to the larger building at 90 Parent Avenue. When the CCC began to outgrow the available space towards the end of 1960, Archbishop Marie-Joseph Lemieux undertook to build an extension in return for a long-term CCC lease.[52]

When that lease was due for renegotiation ten years later, the CCC faced many new questions. Even the enlarged Parent Avenue building was short of suitable space. Besides, the CCC faced a budget deficit and rent was the largest recurring item. A relocation committee was set up, with Marrocco as chairman. Several options were set out in a report that he brought to the November 6-8, 1968, board meeting. The possibility of the CCC buying the Ottawa major seminary should not be considered, he advised. It would cost too much. At the same time, because the then proposed national pastoral council might take over some CCC projects, the conference, he said, should not enter a new ten-year lease for 90 Parent Avenue. The board accepted Marrocco's recommendation that his committee look into buying, building or renting another place.[53] After more study, the September 1969 board meeting decided unanimously that the best solution was to build.[54] The fall plenary voted approval in principle. The following March, the board had a financial plan. A 30,000-square-foot building would cost about $635,000. The sum could be taken from the bishops' fund and replaced in a period of three-and-a-half years, the report added.[55]

By the time of the April 1970 plenary meeting, an architect was at work. Many questions were still being asked, however. Should the bishops build a new office for themselves when the image of poverty in the Church was being promoted? Might the CCC be over-building if the Pastoral Council plan went ahead? What would be reported by the Dumont Commission, which was at work in francophone dioceses studying the role of the laity and other aspects of the life of the Church? As well, in Montreal, the Assembly of Quebec Bishops was building up its regional offices, while urging that the other three pastoral regions do likewise. The April plenary ended with a divided vote, thirty-nine to twenty-one, to proceed with a new CCC office.[56] Discussions continued during the summer, and at the September 1970 board meeting, the result of another vote was reported. Thirty-three members were in favour of building, sixteen were opposed, and nineteen abstained. As the board struggled with the question, Archbishop Joseph-Aurèle Plourde of Ottawa indicated that another diocesan building might be for sale.[57] The building committee gave a progress report to the December board meeting, at which Plourde also mentioned that 90 Parent Avenue might be available for a five-year lease.[58]

Marrocco's report to the March 1971 board meeting reflected the frustration of the building committee. "The Committee unanimously continues to believe," he reported, "that from an economic point of view it would be advantageous to the CCC – both in the long and short term – to construct a much more functional building and see to its maintenance." However, "taking into account the evolution of the study underway on this subject – particularly during the past year," the committee believed that "for all practical purposes" there was only one solution: to rent 90 Parent Avenue for another five years.[59] The membership subsequently confirmed the decision.

At the same March 1971 board meeting, the general secretaries, Rev. Charles Mathieu and Rev. Everett MacNeil, were mandated to undertake a major evaluation of the CCC. They later assessed the decision not to build as "a very unfortunate financial calculation on the part of the CCC.... When the history of the conference is written, this decision will be severely judged." Whereas the building committee had indicated a saving of about $240,000 over ten years, "this estimate is very much less than the reality," the general secretaries said. "We should have been talking of a saving of $500,000." Even if the proposed building had been larger than the CCC eventually needed, any extra space could have been rented out to give the conference a regular revenue source.[60]

The whole process seemed to be starting up again when Plourde told the April 1975 plenary that the Ottawa archdiocese faced some building needs, for which the simplest solution would be to reoccupy 90 Parent Avenue.[61] The first reaction of the CCC executive was to explore whether Ottawa might be willing to sell the property. By August, the executive had moved on to negotiations with the Oblate Fathers for Clegg Street land near the University Seminary. Within the next few months, however, the Oblates decided not to sell and several other sites proved unsuitable. The October 1976 board meeting decided that the CCC should continue renting, and took "grateful note" of a letter from Plourde that the Ottawa archdiocese was prepared to continue renting 90 Parent Avenue "for a period of up to 10 years."[62]

Indeed, this arrangement would continue into the 1990s, and Archbishop Ouellet would not be alone in looking back with second thoughts on what might have been.

CHAPTER THREE

Vatican II – The Great Divide

I. CCCB and Vatican II

Everyone was surprised when, on January 26, 1959, Pope John XXIII announced that he was calling all the bishops to meet with him in an ecumenical council. Even the Pope was surprised by the idea which, he said, "struck us like a sudden and unexpected blow...like a full-blown flower of an unexpected spring."[63]

The commission named to prepare for Vatican II called for ideas from every bishop and from superiors of religious communities, heads of Catholic universities, and the like. Bishops in Canada sent sixty replies – fifty-nine Latin texts of varying lengths and nineteen pages in French from Cardinal Léger.[64] Altogether, there were 1,998 submissions from the world's bishops and others.

On Pentecost Sunday, June 5, 1960, Pope John announced the setting up of eleven commissions and three secretariats to prepare for the Council, which he called a "new Pentecost." Named to them were fifteen Canadian bishops and eleven Canadian priests.

On the central co-ordinating committee were Cardinals McGuigan of Toronto and Léger of Montreal, and Gaspé's Archbishop Paul Bernier, who was CCC president when named.

Members of the theology commission included Archbishops Maurice Roy of Quebec and Maxim Hermaniuk of Winnipeg (Metropolitan for Ukrainian Catholics in Canada), and Auxiliary Bishop Lionel Audet of Quebec. Canadian priests named were Rev. Marcel Bélanger, vice-rector of Ottawa University, as consultant, and Rev. Léo Laberge, an Oblate working in Rome, as a member of the commission's secretariat.

Bishop Georges L. Pelletier of Trois-Rivières was named as a member of the commission for bishops and dioceses and Archbishop Lemieux of Ottawa as a consultant. Members of the commission for religious were Archbishop George B. Flahiff of Winnipeg and Father Van Den Broeck of St. Bernard de Lacolle, Quebec. Two Canadian Oblate priests in Rome were also named: Rev. Joseph Rousseau as secretary and Rev. André Guay as consultant.

Coadjutor Archbishop Philip Pocock of Toronto and Bishop Arthur Douville of St. Hyacinthe were consultants for the commission for clergy and lay people. Auxiliary Bishop Valérien Bélanger of Montreal was a consultant for the commission on sacraments, along with Franciscan Rev. G.M. Brisbois, a Canadian teaching in Rome. Retired missionary Archbishop Louis-Joseph Cabana was named consultant for the missions commission. Bishop Alexander Carter of Sault Ste. Marie and Monsignor G.E. Bourgeois of Trois-Rivières were consultants for the lay apostolate. Theologian Rev. Gregory Baum of Toronto served as consultant for the secretariat for promoting Christian unity. Bishop Émilien Frenette of St. Jerome and Rev. J.M. Poitevin, P.M.E., were consultants for the secretariat for media questions.

Only two preparatory commissions – for seminaries and for Oriental Churches – had no Canadian members.

These twenty-six Canadians joined in the work of compressing the suggestions received into seventy documents intended for study during the Council. The documents, which were prepared for the world's bishops in the spring and summer of 1962, amounted to 2,060 pages in nineteen booklets. Although they were the fruits of serious work, not one of these texts was accepted as such by the Council. Completely recast, rewritten, telescoped or combined, they are unrecognizable in the sixteen documents finally promulgated at the end of the Council.

When the Council opened in October 1962, a total of eighty Canadian bishops checked into nineteen hotels and religious houses in Rome. They joined 2,460 other Council fathers in the elaborate opening ceremonies. They went to the first working session on October 13 – and in fifteen minutes were coming out again.

It is impossible to overemphasize the importance for the rest of the Council of those first fifteen minutes. It had been announced after the opening Mass that the Council fathers would be asked to vote at once for members of the all-important commissions to direct the Council's work. However, France's Cardinal Achille Liénart, seconded by Germany's Cardinal Joseph Frings, immediately moved that time be allowed for consultation and the study of lists from each country so that all attending could have a better idea of the best possible candidates. The assembly agreed.

Led by Archbishop Maurice Baudoux of St. Boniface, then CCC president, work began that same morning to prepare a list of Canadian nominees. It was decided to propose twelve Canadians for the ten commissions. In general, those who had served on preparatory commissions were named. Suggestions had to be gathered from the Canadian bishops' nineteen different residences and compiled into one list, which was ready the next day. In all, 1,655 copies were made for distribution to other bishops. The Canadians also gathered the proposals of other national conferences and compiled a composite list of those from all over the world who seemed best qualified for the various commissions. With a page for each commission, this overall Canadian list was ready on October 15, the day before the voting.

Each commission was to have sixteen members elected by the Council and eight named by the Pope. At the end of the process, which included a second vote late in the second session in 1963, eleven Canadians were elected and two named. Canadians made up more than four per cent of the commission membership, although they formed just over two per cent of Council membership. Cardinal Léger and Archbishop Roy were elected, and Bishop Georges Pelletier named, to the commission for faith and morals. Bishop Marius Paré of Chicoutimi and Bishop John C. Cody of London were elected to the commission for seminaries and Catholic education. Elected singly were Bishop Albertus Martin of Nicolet to liturgy, Archbishop Lemieux of Ottawa to government of dioceses, Archbishop Pocock of Toronto to discipline of clergy and people, Archbishop Flahiff of Winnipeg to religious, Bishop Bélanger of Montreal to sacraments, Archbishop Baudoux of St. Boniface to

Oriental Churches, and Archbishop Hermaniuk of Winnipeg to the Secretariat for Promoting Christian Unity. One Canadian priest, Rev. Léo Deschâtelets, superior general of the Oblates of Mary Immaculate, was named by the Pope to the missions commission.

Only the joint lay apostolate/modern media commission had no Canadian member. Other Canadians served in different capacities, however. Bishop Henri Routhier of Grouard, Alberta, was appointed to a special fourteen-member committee for Council media relations. Gregory Baum continued as consultor to the Secretariat for Christian Unity. Later, Pope John XXIII appointed a special mixed commission to revise the document on divine revelation after its original draft had resulted in a stalemate in debates during the first session. Cardinal Léger, Archbishop Roy and Bishop Pelletier were named as members of this same special commission and Baum was named a consultor.

This process of preparing lists of nominees gave the bishops' conferences a key role at the very beginning of Vatican II that had not at all been foreseen. A number of conference presidents, Archbishop Baudoux of the CCC among them, then organized themselves as a group that came to be called Inter-Conference. They met almost every Friday afternoon at the Domus Mariae to compare notes on each week's Council events and to organize future plans and strategies. When Archbishop Flahiff succeeded Baudoux as CCC president, he also took his place at Inter-Conference.[65]

II. CANADIAN OFFICE IN ROME

One of the last decisions made by the Canadian bishops before leaving for the Council was not to organize an office in Rome.[66] The Council had its own vast secretariat. There had been no indication that conferences would have any role. When the Canadians emerged from the fifteen-minute first session, however, they had the task of compiling a list of candidates for Council commissions. As president of the CCC, Baudoux had to set up an improvised "office," which amounted to a briefcase, a small car and a telephone. The briefcase belonged to Baudoux himself. The rented car was driven by Monsignor Cyrille Contant, who had come to Rome as secretary to Bishop Brodeur of Alexandria. The telephone was at the Canadian College, and was attended for the most part by Rev. Bernard DeMargerie of Saskatoon, then a student at the college. The CCC "office" was never out of business during the rest of the Council.

For the second session, Monsignor Raymond Limoges, CCC French general secretary, came to Rome for the first half and Monsignor John Carley, his English counterpart, for the second. They were both there for the CCC general meeting, around mid-session. The CCC office consisted of two rooms at the Canadian College. Hélène Masson of Chicoutimi, Quebec, who had been working in Rome, served as secretary.

At the beginning of the third session, Carley located and organized two large rooms just three blocks from the Council in St. Peter's. Nora Smith and Marie Clusiau from the CCC Ottawa staff came to Rome as secretaries. A young Roman with a motor scooter was hired to run errands. Each evening he went to every hotel or house where Canadian bishops lived to bring them mail, Council information and draft texts on which one or another Canadian wanted comments or support from his confreres. Charles Mathieu, the new French general secretary, joined Carley for the CCC general meeting at the mid-point of the session and stayed on to close the office. Mathieu returned for the final session, joined by Rev. John Shea, director of the CCC social action department. Shea was substituting for the newly-named English general secretary, Jesuit Rev. Gordon George, who would be taking up his duties at the end of the year. Two Canadian secretaries – Marie MacNeil of Ottawa and Thérèse Rainville of Montreal – joined several local helpers.

III. CANADIAN INTERVENTIONS

Of the 2,205 oral interventions (ten-minute Latin statements) made during the Council's four sessions, sixty-three were by Canadians: eleven in the first session, fourteen in the second, twenty-five in the third and thirteen in the final session. (There was a total of 4,229 written statements, double the number of oral ones.) Cardinal Léger spoke twenty-four times during the four sessions; Archbishop Hermaniuk, eight; Archbishop Baudoux, six; Bishop Remi De Roo, four; Bishop Gérard-M. Coderre of St. Jean, Quebec, three; and Cardinal Roy of Quebec, Bishop P.-É. Charbonneau of Hull and Auxiliary Bishop Antoine Hacault of St. Boniface, twice each. Single interventions were made by Archbishop Georges Cabana of Sherbrooke; Archbishop Pocock of Toronto; Archbishop Flahiff of Winnipeg; Archbishop Anthony Jordan of Edmonton; Bishop Albert Sanschagrin of Amos, Quebec; Bishop Alexander Carter of Sault Ste. Marie; Ukrainian Bishop Andrew Roborecki of Saskatoon; Bishop William Power of Antigonish; Bishop Michael Rusnak of Toronto, spiritual head of

Slovakian Catholics in Canada; Bishop Vladimir Malanchuk, a Canadian priest who had been named to head Ukrainian Catholics in France; Father Léo Deschâtelets, superior general of the Oblates of Mary Immaculate; and Rev. Germain-Marie Lalande, superior general of the Holy Cross Fathers.

Space limitations do not permit a detailed presentation of what Canadians said at Vatican II.[67] The topics on which they intervened forecast, in a way, the conference's later major program concentrations. There were fifteen interventions on the text about the Church in the modern world; nine on Christian unity; seven on the nature of the Church; five each on Revelation and priests; four each on liturgy, laity, and bishops; two each on the media and on relations with Jews; and one each on religious liberty, the Blessed Virgin, religious life, Catholic education, missions, and non-Christians.

CHAPTER FOUR

Implementing Vatican II

I. MISSIONS

The minutes of early conference meetings group a number of items about missionary activity under the heading "Propagation of the Faith."[68] There was no bishops' commission or office for missionary work until 1959. It came about then largely through an initiative of Pope John XXIII and is another example of how directly the Holy See was involved in conference activities before Vatican II.

When Archbishop Sebastiano Baggio came to Canada as Apostolic Delegate in 1959, one of the people who met him at the Montreal airport was Bishop Albert Sanschagrin of Amos, Quebec, who had been in Chile as an Oblate missionary and knew Baggio from that experience. Baggio asked Sanschagrin to meet him in Ottawa as soon as possible. There, Baggio unveiled Pope John XXIII's plan for helping Latin American dioceses. Sanschagrin told Baggio that if Rome really wanted action it should ask the CCC to create a permanent commission for the purpose. Archbishop Paul Bernier was then CCC president. He was resisting the idea of creating a new commission because this would call for a change in the CCC constitution, which had been approved by Rome, and which he regarded as untouchable. Following Sanschagrin's advice, Baggio saw to it that a request for a new commission came promptly from Rome. The CCC just as promptly set up the Canadian Catholic Commission for Latin America.

To get action on his plan, Pope John called a November 1959 meeting in Washington, D.C. Archbishop Antonio Samorè, secretary of the Pontifical Commission for Latin America, came from Rome to preside. Bernier led the Canadian delegation of Archbishops Marie-Joseph Lemieux of Ottawa and Georges Cabana of Sherbrooke, Auxiliary Bishop Thomas Fulton of Toronto and Bishop Sanschagrin. Baggio accompanied them. They were joined by a similar U.S. delegation and one from CELAM, the umbrella organization of Latin American bishops' conferences.

About a thousand Canadians, members of the traditional missionary communities of men and women, were working in Latin America at the time. An increase in their numbers and more lay volunteers would be welcome, but the Pope's novel plan was that U.S. and Canadian bishops should send priests from their dioceses to work in Latin American dioceses under bishops there. Bernier enthusiastically promised another 2,000 Canadians. Sanschagrin thought that target unattainable, as in fact it proved to be, although twenty-seven Canadian dioceses eventually signed agreements with Latin American counterparts.

There was a second part to the Pope's plan. It called for Canada and the U.S. each to build and operate a seminary, one in Central America and the other in northeast Brazil. Sanschagrin, one of the Canadians at the meeting who could argue in French, English or Spanish, suggested that Central America was too close to the U.S. and that there might be questions about U.S. imperialism. The U.S. bishops should take the one in Brazil, he suggested. They agreed and followed through by giving the Holy See $1 million to have it built and staffed.

Rome decided that the second seminary should be in Honduras, at Tegucigalpa. The CCC sent Sanschagrin there in the spring of 1960. He found the local bishops still unaware of the plan but enthusiastic when he told them about it. Back in Ottawa, the CCC's October plenary meeting approved the commission's plan. Four priests from Canadian dioceses, headed by Monsignor Gérard Cambron of Sherbrooke, would direct the seminary. In January 1961, Sanschagrin was back in Honduras with Cambron to sign a $200,000 contract for the seminary that would be owned by the bishops of Honduras and built and managed by Canadians. Despite initial delays and cost overruns, the doors opened in 1962. Since 1966, Quebec's Pont-Viau Foreign Missions priests have run the seminary, replacing the original team of diocesan priests. Canada's financial responsibilities towards it ended in 1977. The seminary celebrated its twenty-fifth anniversary in 1987, and in 1991 reported eighty-five students, of whom thirty-five to forty per cent were expected to continue to ordination as priests. (That same year, the seminary in Recife, Brazil, which the U.S. bishops had helped with initial funding, was closed at Rome's request on the grounds that it had failed to maintain an adequate program of studies.)[69]

Soon after Vatican II, other missionary concerns began to assert themselves at the CCC. Without reducing the Latin American commitment, increasing attention was given to the mission needs in other lands and in Canada itself. In the early 1970s, the commission and office for Latin America were given more inclusive names: missions commission and missions office.[70] Their mandates at the time were expanded to include world-wide missions as well as those in Canada's inner cities and far North. As well, at its 1973 annual meeting, the CCC established the Canadian Pastoral Fund for Evangelization. Its terms of reference dedicated the fund as the instrument of the Canadian bishops' conference to come to the aid of other conferences in their tasks of evangelization. The new fund was formed by merging the Latin American Fund that had developed after 1961 and the much older Canadian Missions Fund.

Northern Canada

Pastoral work in Canada's far North had been historically assigned to the Oblate Fathers, who pioneered among the Inuit and Indians. Vatican grants from world mission collections aided their work. Oblate bishops from northern dioceses brought awareness of this work into CCC meetings. During the 1970s and early 1980s, these bishops became increasingly insistent that responsibility for northern dioceses be shared with southern dioceses. This was a domestic application of the Vatican II theme about each bishop's universal role.

One response at the CCC was to give the missions office the task of preparing sessions on "The Missions of Northern Canada" as the special theme of the 1983 plenary meeting. It drew attention to the growing insistence by Canadian native people that their traditional religious rites should be appreciated by the Church and integrated into Church ceremonies. It also launched a process, still not completed as the 1990s dawned, to transfer from Rome to Canada total financial responsibility for the northern dioceses.

The movement to give more place to traditional native rites did not begin at the CCC, nor entirely from outside the Church, either. To some extent, the demand for recognition of native rights and customs resulted from the general increase in native self-awareness. Political efforts to establish broad aboriginal rights and settle land claims both accompanied and aided the renewal of native spirituality. These native movements were met by some positive response from the Canadian Churches on both the political and spiritual fronts. Oblate missions in western and northern Canada and Jesuit missions in Ontario have become leaders of the Catholic response to renewed native spirituality. The CCC's National Office of Religious Education designated a specialist for native catechetics. Some dioceses with native populations have initiated programs to appreciate and enhance native rites. Also, Catholic native people have emerged as leaders in their own struggles for respect and recognition. Considerable aid for this work has come from the Catholic Church Extension Society, based in Toronto. As well, the CCCB missions office was supporting this movement as the 1990s began, and was trying to help the bishops keep abreast of it.

Mission Finances

The question of financial support of mission areas in Canada involves Church history from the nineteenth century. An international collection of money was started in 1836 under the title "Propagation of the Faith." The bishop of Quebec sought and obtained the right to retain part of the funds collected under this title and to use the money for missions of his own vast diocese, in the Northwest Territories, British Columbia, Oregon, Hudson Bay and northern Quebec.

Over the years, the mission organizations launched by the Vatican evolved. They are now grouped in Canada under the general title of Pontifical Mission Aid Societies,[71] with national offices in Toronto and Quebec for their English and French sectors. Their constitution makes them responsible both to Rome and to the bishops of Canada through the national conference. They are familiar to Canadian Catholics through their materials to promote awareness of the missions and through their annual fundraising efforts, which are centred on Mission Sunday.

Some of the funds collected by these societies have been held for use in Canada – since 1836 by the diocese of Quebec, and since 1943 by the bishops' conference. The money has helped different groups through the years: 1933, western dioceses poverty-stricken by the drought; 1943, other dioceses in deep debt; 1959, Latin America; and after 1973, the Canadian Pastoral Fund for Evangelization and other mission-aid projects growing out of the work of the CCCB's commission and office for missions. Over the years, the formula for calculating the share of the collection to be retained in Canada has varied, but in Canadian eyes the right has been firmly in place since it was granted in 1836.

There was dismay among CCCB members, therefore, when a March 26, 1988, letter was received in Ottawa from Cardinal Jozef Tomko, prefect of the Vatican's Congregation for the Evangelization of Peoples. He asked the CCCB to discontinue retaining twenty per cent of Mission Sunday revenues and to remit the total collection to Rome. The CCCB's response came in stages. Because the Tomko request would remove the revenue base of the CCCB's Pastoral Fund for Evangelization, the rationale for this fund was re-examined. The bishops agreed that they wished to retain it so they could give concrete expression to their sense of collegial solidarity through occasional grants to other bishops' conferences. The work of the CCCB missions office was then reviewed and rearranged, with some staff reductions. In light of these studies, the CCCB's October 1989 plenary meeting agreed that it needed to retain fifteen per cent of the gross revenues of the annual Mission Sunday collection. This would maintain the Pastoral Fund and finance the missions office and its projects.

An agreement was reached during January 1990 meetings in Rome between Cardinal Tomko and CCCB representatives – the president and vice-president, Bishops Robert Lebel and Thomas Fulton, and Rev. William Ryan, English general secretary. The CCCB would retain the amount proposed. The Vatican would reduce and eventually eliminate its annual grants to Canada's northern dioceses. These dioceses would become fully responsible for meeting their own needs, with the help of other Canadian dioceses. Other parts of the agreement included plans for closer collaboration between the Vatican and the CCCB in co-ordinating, supervising and managing the Pontifical Mission Aid Societies.[72] Guiding the agreement were the Vatican II principles of collegiality that are renewing the Church's approach to missionary activity everywhere.

II. LITURGY

The Vatican II Constitution on Liturgy was promulgated during the second session of the Council, in 1963. Things moved quickly after that. The final Council vote took place on November 21. Two months later, on January 25, 1964, Paul VI established a new body – the Consilium for the Implementation of the Constitution on the Sacred Liturgy – to facilitate and oversee the reform program. The Consilium, in turn, issued an official instruction the following September.

Already before that, the Canadian bishops had decided on the first liturgical changes for this country. Meeting in Ottawa on February 14, 1964, the ten-member CCC board approved the reading of the lessons – Epistle and Gospel – in English or French instead of Latin. Other changes followed. The CCC's April 1964 plenary meeting agreed on the use of English or French in all parts of the Mass up to the Canon, except the Preface; and from the Lord's Prayer to the dismissal, except the priest's communion prayers. At another plenary meeting in Rome on October 3, during the third Council session, the finishing touches were put on these plans.

Approval of each proposal by the conference had to come from the Consilium. It got to work promptly. The decisions of the CCC's April 1964 meeting were confirmed two months later, and those of October within six weeks. The Canadian bishops, therefore, were in a position to put some of their decisions into effect on January 1, 1965. The major changes in the Mass, however, were introduced on the first Sunday of Lent, March 7, 1965. At Easter 1966, there were further changes when English and French came into use in Canada for the Preface of the Mass.

The Consilium was, in effect, the Council's commission on liturgy, transformed by Pope Paul VI into a post-Council body. Bishop Albertus Martin of Nicolet, Quebec, who had been a leading member of the Council's commission, was immediately confirmed as a Consilium member; Bishop Emmett Carter of London, Ontario, was named to it at the end of the Council. Two Canadian priests were named as consultants: Rev. Vincent Kennedy, a Toronto Basilian teaching in Rome, and Rev. Gaston Fontaine, who had been director of the national liturgy office for French Canada, and who had gone to Rome during the summer of 1965 as a member of the Consilium secretariat.

Given the need to adapt the liturgical changes for each language and for varying cultural needs, the CCC set up separate English and French commissions of bishops to oversee and direct work. Each commission brought proposals for changes to CCC plenary meetings. The Vatican's post-Council implementation norms and CCC bylaws set out the procedures. Each commission first submitted its proposals to bishops of its own sector, English or French. After agreement in each sector, both sets of proposals were submitted for approval by the entire CCC in plenary assembly. The process of reaching agreement might have taken years but was accomplished in months, thanks largely to the procedure for voting by mail that had been developed by the CCC general secretariat immediately after the Council. In this way, each commission's proposals could be mailed to the bishops. By return mail, the bishops could indicate agreement or disagreement and suggest changes. On the basis of these comments, the commissions could direct further work, so that the proposals that came to actual plenary meetings were usually accorded ready approval.

One major decision was that Canada's English and French texts would be harmonized with those for other countries that used these languages. The International Commission on English in the Liturgy (ICEL) began work on common English texts, with Archbishop M.C. O'Neill of Regina as the first Canadian member. Archbishop Maurice Baudoux represented Canada on the Commission internationale francophone pour les traductions et la liturgie (CIFTL). Linguists and other experts on both of these teams constantly had to take into account the post-Council revisions that were being developed by international specialists who were working under the direction of the Consilium in Rome. The new Order of the Mass in the *Roman Missal* promulgated by Paul VI in 1969 was one such major change.

Once the liturgical changes had been approved in Canada and Rome, a major task was to prepare English and French versions of the official books needed on altars, in pulpits and elsewhere. Each CCC liturgy office became the centre of a huge publishing venture. The CCC decided to organize itself to edit, publish and market the new English and French books for churches and chapels across the land. To this end, the CCC Publications Service was organized in 1966. This initiative has given the conference direct control over the content and style, timing and pricing of all official English and French liturgical materials used in Canada. It also has been a source of revenue for the conference.

Under the direction of the bishops' commissions for liturgy, the CCC's national liturgical offices, English and French, also undertook to inform and educate priests and other church members about the changes.

An important instrument for the two liturgy offices' educational work has been their *National Bulletin on Liturgy* (*Bulletin national de liturgie*). Each office has also developed a national advisory council, networks of diocesan directors of liturgy, and long lists of achievements in summer schools, topical workshops, lectures and conferences, the encouragement of liturgical arts and the development of library resources.[73] There is no end in sight for the process of enhancing the liturgy as directed by Vatican II.

III. ECUMENISM IN CANADA

The Council's decree on ecumenism was promulgated during the last days of the 1964 third session. In anticipation of the text and in light of increasing ecumenical activities in Canada, the CCC annual meeting in Rome in the fall of 1964 established a bishops' committee for ecumenical activities, and the next fall made it a full commission.[74] Two fields of interest and concern converged in these initiatives. During the 1940s and 1950s Canadian Christians, including Roman Catholics, began to take an interest in dialogue to overcome denominational differences. One sign of this new ecumenical spirit was the formation in 1944 of the Canadian Council of Churches. The Catholic Church was not a member but, here and there, Catholics began making contacts with local ministerial associations. Here and there, too, priests and other pastors had informal discussions about common pastoral problems, such as how to minister to couples in mixed marriages. However informal and unofficial at first, some of these dialogues and exchanges became increasingly structured in the late 1950s. Catholic ecumenists such as Rev. Irénée Beaubien in Montreal began to be recognized for their pioneering work.

Other Catholics were beginning to meet with fellow Christians to discuss working together on social justice issues. Priests Peter Nearing, Jack Shea and Bill Ryan, directors in turn of the CCC social action department in Ottawa, were among them. Succeeding Nearing in 1963, Shea, who was joined in 1964 by Ryan, worked actively with counterparts in the Toronto national offices of other Churches to build up the National Committee on Church and Industrial Society. They also explored mutual concerns through the Toronto-based Religion-Labour Council headed by Dr. David Somers, on which conference representatives had observer status.

Before the end of Vatican II, there were plans for high-profile ecumenical collaboration to build a Christian Pavilion at the 1967 World's Fair in Montreal. The joint venture by seven Churches was announced on

December 22, 1964. Signers were Cardinal Léger; United Church Moderator E.M. Howse; Montreal's Anglican Bishop Kenneth Maguire; Dr. Ritchie Bell for the Presbyterians; Rev. Emrys Jenkins for the Federation of Baptist Churches; Bishop Timothy Rodostolou, Greek Orthodox bishop of Canada and Alaska; and Dr. Earl Treusch for the Lutheran Church. It was heralded as "the first time in history all these churches unite to bear a common Christian witness to the world in erecting a common building." The decision to proceed was made easier when Canada's Catholic bishops "received a formal assurance from the Vatican that there would be no Vatican pavilion at Expo '67. This way, the Catholic Church will be able to participate in the Christian Pavilion, the initiative and responsibility for which is left to the Canadian Bishops."[75]

Joint Working Group

Soon after the Christian Pavilion and Expo '67 closed in the fall of 1967, a new project for structuring the ecumenical dialogue was undertaken. At the international level, a Joint Working Group (JWG) was set up by the Vatican and the World Council of Churches. The idea of having a similar group in Canada quickly developed, and in 1968 the Joint Working Group of the Canadian Council of Churches and Canadian Catholic Conference was formed. The representatives named to it soon moved beyond friendly dialogue about theological differences dividing their Churches. One of their projects was a study of baptism as each denomination understood and practised it. The participating Churches agreed that each could recognize baptism performed by the minister of another provided an agreed upon formula was used. In related studies and discussions, the JWG made progress in developing programs for pastoral care of couples in mixed marriages. Ecumenical education was also promoted. Common prayer was encouraged, especially through the use of materials prepared since 1969 by an ecumenical committee for the annual Week of Prayer for Christian Unity.

New Structure

The Joint Working Group in 1969 agreed in principle that Canada's Churches should look to a closer structural relationship. The Catholic Church was not a member of the Canadian Council of Churches. The JWG set up a committee to explore a new, broader ecumenical structure. The Council of Churches and the bishops' conference agreed to sponsor a national consultation, which was held in Montreal in 1973. After lengthy discussions, which explored old differences and new hopes, the one hundred members of various Churches agreed to recommend the formation of a new Canadian Christian Council.

The JWG then set up a Wider Ecumenical Fellowship (WEF) committee. It uncovered two kinds of questions. How did members of the Canadian Council of Churches, formed thirty years earlier, feel about abandoning it for a new structure? Since Catholics made up more than half of Canada's Christians, would they have more than half the seats on every board and committee of a new body – and pay more than half the total budget? Catholics and representatives of other interested Churches met in 1980 and 1981. They agreed to proceed gradually by setting up an Inter-Church Committee (ICC). As the study of various options continued, the bishops' conference decided that associate membership in the existing Council of Churches would be preferable to proceeding further with a new ecumenical body. During 1984, therefore, the Council of Churches began to deal with the CCCB's request for associate membership. The process continued throughout 1985. Monsignor Basil Meeking, from the Vatican's Secretariat for Promoting Christian Unity, attended the January board meetings of both the Canadian Council of Churches and the CCCB to facilitate and encourage the negotiations. The signing of a formal agreement took place in April 1986, to come into effect in May of that year. A number of structural adjustments followed. In October 1987, the Canadian Council of Churches' General Board adopted revised bylaws and in November 1991 an amended constitution was approved.[76] With CCCB involvement, the Canadian Council of Churches has also increased its capacity to work in French as well as English.[77]

Meanwhile, several bilateral dialogues have been initiated between the bishops' conference and representatives of other Churches. The first of these, the Canadian Anglican-Roman Catholic Dialogue, was established in 1971. Eight representatives from each Church and one observer from the United Church meet three times a year. As well, nine bishops from each Church meet once a year to discuss practical pastoral and theological questions. These meetings have been a Canadian forum for discussing the work and reports of the Anglican-Roman Catholic International Commission (ARCIC), which is directed by Canterbury and Rome. Practical results of the Canadian dialogue have included its *Pastoral Guidelines for Interchurch Marriages between Anglicans and Roman Catholics*, published in 1987, and a text on *Pastoral Guidelines for Churches in the Case of Clergy Moving from One Communion to the Other*, completed in 1991.

A formal Roman Catholic-United Church Dialogue was initiated in 1974. Six members of each Church, with one Anglican observer, meet twice a year. Early topics included the position of each Church on abortion. Discussion of abortion led the group to reflect on the nature, purpose and methods of dialogue itself. It went on to explore the role and exercise of authority in each Church, and the meaning of "evangelism/evangelization" for each.

Dialogue between the CCCB and the newly constituted Evangelical Lutheran Church in Canada (ELCIC) began in 1986. Each Church names seven members; there is one Anglican observer. Discussions began with a review of agreed upon statements from earlier Lutheran-Catholic dialogues. Other topics since 1986 have included the understanding in each Church of ordination, priesthood, eucharist and episcopacy. Members of the national group have sponsored study days for clergy and others in their respective regions, a process that involved about 800 persons during the national dialogue's first five years.

Another dialogue in which the CCCB has taken an interest has been the Canadian Christian-Jewish Consultation. Since 1977, a liaison committee named by the Canadian Council of Churches, the CCCB and the Canadian Jewish Congress has met four or five times a year. Discussions focus on such issues as refugees and immigration, African famine relief and proselytism on university campuses. The group plans and hosts an annual seminar to promote improved relations between Jewish and Christian communities. A two-day conference on "Faith Communities Confronting Racism" was held in Winnipeg in May 1990.

There are no formal CCCB dialogues with other non-Christian faith groups, but there have been occasional meetings.

IV. 'CHURCH IN THE MODERN WORLD'

In Quebec, the 1960s saw vast social changes that have been called the "Quiet Revolution." In other parts of Canada, too, the reorganization and extension of governments' presence in such fields as welfare, education and health care gave rise to dramatic incidents, such as the 1962 doctors' strike in Saskatchewan. Information and education have been major components of the initial response to these social changes by the bishops and their co-workers. CCC French social action department directors Rev. Charles Mathieu and Rev. Jean-Guy Hamelin organized and led hundreds of study sessions and workshops for priests, religious brothers and nuns.[78] English bishops and directors – Smyth, Nearing, Shea and Ryan – were equally busy promoting education programs in the different situations faced by English dioceses. Until the final one in Montreal in 1965, the Social Life Conferences were major teaching events. There were also numerous study days for priests and religious. Then, gradually, from 1964 on, Vatican II teachings began to make a great difference.

Developments in Social Teaching

The influence of Vatican II on the Church's social teaching and on that of the CCCB was manifold. Pope John Paul II later wrote that in the mid-1960s, the emphasis shifted from class questions to world issues.[79] A Canadian theologian's analysis of CCCB statements showed that there was also a shift in how social problems were perceived. The bishops' messages of the late 1950s pointed to religious and spiritual causes of injustice, and those of the early 1970s began to turn attention to social causes. To earlier calls for personal conversion were added calls for structural changes.[80] There was also a change in teaching methods. Earlier messages set out principles of Catholic social teaching to be applied to social realities. Soon after Vatican II, CCC statements began to describe in detail the social realities of deprivation and injustice to which the social teachings could be applied.

Some of the ingredients that went into these changes can be discerned in the agenda of a meeting of the English section of the social action commission in Edmonton on February 2, 1966. The staff reported on their work for the November 28-December 1, 1965, national conference on "A Health Charter for Canada." More than twenty national organizations had co-sponsored the conference, which aimed at increasing support for the proposals of the Hall Commission on Health Care.[81] This was an example of "Church in the world," something quite different from a social life conference by Catholics for Catholics. Meanwhile, ecumenism was opening up other new avenues. Interchurch collaboration on social issues had begun. English social action department directors John Shea and William Ryan were meeting regularly with their counterparts from the national Church offices in Toronto as the National Committee on Church and Industrial Society.[82]

While this change of orientation was proceeding – from inside the Church to the outside world and other Christians – a policy change was also under way. In 1966, the social affairs commission and staff began to shift teaching priorities and methods. Conferences and publications on Catholic social teaching gave way to consultations, research, educational activities, ecumenical collaboration and outreach into Canadian and international society, public statements and interventions, and publications. The shift, in a sense, was from trying to help only Church members to trying to serve all of society.[83] At this same time, the bishops and staff of the CCC's French sector were reaching out to a group of lay leaders and priests who had been invited to work with them on social questions. This Conseil national d'action social (CNAS) was constituted as "a tangible expression of the co-operation of members of the people of God who are working together to help the Church to accomplish even better its mission in the modern world."[84] The CNAS met every few months from December 1966 to June 1972.

The CCC's 1966 Labour Day statement ushered in a quarter-century of post-Council social teaching by the Canadian bishops that can be divided into four phases. Common to all four phases was the three-step teaching method of looking in detail at social realities, judging them in light of principles drawn from the Gospels and other Christian teachings, and suggesting actions to be taken. Other CCC messages, pastoral letters, briefs and press releases covered a wide range of issues.[85] Increasingly after Vatican II there were statements, briefs and position papers co-signed by the bishops and leaders of other Churches.

Phase One: Economic Realities of Poverty

"Poverty in Canada," the 1966 Labour Day statement, introduced a major focus on poverty in Canada and abroad. It stressed that because God intended "the earth with everything in it for the use of all human beings and peoples," social justice required that everyone work together "to eliminate those social conditions that foster poverty and deprivation."[86] The 1967 Labour Day statement on the economic conditions faced by Canadian families noted, in turn, that "misery, poverty, privation is the lot of more than a third of a population that lives in a very affluent country."[87] In a March 1968 pastoral letter, the bishops announced a project directed against world poverty, later to be called the Canadian Catholic Organization for Development and Peace (CCODP). In May, 500 people gathered in Montreal for a Church-sponsored national conference on the theme of "Christian Conscience and Poverty."[88] The 1968 Labour Day statement again dealt with the struggle against poverty and injustice. It called for "strategic and sustained cooperative action" by all levels of society."[89]

The report of a strategy committee[90] that proposed "A Coalition for Development" to take action on the Montreal poverty conference was submitted to the bishops' conference and the Canadian Council of Churches in May 1969. To win the long war against want, "a partnership of public, voluntary and religious agencies is necessary," it said.[91] A coalition secretariat was located in the CCC's social action office in Ottawa and work began to recruit non-Church members.[92] Representatives of more than thirty national organizations and citizens' groups met in Ottawa on March 13, 1970, for the founding forum of the Coalition for Development.[93]

A joint Church brief was presented to the Senate Special Committee on Poverty in June 1970. It recalled the 1968 Montreal poverty conference and told about efforts to organize the Coalition for Development. However, even the strategy report for the coalition did not go far enough, the representatives of the bishops' conference and the Canadian Council of Churches told the senators. It did not point out that existing social systems have built-in biases that tend to perpetuate inequities. The Church representatives said that they now preferred "to speak of humanity's escape from poverty in all its forms as a gradual *process of liberation*." This process, they added, had to start with liberation from myths about what causes poverty and go on to new power groupings, new attitudes and new social structures and methods.[94]

Phase Two: Political Realities of Poverty

The 1969 Labour Day message again dealt with poverty, but focused on political signs of injustice. Entitled "New Power," the text was influenced by two social processes. One was the study launched by the Quebec bishops into new ways for the Church to be present in the modern world. The other was the work being done to found the Coalition for Development. The statement defined "new power" as "the ever-widening participation in public dialogue and policy-making." The Christian criterion, it noted, is always whether a particular exercise of power contributes "to the fashioning of a just and humane society in Canada and the global community."[95]

A few weeks later, the principles of this statement were applied to the empowerment of native communities. On November 28, the bishops commented on a federal "Statement of Indian Policy." The government invited Indian organizations to discuss their role in implementing the new policy, but these groups lacked the means to be equal partners in such a dialogue, the CCC noted. The bishops pledged support for native efforts to negotiate "an equitable settlement of treaty, land claims and other rights," and asked the government to give native groups the financial aid needed "to enable them to do research and acquire the means necessary for a meaningful dialogue."[96]

The June 1970 interchurch brief to the Senate poverty committee was echoed directly in the CCC's 1970 Labour Day message. On every continent and in most nations, it said, "anguished voices are crying out for liberation from the slavery of war, economic want, political tyranny, sterile legalism, social discrimination, stifling paternalism, cultural disparity and spiritual alienation."[97] Within weeks of the publication of the message, the Front de liberation du Quebec triggered the October FLQ crisis. The formal episcopal comment about it came from Cardinal Roy as president of the Assembly of Quebec Bishops. Rejecting violence, he emphasized the theme that "injustice breeds violence."[98]

Continuing that theme, the 1971 Labour Day message said that it was urgent "that Canadians identify and begin to root out the underlying causes of violence; mere condemnation of violent symptoms is never enough." "Injustice breeds violence," it added, quoting Roy's statement. "The process is well known: deprivations, misery, humiliation, arbitrary restraints bring about a revolt of the oppressed, and also the revolt of others who are determined to fight for a just, humane world. This in turn elicits restraining action by the forces of law and order which sometimes leads to physical and psychological excesses...."[99]

The basic concepts of liberation from poverty and injustice were also discussed earlier in 1971 in the first of only two statements ever to come from an Inter-American Bishops' meeting. These annual meetings bring together representatives of the bishops' conferences in Canada and the U.S. and of CELAM, the umbrella organization of the conferences in Central and South America. Their informal discussions are not usually recorded or reported, so the 1971 statement was an important exception. It reviewed dealings of Canadian and U.S. governments and corporations with Latin American countries. "North American countries, like all rich nations, separate their aid from their trade relations with Latin American republics," it said. "This hides contradictions in the present system, wherein most aid is not genuine assistance; and even if it is, this aid is usually wiped out by unfair trade practices in which powerful nations indulge."[100]

Plenary Follow-up to the 1971 Synod

The April 1972 plenary, as a follow-up to the 1971 Synod on justice, published texts dealing with social justice in the Church, sharing national income and the issue of Quebec's self-determination.

On justice in the Church, the plenary noted that "most of us – bishops, priests, religious and laity – are challenged to practise more voluntary penance, such as greater *restraint* in the use of goods, and more *generous sharing* in the spirit of stewardship, even to the point of sacrificing what many people think is their due." As steps to this end, the text mentioned social education and research; periodic review of the treatment of Church personnel; sharing of personnel and resources among dioceses; financial openness throughout the Church; social usefulness as an investment norm; collaboration with the unorganized poor; support of local credit unions and co-operatives, and local coalitions of Churches and other voluntary organizations. It also proposed that the 1972 Labour Day statement deal with these themes.[101]

"The riches of Canada are unequally shared," the second text affirmed. "This inequality, which keeps so many people poor, is a social sin." Without espousing any particular program, the bishops invited Canadians to accept the social goal of an equitable redistribution of income. They also called for "acceptance of the principle that each Canadian should be assured that level of income necessary for decent human living and for full participation in society."[102]

Regarding the debate about Quebec's political future, "we wish to state," the bishops said, "that all options which respect the human person and the human community are a matter of free choice on the individual as well as the collective level. This is in keeping with the most recent teaching of the Church." The teachings cited included Paul VI's letter, *Octogesima Adveniens*, to Cardinal Roy, and the text from the 1971 Synod, that "peoples should not be hindered from attaining development in accordance with their own culture," and that "all peoples should be able to become the principal architects of their own economic and social development." The bishops concluded with their own assurance "that the Bishops of Canada will be at the service of the people of God, whatever political, economic, social and cultural situation they choose."[103]

As directed by the April plenary, the 1972 Labour Day statement revisited the subject of justice in the Church, through a message on "Simplicity and Sharing." The disparities of poverty and wealth, it insisted, did not come about because of fickle fate, nor because it was "the Father's will that the majority of his divided family should be denied basic necessities of life while a minority prospers." The problem, the text stressed, "is the abuse of power, the coercion of the weak by the powerful" – internationally, nationally and locally.[104]

Phase Three: Interchurch Coalitions

The year 1973 marked a turning point for the social justice work of the CCC. As one of several structural changes at the time, what had been two social affairs offices, English and French, became one bilingual "desk." Also, from 1973 onward the research work of the interchurch coalitions became an increasingly important source of empirical evidence of social disparity and injustice in Canada and elsewhere. The bishops' social teachings reflected the new information coming from the coalitions. At the same time, the coalitions developed as new channels through which Catholic social teachings became more widely known by members of other Christian Churches.

At the beginning of 1973, the CCC entered the debate on extending the suspension of capital punishment in Canada. The case for retaining the death penalty had not been proven, they said, and called for further research during a second period of suspension. Those who favoured the death penalty, they said, bore the burden of proving that it was an absolutely necessary deterrent, required for good order in the country.[105]

Meanwhile, plans were going forward for CCC participation in a major interchurch social justice education project. Church leaders, including Bishop William Power as CCC president,[106] would present a brief to the federal government and then travel across Canada to give it a "grassroots" launching. The strategy marked the beginning of the "Ten Days for Development" program of Church development and relief agencies, including the Canadian Catholic Organization for Development and Peace. The brief also announced the start of two interchurch research coalitions: the GATT-Fly Project and the Inter-Church Project on Population (ICPOP). For each, the Churches pooled money to provide a budget for a small, permanent staff for research and action regarding a specific social problem. Eventually, there would be more than a dozen of these interchurch coalitions – a unique Canadian model for ecumenical co-operation in efforts to apply Gospel values in temporal affairs.[107]

"Development Demands Justice," the Church leaders' brief proclaimed in its title. It quoted the 1971 report of the Special Senate Committee on Poverty in support of the view that "it is our economic system which is primarily responsible" for the inequitable distribution of resources and services. Poor countries wanted far-reaching changes regarding international trade, corporate investment and foreign aid. The brief asked Canadians if they were prepared to help make such changes possible – by paying more for such products as coffee, cocoa, rice and sugar; by giving trade preferences to Third World products; by demanding less return on investments; by improving the amount and kind of aid. The Canadian government, in turn, was asked to incorporate similar principles in the policies it was then preparing for the 1973-74 round of international negotiations on the General Agreement on Tariffs and Trade (GATT) and the International Monetary Fund (IMF), and for the 1974 United Nations World Population Conference.[108]

Later, the 1973 Labour Day statement stressed that "Inequality Divides: Justice Reconciles." In Canada and elsewhere, the message noted, people did not have equal opportunities for human development. "Such inequalities are the work of men and the political-economic systems they fashion," the text affirmed. It added that "as yet, comparatively few Christians appear prepared to become prophetic witnesses to the fraternal harmony promised in the Beatitudes – even though such co-operative interdependence is now a practical necessity for global survival as well as a moral necessity for wholeness of life."[109]

PLURA

An interchurch association to promote justice in Canada was one of the results of the heightened awareness of poverty in Canada that developed during the late 1960s and early 1970s. Known as PLURA, its name came from the first letter of the names of the participating Churches: Presbyterian, Lutheran, United, Roman Catholic and Anglican. Senior executives of these Churches began meeting in 1970 as ICCCDR – the Inter-Church Consultative Committee on Development and Relief. Both the bishops' conference and the Canadian Catholic Organization for Development and Peace sent staff to represent the Catholic Church. One of the projects they discussed was joint action on domestic poverty. Some ideas on possible actions also came from the National Welfare Council, formed in 1970 as a private-sector advisory body to the federal Minister of Health and Welfare. During 1973, the Churches agreed to commit money each year to a common fund for projects to combat poverty in the country. From this fund, grants would be made in modest amounts to local anti-poverty and self-help initiatives, and to groups of low-income/disadvantaged citizens. The aid often has been in the form of seed money to help launch a local project. Through the constitution given to PLURA by the participating Churches, its administrative board is predominantly made up of representatives of local groups from across the country who are joined by Church representatives in managing the organization and selecting projects. A global figure for the money distributed in this way by PLURA in its first 20 years is about $3 million.

World Conferences

During the early months of 1974, CCC social action staff members, working with specific episcopal mandates, were active in two interchurch coalitions that monitored the Canadian government's role at the world conferences on population and on food.[110] The 1974 Labour Day message reflected the involvement of CCC staff in Project GATT-Fly's preparations for the Rome food conference later that year. The text examined causes of the worsening world food situation. The underlying causes of the food problem, the bishops stressed, "generally are found in the consuming and marketing practices of economic systems – practices which continuously widen the gap between humanity's rich minority and poor majority."[111]

The CCC took up a wide range of social issues during the year between the 1974 and 1975 Labour Day messages. The September 1974 plenary meeting issued a short statement for International Women's Year (1975).[112] Before year end, CCC president Archbishop Jean-Marie Fortier wrote to Prime Minister Pierre Trudeau to appeal to the government to find "a just and human solution for the serious problems of Haitians now in this country who are facing deportation."[113] The first statement of 1975 was made by the CCC executive committee in support of "recent initiatives by our Federal and Provincial governments to draft legislation on guaranteed income."[114] Two 1975 statements by the social affairs commission, meanwhile, dealt with immigration. In a July 11 pastoral letter, they noted that Canadians had been opposing controls on prices, wages and other elements of the economy. Yet, there was a preoccupation with controlling immigration. "What does this mean," they asked, "if we seek to keep markets free and migrants controlled?" Fear of newcomers, they urged, should be replaced by fraternity, sharing, openness, hope and love. In a similar vein, the commission's September brief urged that "instead of designing a legal stockade to keep Canada as it is," the joint parliamentary committee "aim at contributing to a global policy intended to help move all peoples to full realization of their capacities and worth as persons."[115]

To start work on the 1975 Labour Day message, diocesan directors of social action were consulted about possible themes. Their concerns about northern resource development and the rights of native people were taken up in the message "Northern Development: At What Cost?" The critical issue, it said, "is how these northern energy resources are to be developed – by whom and for whom." The text developed two ethical principles: justice for northern native people and responsible stewardship of the North's non-renewable resources.[116] The interchurch coalition Project North (later called the Aboriginal Rights Coalition) was launched after publication of the message.

Just as in March 1973 Church leaders had given the federal cabinet a brief, "Development Demands Justice," so on March 2, 1976, they went to cabinet with "Justice Demands Action." This brief dealt with five public policy areas on which the government had previously been pressed for action: international development; transnational corporations; northern development; income distribution; and policy on immigration, population and refugees. The basic issue, the brief argued, is "who shall control and benefit from the earth's natural resources?" Would they be used to enrich a minority or to meet the unfulfilled needs of the majority?[117] The social affairs commission took up similar concerns in a May 21 statement on the eve of the United Nations Habitat Conference in Vancouver. It outlined their "pastoral preoccupations with housing problems in the world and in this country.... It is not that economic means are lacking: the problem is to find the will to reconstruct our society and reorder its priorities," the bishops said.[118]

As the bishops and staff approached the task of selecting a 1976 Labour Day theme, they were urged not to launch another major theme study. The two previous messages, on food and northern development, were just being acted upon by many local groups who needed time to get organized. The bishops, too, wished to avoid giving the impression that they were "issue hopping." As a result, the 1976 message, "From Words to Action," took up no new issue. It emphasized six guidelines for converting words about social responsibilities into actions on behalf of the poor and oppressed: 1. Understanding the Gospel message of justice; 2. Modifying our more affluent life styles; 3. Listening to the victims of injustice in our communities; 4. Denouncing injustice in our communities; 5. Collaborating to change the causes of injustice; 6. Assisting the poor and oppressed.[119]

Phase Four: Towards New Approaches

It had not been foreseen when it was written that the 1976 Labour Day message would be the last of its kind. In its report to the April 1977 plenary meeting, the social affairs commission proposed a new approach. Instead of a major statement, a short message would try "to help Christians in the search for a new socio-economic order based on justice." The commission would also prepare a "primer" or guidelines, designed to raise questions and stimulate local discussions and actions. In addition, the bishops of the four pastoral regions would be invited to sponsor regional conferences.

The announced CCCB statement, "A Society to be Transformed," was issued during the 1977 fall plenary meeting. It urged people to get involved in reshaping society and it pressed a particular kind of involvement. "Christians," the bishops said, "must be leaders in identifying and promoting the solutions that come only through new or renewed values, attitudes and relationships." The statement found both modern capitalism and the Marxist alternative lacking. It foresaw tensions and debate at the local level as some tried to reform capitalism and others opted for socialist solutions. Tension and disagreement could be part of a healthy process for change but, it said, "no option is valid that does not unite people in efforts for the creation of a society based on justice." It concluded: "Different models of society can be built from Gospel values of love, justice and equality, but no social order built without these values can meet fully the legitimate aspirations of all mankind."[120]

The publishing highlight of 1979 was the promised "primer," *Witness to Justice: A Society to be Transformed* – a book of 135 large-size pages. It contained three working papers: "Faith and Justice," which outlined biblical and Church teachings on the social justice responsibilities of Christians; "Justice in Canada," which surveyed this country's social and economic ills and injustices; and "Justice in the Third World," which analyzed problems in developing countries and Canadian involvements in them. It also proposed action projects and had a bibliography suggesting possibilities for further study. The divisions chosen for the book later became an organizing framework for the CCCB's social justice work for the next decade and into the 1990s.

"Unemployment: The Human Cost," a January 4 statement by the CCCB board, opened 1980. It analyzed unemployment as a phenomenon that afflicts different social classes and regions of Canada in different ways. There are both material hardships and psychological strain for those most affected. A major long-term task, the bishops said, is the development of alternative industrial strategies designed to serve the needs of all people in the country. This would require effective measures to increase the self-sufficiency of Canada's industries, strengthen the manufacturing sector and other job-producing industries, redistribute capital in favour of underdeveloped regions, and enhance community ownership and control of local industries.[121]

The statement opposing the neutron bomb by the CCCB's November 1981 plenary was the first of a series of messages about disarmament.[122] Opposition to nuclear weapons as a threat to human survival was reiterated in a CCCB presentation to the federal Standing Committee on External Affairs and National Defence. The February 16, 1982, brief also referred to the build-up of armaments as a cause of social injustice and criticized military regimes for increasing repression.[123] Then, on December 14, the CCCB president joined other Church leaders in a presentation to Prime Minister Pierre Trudeau. They noted that although Trudeau and other members of his government had spoken out against nuclear arms, there was concern "that Canada is at the same time a willing participant on a path that we believe promises only destruction and defeat of the struggle for justice."[124]

The social affairs commission began the 1980s with a plan for subdividing its work for bishops and staff into eight portfolios: frontier development, civil/political liberties, food production, resource development, industrial production, poverty/disparities, refugees/immigration, and political/constitutional development. The commission's 1982 report noted the further distinction between teaching projects and action/research projects. Teaching projects centred around promotion of the 1979 document *Witness to Justice: A Society to be Transformed.* Action/research projects, in turn, were associated with each of the eight portfolios into which the commission's work was divided.

Towards the end of 1982, the commission completed work on the teaching project that was greeted with a burst of publicity of such magnitude that for many people the CCCB's public image is defined by this one text. As one measure of its immediate appeal, just eight months after it broke into news headlines on December 31, 1982, the commission reported that the text was available in six languages and that 206,000 copies had been sold. As a measure of its durability, ten years after its appearance "Ethical Reflections on the Economic Crisis" was still capable of sparking debate both outside the conference and among CCCB members themselves. There was even debate about what made it debatable at all.

There is space here for only an overview of the ensuing debate. One aspect of it had to do with CCCB procedures. Cardinal Emmett Carter called a New Year's Eve press conference a few hours after the *Toronto Star* published the full text. Carter insisted that it was a statement of the social affairs office, not of the Canadian bishops, because proper consultation procedures had not been followed. Archbishop Henri Légaré, the CCCB's president, maintained at the time – and still insisted in a 1992 interview[125] – that in authorizing release of the statement he had fully respected the CCCB's code of procedures for texts that contain no new policies – that is, no principles not previously presented in such texts as "A Society to be Transformed" and "Unemployment: The Human Cost." Whatever else it accomplished, Cardinal Carter's protest resulted in immense publicity for the text. Others who were less concerned about CCCB procedures moved the debate to a political level. Despite its disavowal of any political option, the text favoured a New Democratic Party agenda, some said. Still others launched what was probably the most extensive discussion, about the merits of the text's economic analysis and proposals. More successfully than any other CCCB statement, it achieved its aim of stimulating serious, sustained debate about the Canadian economy and about ethical considerations as well as technical factors. Throughout 1983, commission members and staff could do little else than try to cope with demands placed on them in response to the message.

During 1984, the commission reorganized its work according to the 1979 working document *Witness to Justice*, which set out three categories: faith/justice perspectives, justice in Canada, and justice in the Third World. In May, too, a new working instrument, "Ethical Choices and Political Challenges," was published – but without the media response accorded its predecessor on the economy. On May 1, 1985, and again a year later, statements were issued in support of labour unions.[126] The social affairs commission's report to the 1986 plenary meeting noted staff efforts to work in a widening network of local, diocesan, regional and national organizations. These staff efforts were similar to efforts that brought some twenty other national organizations for the 1965 national medicare conference or for the Coalition for Development in the early 1970s. The report said that "the commission is putting a priority on developing more popular methods for communicating the Gospel message on social justice to a broader spectrum of people, both inside and outside the Church."

The elections of commission members during the 1985 and 1987 CCCB plenary meetings gave rise to a dispute among close followers of the work of the social action commission. The conference has adjusted its rules for the election of commission members many times. It did so in April 1976 and again in September 1983 when it adopted Bylaw 4.5, which specified that "Members of Commissions are named for a two-year mandate, renewable once." The practical results of this bylaw came into effect gradually during the 1985 and 1987 elections of commission members. Bishop Remi De Roo had been re-elected chairman of the social action commission in 1983. As he approached the 1985 elections, he had been a member of the social affairs commission for eleven years and its chairman for five. He was renamed a member of the commission in 1985 but was replaced as chairman by Bishop Paul O'Byrne of Calgary. Then, in the 1987 election, De Roo was named instead to the theology commission, where he served for four years before being re-elected to the social affairs commission in 1991. Supporters and opponents of the conference's social justice teaching argued publicly about whether the results of the 1985 and 1987 elections represented a political defeat for De Roo or just a procedural adjustment that affected him along with many other bishops.[127]

An interchurch initiative in support of native people was an early preoccupation of 1987. The CCC president, Bishop Bernard Hubert, cosigned an ecumenical pastoral letter entitled "A New Covenant." It called for the constitutional recognition of self-government for aboriginal peoples in Canada. The president also joined in protesting proposed new legislation to restrict entry of refugees into Canada. The social affairs commission and staff also began to enter the debate over a United States-Canada free trade agreement. "Free Trade: At What Cost?" – which raised discussion questions – was published in June. This was followed in 1988 by work on an analysis of the possible impact of United States-Canada free trade on developing countries – a study published by the Canadian Catholic Organization for Development and Peace in July 1988.[128]

The social action commission and office maintained their threefold focus during 1989, 1990 and 1991: faith/justice teaching, justice in Canada, and justice in the world. Social problems persisted, too: unemployment, crises in the fishing and farming sectors, neglect of native rights, the Goods and Services Tax. Also, two major new projects emerged. One that held great hope for local response but lost momentum during 1991 was the "Work and Solidarity" project. The commission tried to launch a local study of "the crisis of work" in each diocese, putting together empirical findings and the principles outlined by Pope John Paul II in his 1981 encyclical on work. A poor response to it illustrated once again the difficulty of attempts at national pastoral animation in all dioceses. In contrast, commission and staff were fully successful in preparing the major theme study for the 1991 plenary meeting to celebrate the one hundredth anniversary of Leo XIII's encyclical, *Rerum Novarum*. Indeed, the occasion was equally a celebration of fifty years of CCCB social teaching.

V. RELIGIOUS EDUCATION

The beginning of the Canadian Catechism is recorded prosaically in a 1966 CCC minute: "At a joint meeting of the French and English Episcopal Committees on Religious Education, both the French and English versions of *Viens vers le Père* and *Come to the Father* were approved in principle as a 'Canadian' Catechism."[129]

A project of this kind had been on the minds of the bishops for years. Meeting in Quebec City in 1938, five years before organizing themselves as an episcopal conference, the bishops had noted that "the problem of obtaining certain uniformity in the Catechism Text Books was taken up at the last Council and a committee appointed to study the matter without however any tangible results."[130] Again in 1954, failure was recorded. The Commission on Education, Press, Radio and Cinema told the CCC plenary meeting that "The suggestion to have a uniform or the same catechism both in French and English for the whole of Canada is excellent. But to find a catechism which would be satisfactory and accepted by all seems impossible. For the time being the Baltimore Catechism is suggested by this commission as the more practical." The General Assembly took no action in this matter, the minutes add.[131]

It was no accident that the 1966 agreement on *Come to the Father* was announced just weeks after the conclusion of Vatican II. Even before the Council, along with movements to renew the liturgy and promote the study and use of Holy Scripture, there had been organized efforts to update the teaching of religion, integrating the latest theological insights with the findings of modern psychology about how people learn at various age levels.

Meanwhile, the social context for religious education was changing in Canada. Constitutionally, education was a provincial responsibility. Across the country, as the 1960s dawned, the situation of Catholic schools in which religion could be taught varied markedly. The bishops, as official teachers of the faith, were accepting a real challenge when, as in 1938, they took up the problem "of obtaining certain uniformity" in catechism textbooks. The Quebec bishops faced special difficulties as the Quiet Revolution of the 1960s began to sweep away the province's Church-run schools. To meet these needs, the Quebec bishops established the Office catéchistique provincial (OCP). The OCP, in turn, launched the research and development project that resulted in the *Viens vers le Père* program that was central to the 1966 Canadian Catechism agreement.

The bishops of the rest of Canada came to the same agreement after exploring the Confraternity of Christian Doctrine (CCD) as a way to renew catechetics. The CCD program was appealing from several points of view. First, it had the aura of highest Church approval, as the "venerable archconfraternity" had been established in Rome. In 1905, Pope Pius X had requested that it be established in every parish, and Canon 711 in the 1917 Code of Canon Law incorporated his directive. At a more practical level, the confraternity had taken root in the United States, and U.S. aid, including books and field workers, was available to Canadian bishops.

During the years 1925-1935, the CCD made its appearance in Canada, especially in western dioceses. With U.S. aid, five regional conferences were held – in Saskatoon (1950), Nelson (1951), Edmonton (1952), Regina (1953) and Calgary (1954). Then, in 1954, U.S. aid was withdrawn. Concern had developed that, without an official invitation to enter Canada, promoters from the U.S. might be accused of trespassing. There was no Canadian national CCD centre to issue such an invitation.

Serious tension developed between some English-sector bishops and the CCC over the issue. In 1953, the English section of the Commission on Catholic Action and the Lay Apostolate, led by Bishop Francis P. Carroll of Calgary and Bishop Malcolm MacEachern of Charlottetown, began to recommend that the CCD be established nationally by the bishops' conference. The 1958 plenary agreed to the formation of a CCD committee with English and French sections made up of three bishops each. The committee was asked to propose a constitution for study at the 1959 plenary, to be followed up thereafter by the commission on education.

The minutes of the 1959 plenary meeting record the annoyance expressed by Carroll and MacEachern. Why, after the 1958 plenary, they asked, had the CCC board called for still more study of a national CCD? The necessary study had been done by their commission prior to the 1958 plenary. The decision at that plenary to switch responsibility for the CCD from their commission to the commission for education was no cause for delay. It was interesting to note, they added, "that the project for a National Confraternity has shifted back and forth between the Episcopal Commissions on Education and Catholic Action since 1953, and that the project, since that date, has appeared six times in the minutes of the Canadian Catholic Conference without any results."

Carroll and MacEachern concluded their report with two proposals. If the CCC did not wish a national CCD, nothing seemed to prevent interested bishops from organizing one for themselves. Also, if the CCC constitution were ever revised, "some consideration should be given to the inclusion of the Chairmen of the various Episcopal Commissions on the Administrative Board in order that the latter may thoroughly understand the opinions and decisions of the Commissions."[132] This latter question – how best to link the episcopal commissions with the CCC's board and executive committee – would be studied for every CCC restructuring, including the latest in 1989.

Carroll and MacEachern did not drop the CCD question after their reproachful 1959 report. The minutes of the 1960 CCC annual meeting record that their commission once more requested that a national CCD organization "be implemented without delay." On February 1, 1961, the board decided to appoint a bishop as national director of the English section of the CCD. Bishop Carroll, the minutes added, "will be asked to suggest a nomination for this office if he feels he cannot accept same himself." The next public event on the matter was the April 7, 1961, announcement that the CCC board had named Bishop Emmett Doyle of Nelson to be the national English CCD director.[133]

Doyle moved quickly. He soon informed the bishops that a national CCD office had been opened at the CCC secretariat in Ottawa. Temporary arrangements had been made for Romeo Maione to act as CCD secretary. Maione, after six years in Brussels as international president of the Young Christian Workers, was back in Canada as assistant to Peter Nearing in the CCC's social action office.[134] Then, on June 25, 1962, Rev. Gerald Fitzpatrick of Calgary was announced as the first executive director of the

CCD's national Canadian office.[135] Minutes of a meeting between Doyle and Fitzpatrick just over a year later show how ideas were evolving. "The name 'Confraternity' will likely be dropped," it was noted. "The important thing is that we are all concerned about the same problem – religious instruction. The French bishops and educators will be more interested in a national office if not restricted to confraternity."[136]

During the CCC plenary meeting in Rome in the fall of 1963, the CCD's name was changed. It was now referred to as an office of religious education. Interested English and French bishops were asked to confer further about the office. On the final day of the plenary, Doyle and Bishop Gérard-Marie Coderre of St. Jean, Quebec, won approval for budgets of $12,000 each for English and French offices of religious education. The French sector's Office national de l'éducation chrétienne was established in July 1964. Its temporary director was Abbé Robert Gaudet of Quebec's Office catéchistique provincial (OCP). Abbé Claude Michaud of Edmundston, New Brunswick, was named full-time director in January 1966.

The first-year catechism, *Viens vers le Père*, was published in 1964 by the OCP in Montreal. By September the next year, an English translation was being prepared, and the OCP was in contact with a publisher to print and distribute it.[137] Thus, the French and English texts that the CCC approved in 1966 as a basis for a Canadian Catechism were the product and property of the Quebec bishops' office.

The decision to launch the Canadian Catechism resulted in a burst of creativity similar to that surrounding the production of new vernacular texts for the liturgy. Basilian Rev. David Megel came to the English National Office of Religious Education (NORE) in Ottawa as Fitzpatrick's assistant. A committee of ten catechists collaborated with the Quebec office to adapt English versions for the first three grades. Rev. Martin Jeffery of the Timmins diocese worked with the French team in creating material for grades 4, 5 and 6, which was later revised and adapted for the English version. [138]

Rev. Dennis Murphy of the Sault Ste. Marie diocese was named in April 1967 to a three-year term as Fitzpatrick's successor as director of NORE. Towards the end of 1967, Martin Jeffery was named assistant director. In March 1970, the commission recommended that the office needed four full-time specialists to collaborate with the permanent staff of sixteen at the OCP, who were "justifiably requesting further collaboration." NORE's continuing growth was assured by the report that, for the first time, the fiscal year 1970 had ended with an excess of revenues over expenses.[139]

The question of revenue led to tense and protracted negotiations between the OCP and NORE. The original agreement, signed in mid-1966 by Bishop Coderre for the OCP and Bishop Doyle for NORE, was not a detailed legal document. After the bishops had reached general agreement, others began to define the fine points. Negotiations continued to the end of 1968, when a three-year agreement was reached.[140] The OCP was renamed Office de catechèse du Quebec (OCQ); in June 1970, the OCQ made known the changes it wanted in a renegotiated contract. After meetings in January and February 1971, the OCQ-NORE negotiations seemed deadlocked. Questions of copyright and royalties were in dispute. Finally, by October 1972, an agreement to last until June 1977 was in place.[141]

Midway through the 1972 contract period, both English and French versions were subjected to extensive content evaluations. The evaluations indicated that "the orientation of the *Come to the Father* series is basically sound, and in conformity with the renewal required by Vatican II." At their September 1974 plenary meeting, the bishops agreed to retain a unified catechetical program across the country, reaffirmed their 1966 endorsement of the *Come to the Father* series and officially granted it priority for use in Canada.

When the five-year 1972 contract ended, the CCC Publications Service had developed to the point that it could be the successful bidder for the new contract, to include both production and distribution of NORE's publications. Rev. Peter Sanders, by then NORE's director, could rejoice "that the English Canadian Catechetical program has come home to the Conference."[142] Since then, NORE's growth has been constant. A 1985 market study led to the decision the following year to expand into the production of English catechetical materials for classes from kindergarten to the end of high school, as well as materials for adult religious education.

Because the production of French materials has been centred in the OCQ, the life cycle of the CCC's French catechetical office has been quite different from NORE's. Established in 1964, it was directed full-time from 1966 by Claude Michaud. He worked to promote catechetical renewal in francophone dioceses outside Quebec. The office was a main channel for reporting the needs of these dioceses to the OCQ, where new French materials were being produced. Then, in 1974, the office was one of those that were suppressed when the CCC was restructured. Responsibility for catechetical animation in the francophone dioceses outside Quebec, and for liaison with the OCQ, was assigned to one member of the six-member CCC Pastoral Team, developed in 1974. This responsibility was assumed, in turn, by Rev. Léonard Rochon of Ottawa and Rev. Jean-Noël Gagné of Chicoutimi.

Growing dissatisfaction with this arrangement on the part of the bishops it was supposed to be serving reached a peak ten years later. They complained they were getting only part-time service because the team member assigned for French religious education also had other responsibilities. At the 1985 CCCB plenary meeting, it was therefore agreed "that at the national level, in particular for francophones outside of Quebec, a CCCB employee be assigned full-time, and recognized by all the bishops, as responsible for organizing, gathering information, and fostering collaboration and/or concerted efforts on behalf of religious education, animating diocesan and regional personnel if necessary." A review after three years was also specified. The eventual outcome of the review was that in 1991 the office was, in effect, restored to its 1966 status, with Brother Jean-Claude Éthier as director.

VI. PERMANENT DEACONS

One of the decisions made at Vatican II was to restore the order of permanent deacon. The term "permanent deacon" was used to distinguish this order from those who are deacons as a step towards ordination as priests. In the Latin Church, a deacon can be assigned to read the Gospel and preach, administer solemn baptisms, bless marriages, bring Viaticum to the dying, officiate at funerals and burials, and perform certain other pastoral tasks. Vatican II empowered bishops' conferences to decide, with papal approval, whether to name permanent deacons. Deacons might be married men, "provided they be of more mature age." They also could be "suitable young men, for whom, however, the law of celibacy must remain in force."[143] The final Council vote came during the 1964 third session. In June 1967, Pope Paul VI published norms and procedures to guide any conference that might wish to proceed.

The Canadian bishops discussed the question during their 1966 fall plenary meeting. At the beginning of the following January, the administrative board set up a special committee to study the possibility of restoring the permanent diaconate for Canada.[144] Bishops Remi De Roo and Albert Sanschagrin were named its co-chairmen. Sanschagrin soon afterwards was invited to a meeting of seventeen bishops in Rome to discuss the final draft of the Pope's proposed norms and procedures, which was published four months later. Sanschagrin recalls that when Paul VI met them, he said that he thought it a very happy development to have diocesan bishops working on the draft of his text. It might well be done for other texts, the Pope added – but, as far as Sanschagrin knows, it never was.[145]

During the CCC's plenary meeting in Winnipeg, the fall of 1968, the De Roo-Sanschagrin committee reported. It proposed that the permanent diaconate be restored in Canada with both married and unmarried deacons. The vote was fifty-seven to three in favour, with another seven voting yes with amendments. The committee then proposed a gradual start, "by beginning perhaps with some pilot projects in a few dioceses with special needs, and under the guidance of some Conference body such as the commission for clergy."[146] Pope Paul VI's approval was given on January 20, 1969.[147] In November 1969, at the CCC plenary meeting, a report from the office for the clergy was accepted and the bishops received the first draft of "Guidelines for the Restoration of the Permanent Diaconate in Canada," which was prepared by the office. In the following years, permanent deacons were ordained in about half of the dioceses in Canada.

VII. ROLE OF WOMEN IN THE CHURCH

The first recorded discussion by Canadian bishops about the role of women appears in the minutes of the 1938 meeting of the episcopacy at Quebec City, five years before the CCC was established. One topic concerned the discipline of seminarians and priests. "Concerning women working in seminaries," it is recorded, "the bishops unanimously felt that lay women must never work in seminaries, and religious only in accordance with the prudent regulations of the Holy See." As for the use of automobiles, it was added, a priest was "strictly forbidden to travel alone in an automobile with one woman, and also forbidden to sit in the same seat with a woman."

When he went to the microphone in the Vatican Council hall on October 28, 1964, to speak about the dignity of the human person, Bishop Coderre of St. Jean, Quebec, took a different approach. "The Church in this unique period of her history," he urged, "should invite men, and especially Christians, to do all they can so that women may attain their proper place in the life of human society and in the life of the Church." The Council was discussing the draft text on the Church in the modern world. Coderre spoke on behalf of forty Canadian bishops. The Council text, he urged, should be stronger about two affirmations: that woman "has a unique and necessary role in the realization of God's plan," and "that without the real contribution of woman, human society and even the kingdom of God could not attain either its perfection or fullness, and that mankind would be unfaithful to God's very plan for it."[148]

Time moved on. In 1971, the CCC was wondering how to react to the report of the Royal Commission on the Status of Women and to related general questions about the role of women. Those planning the April plenary decided to invite a group of women "representing various groups and personal positions" to come to Ottawa. It was suggested that they meet for two days to discuss subjects of their own choice and to prepare for a workshop with the bishops, in English and French sectors. A questionnaire was sent out, seeking suggestions about whom to invite and what to discuss. Mary Matthews of Toronto and Hélène Poliquin of Ottawa were asked to analyze the results. The most insistent brief came from a group in Edmonton. "Declare, clearly and unequivocally, that women are full and equal members of the Church," they recommended. "Make strong, immediate representations to the Vatican, asking that all discriminatory barriers against women be removed."

Thirty-two anglophone and twenty-six francophone women responded to the invitation to come to Ottawa for two days of discussion among themselves prior to the April 1971 CCC plenary meeting. They met in small groups by language and in bilingual forums to decide what they wanted to say in later workshop sessions with CCC members. Their presentations to the bishops differed somewhat by linguistic sector, but all endorsed similar recommendations about Church and society. Two of their proposals about the Church echoed the concerns of the Edmonton women. Others called for the ordination of qualified women for the ministry, the presence of qualified women on all bodies dealing with matters that concern all Church members, and measures to ensure "that the attitude of the clergy towards women, sexuality, and marriage, respects the inherent dignity of women." Regarding society, they endorsed all the recommendations of the Royal Commission of the Status of Women that dealt with disadvantaged women.[149] The bishops listened to the proposals and discussed them with the women.

Formal CCC reactions came later that year. The September plenary meeting voted to accept the proposal that at the Synod "the CCC representatives recommend to the Holy Father the immediate setting up of a commission made up of bishops, priests, lay people, both men and women, and religious to study in depth the question of ministries for women in the Church."[150]

Speaking in the Synod just three weeks later, when the priesthood was being discussed, Cardinal Flahiff of Winnipeg presented the CCC recommendation. The specific topic that day was the diversification of ministry, "but no one has raised the question of the possibility of a ministry of women in the Church," Flahiff pointed out. "Are new or changing ministries to be limited to men?" Everyone knew the standard answer to that: "Ministry is a man's work. Let the women...be faithful and obedient servants." But as far as he knew, Flahiff continued, "there is no dogmatic objection to reconsidering the whole question today." Vatican II had made "categorical statements against all discrimination against women in the Church," but many women and others "find that no notable effort has been made to implement this teaching.... We would be failing in our duty towards more than half of the Church if we did not at least speak of the subject."[151]

The CCC board returned to the question five months later. At their March 1972 plenary meeting, the bishops called for "a committee of about twelve people – bishops, experts, religious and lay people" to prepare a working document for diocesan and regional study on the role of women in the Church. The board specified that the committee should also "try to take further steps regarding this question in special follow-up to the recent Synod and the 1971 Plenary discussions."[152]

In Canada, as elsewhere, continuing discussion of this topic was influenced by two subsequent initiatives of the Holy See. On August 15, 1972, Paul VI issued *Ministeria Quaedam*, which reformed the Latin Church's minor orders – steps prior to diaconate and priesthood. It also specified that official installation into the ministries of lector and acolyte remained reserved to men. In May of the following year, the Holy See's International Study Group on the Role of Women was established – with the constraint that it should do no research on the possibility of conferring sacred orders on women.

Early in 1974 the CCC received French and English reports from the members of its study committee on the role of women in the Church. The French report urged that the study be continued by professionals and extended to matters not strictly related to women's questions. The English report reiterated some previous recommendations made by women and asked that the study be continued at the level of the four pastoral regions into which CCC members were organizing themselves – West, Ontario,

Quebec and Atlantic. The May 15, 1974, meeting of the CCC board decided that the study of the role of women in Church and society and of the various recommendations should be continued at the regional level.[153] Some of these concerns were reflected in the CCC's September 1974 declaration for International Women's Year.[154]

In 1975, the Ontario and Western regions carried out extensive studies on the role of women. The archdioceses of Toronto and Montreal reported that study groups were at work. The April CCC plenary, in turn, took up one aspect of the question. As reported to Cardinal Jean Villot, Vatican Secretary of State, by Archbishop Fortier, CCC president, in a May 15, 1975, letter, "The Canadian Conference of Catholic Bishops recommends to the Holy See that the non-ordained ministries foreseen for men in *Ministeria Quaedam* be extended to include women."

The October 1975 plenary took up the role of women once more. Emmett Carter, who was elected president at that meeting, conveyed its conclusions to Villot in a February 23, 1976, letter. Carter said that the meeting had unanimously directed him to say that the Canadian bishops "strongly support the Vatican Study Commission in its efforts to enhance participation of women in the work of the Church." The CCC also supported the study commission's call for the appointment of women as members and consultors of Vatican offices, educational efforts to change thinking about women's roles, and further studies. Carter also told Villot that the CCC was launching a study of the number of women in policy-making roles at various levels of the Church in Canada. Canadian liturgists, he added, had been asked to design ceremonies that dioceses might use to install women in non-ordained ministries, and further studies were being encouraged. The 1972 CCC committee, meanwhile, "continues to work at the regional and local levels and has met an encouraging and willing response from the faithful in the Church in Canada," he reported.[155]

Less than a month later, Carter was in Rome with Archbishop Gilles Ouellet of Rimouski for the annual visit to Vatican officials by the CCC president and vice-president. Informing the Canadian bishops about the visit later, Carter summarized the conversation with Pope Paul VI. Carter and Ouellet had raised the question of the involvement of women in the apostolic mission of the Church and

> pointed out the great concern of the Canadian bishops in this connection. As we had done at other interviews [during the visit], we expressed the view that the idea of the ordaining of women to the

> priesthood was not a pressing matter in Canada, even though the question was much discussed. To our surprise, the Pope notified us that a document was in preparation on the subject and that it was near completion. We immediately expressed our great concern. In particular, we insisted that it was of the utmost importance that the document, whatever its nature, be based on sound theological arguments and that it not be published until it had received a fairly wide consultation. We had already made this point with Archbishop Hamer, although we had not been notified that the document was far advanced in preparation. In view of this situation, we humbly but urgently requested His Holiness to make sure that the bishops of the world had a chance to see the draft and to make recommendations. We pointed at all of the difficulties of having a document of such explosive possibilities appear in public without the bishops having had an opportunity to express an opinion on its contents. We stressed the difficultly with which we were faced when the media approached us and asked us if we had been consulted when, as sometimes was the case, we were obliged to respond in the negative. The Holy Father seemed quite interested in our suggestions and made a note to that effect.[156]

Within a month, the Vatican would receive another indication of where the Canadian bishops stood collectively on the matter of ministries for women. In January 1976, the Apostolic Pro-Nuncio in Ottawa asked the CCC for information about how Paul VI's *Ministeria Quaedam* was being applied in Canada. The CCC board discussed this and consulted with the four regional assemblies of bishops. Emmett Carter sent Archbishop Angelo Palmas a reply in mid-April. "A point which is a matter of grave concern to us is that these ministries not be limited to male candidates," the CCC president reported. "I am directed by the Administrative Board to underline very strongly this feeling of ours, namely that it is difficult to implement the institution of ministries of lector and acolyte as long as this institution is restricted to men. As a result of this difficultly, bishops are not implementing *Ministeria Quaedam* for as long as it continues to bar women from these (and other) ministries."[157]

In July 1976, each Canadian bishop received a long CCC questionnaire about the participation of women in official Church pastoral work in Canada. It was the first step in implementing the decision of the 1975 bishops' plenary meeting to find out how many women were involved in Church policy-making roles. The survey was completed a year later and was published in 1979.

While the survey was still in progress, the Vatican's *Declaration on the Question of the Admission of Women to the Ministerial Priesthood*, about which Carter and Ouellet had spoken to Paul VI, was made public on January 27, 1977. There had been no further consultation. However, the bishops had had sufficient advance notice that Carter, as CCCB president (the organization had changed its name from CCC to CCCB on January 1, 1977), was able to issue a statement the same day as the text was published in Rome. The Vatican's conclusion was that the Church, "in fidelity to the example of the Lord, does not consider herself authorized to admit women to Priestly Ministry." Carter cited this statement and analyzed it briefly. "Careful perusal of the document," he said in the name of the CCCB, "strips away much of what might be considered as a rejection of the aspirations of some very devoted women and which could be interpreted as a down-playing of women in general. We do not consider that such is the case and the document opens up many of the horizons which need to be explored in terms of recognizing the true equality of women without, at the same time denying that men and women have different roles to play." He specifically approved the insistence in the text that ordination is not a right of anyone, man or woman, and that the priesthood is not a superior position.

> Finally we wish to state that the Canadian Bishops will pursue their study of the role of women in the Church with even greater interest. Already many ministerial and other roles are opening to women in our midst. Our attempt will be to emphasize and promote the true equality of women, to encourage their positive and special gifts in the leadership of the Church and in the spreading of the Kingdom without necessarily postulating an identity of roles.[158]

In January 1978, the board approved the publication of the survey results and in March, the executive committee accepted proposals for further action. The CCCB commission for the laity was asked to seek a better means to continue the dialogue with women at the regional level. It was also suggested that the president "write a letter to all Conference members recalling the Conference commitment to strengthen the participation of women in diocesan and parish life." The letter was sent the following month.[159]

The survey results showed that almost two-thirds (64.3 per cent) of all Church office directors in Canada were priests. Women directors, religious and lay, made up twenty-seven per cent and men (priests and lay) seventy-three per cent. When office directors and assistants were combined, women reached thirty-six per cent.[160]

Bishop Robert Lebel again took up women's issues when he addressed the 1980 Synod of Bishops. "The state of submission and oppression to which women are subjected in the world constitutes a sinful situation, the result of original sin...and, therefore, something to correct," he began. Vatican II had proclaimed full recognition of the dignity of women and equality with their male partners in the Christian family, he noted. "How can we bring the Church as a whole into accord with the 'Domestic Church' [the family] on this point?" What women want, Lebel told his fellow bishops, "is to see in the Church a serious desire to have them assume responsibilities. Certain negative attitudes in matters of no great importance are still very telling. Why, for example, the desire to keep women and girls far removed from the altar? I grant that it is not cruet-carrying that will enable women to attain their full religious development, but it is a serious matter to them that they are denied even that.... We have a long road to travel in answering our sisters' legitimate desire to employ all their faculties in the service of the Church," Lebel concluded. "We must, of course, avoid embarking on futile projects and must not arouse false hopes. But we must have a basic, positive attitude toward their demands...."[161]

The next January, the CCCB secretariat sent a questionnaire to some seventy women across Canada who had participated in previous projects. It invited replies in the form of stories about women's experiences in the Church. A media release invited others to participate. In March, eight respondents, selected by region, met with CCCB staff and prepared recommendations for further action in light of the replies received. The formation of a committee to study Christian feminism, and a major discussion at a CCCB plenary meeting of the role of women in the Church, were two of the proposals. At its June 1982 meeting, the CCCB board set up an ad hoc committee of five women from across the country, two women staff members and two bishops, Raymond Saint-Gelais of Nicolet and James MacDonald of Charlottetown. The committee was asked to report back in a year.

Meanwhile, at the 1983 Synod of Bishops on reconciliation, Archbishop Louis-Albert Vachon of Quebec discussed male-female relations as one important aspect of the Synod's theme. He warned that appeals by the Church to the world for the advancement of women were "on the point of losing all impact, unless the recognition of women as full members becomes, simultaneously, a reality within the Church itself." Reflecting the survey process then under way, he told the Synod that "in Canada, an ever-increasing number of women are speaking out and revealing their thoughts and feelings. The dualist vision of flesh-and-spirit and the sexist prejudices resulting from it have strongly marked their past and continue to mark their present." He presented the recommendation of the Canadian bishops: "Let there be organized structures for dialogue which serve as meeting places for mutual exchange and recognition, and effective implementation of new bonds of equality between men and women in the Church."[162]

A major discussion of women's issues took place at the 1984 CCCB plenary meeting. It centred on twelve recommendations by the ad hoc committee established in 1982. Their proposals were presented in the form of a draft study kit for parish use. Media coverage of the meeting focused on two incidents. The women members of the ad hoc committee had been invited to make opening presentations to a plenary session and then take part in workshop discussions. However, when the formal debate in the plenary session began, Bishop John Sherlock, the CCCB's president, insisted on observance of the CCCB bylaw that participation in plenary discussion be limited to bishops. The women committee members, he held, had been heard in their initial presentation and in the small groups. This ruling made media headlines, as did the objection of a small group of Ontario bishops to what they said was unacceptable feminist content in the proposed kit.

In the end, the plenary recommended that the kit be published after some revisions. After it appeared in June 1985, it continued to have a high place on CCCB agendas after a group called Women for Life, Faith and Family publicly dissociated themselves from it. They asked the CCCB to approve and distribute an alternate kit that they had prepared. Bishops of the CCCB commission for ministries and associations met with the group in February 1986 and reviewed the women's documents. The bishops decided that while the group's kit might prove helpful to members of the group, the CCCB kit was "the more appropriate instrument to offer local groups at this time for the limited objective sought." The March meeting of the CCCB permanent council reaffirmed the 1984 plenary recommendations, including pastoral use of the kit, with the understanding that it might be adapted to particular diocesan situations. Subsequently, some 15,000 copies of the kit were sold for use across the country, in English and French.

In June 1986, a brief by the CCCB's social affairs commission urged the parliamentary task force on child care to support a high-quality, fully funded, universally accessible, non-compulsory, comprehensive child care system for Canada. "Our study of the situation," the CCCB brief said, "has led us to the inescapable conclusion that Canadians are facing a monumental child care crisis and that concerted government action is urgently required." It specifically argued that such a recommendation was fully in accord with traditional Church teaching about family values.[163]

During preparations in Canada for the 1987 Synod of Bishops on the role of laity in Church and society, women's issues were again raised, as reflected by the October 9, 1987, Synod intervention of Bishop Jean-Guy Hamelin. He called the affirmative movement of women "an outstanding fact of the social evolution in our day...as massive as the industrial revolution in the last century." In Pope John XXIII's language, it was a "sign of the times."

Hamelin outlined a five-point program to the Synod. "We need to find practical ways," he said, "to recall and recognize the contribution of Christian women in every area of vital importance to society." Likewise, he said, the full participation of women in Church life should be recognized in law as well as in fact. "Their voice is essential to the sign-value of the Church as Sacrament and to the witness which the Church is commanded to bear." Third, said Hamelin, the canonical obstacles that block access of lay men and women to positions of responsibility that do not require ordination should be moved aside. Similarly, he added, the rules that keep women away from the altar should be rescinded, and women and men should be made equally eligible for installation and service as acolytes and lectors.

The question of ordination of women "remains a controversial one in our communities," Hamelin continued. "But we observe that the reasoning used so far to explain the reservation of sacred Orders to men has not seemed convincing, especially to young people." The permanent diaconate could represent a new opportunity, he noted, and proposed that particular churches concerned about this question should establish reflection groups including both sexes. "The full participation of women in the life of Church and society is not a new idea," Hamelin concluded. "It is the original intuition of Genesis. According to the heart of God humanity is not humanity without the mutual presence of man and woman to each other, without the original covenant between them."

As the 1990s began, CCCB initiatives on women's issues centred on encouraging inclusive language and opposing violence against women. The bishops on the CCCB Pastoral Team issued a pastoral statement on inclusive language in August 1989. Then a twenty-two-page set of workshops on inclusive language, for use by small discussion groups, was prepared by the Pastoral Team staff and published in April 1990. The same group prepared a sixty-two-page set of workshop outlines on nine human life issues, three of them – pornography, prostitution and violence – arising from the concerns of women. Violence against women was studied in detail in the June 13, 1991, statement "To Live Without Fear," by the CCCB's permanent council. "A healthy and creative society cannot tolerate any form of violence," the statement said. "When this violence is based on the erroneous and insidious premise that men are entitled to dominate women, it is particularly abhorrent and dangerous." The CCCB president, Archbishop Marcel Gervais of Ottawa, was one of eleven leaders of Canadian Churches who signed a March 27, 1992, submission to the Canadian Panel on Violence Against Women. The brief included a list of actions that Churches could take, along with recommendations for government action. "We recognize the need to ensure that the victims of abuse know that their suffering is neither trivialized nor ignored by church and society," the text concluded. "We also recognize an obligation to help abusers take responsibility for their actions and to be truly converted from such action."[164]

The latest stage of the CCCB's work on women's issues was the October 30-November 1, 1992, consultation of more than forty women from all parts of the country. They were representatives of a diocesan network of people working on such issues as women and poverty, violence against women, new reproductive technologies and inclusive language. Their orientation towards the future was indicated by their discussion of means to strengthen the network of diocesan women's groups and to enhance collaboration on women's issues between the CCCB and the dioceses.

VIII. LAY APOSTOLATE AND CATHOLIC ACTION

Two signs can be noted of the early concern of the Canadian bishops' conference about the role of the laity in the Church. A commission for the lay apostolate was one of the first to be set up when the conference was organized. As well, the lay apostolate was one of the topics on which the Canadian bishops intervened in a concerted way at Vatican II. Yet a national office for the laity was short-lived and the effort to establish a Canadian Pastoral Council as a national mechanism for regular, formal lay participation in the work and concerns of the bishops' conference was not successful, as will be seen later.

When the conference was organized, the francophone dioceses already had an immense lay apostolate structure. Catholic Action was an organized movement in itself and separate specialized movements existed for trade unions, employers, students, young workers, farm women and many others. Each movement had its own chaplains, and the chaplains had their own organizations for personal development and support.

Many English bishops wanted to emulate all this in their own dioceses. The February 1944 study days in Toronto, discussed earlier, were an example of early efforts made to transplant the Catholic Action movement into the anglophone milieu. In 1959, the CCC authorized a budget for the bishops to prepare a national organization for Catholic Action and the lay apostolate in English Canada. The Catholic Action and Lay Apostolate commission, English section, found the organizing task difficult. "There are so many quasi-Catholic Action units in the different dioceses across the country," they reported, "and many of them overlap in their objectives and activities." As well, they added that "the distinction between...Social Action and Catholic Action does not seem to be clearly defined."[165] Four regional conferences on the lay apostolate were held in English dioceses in 1963. The bishops were assisted in this by Romeo Maione, who did lay apostolate work as assistant to the director of the social action office. Then, in the fall of 1963, during their plenary meeting in Rome, the bishops approved an English lay apostolate office in Ottawa. Named first director was Tom Johnston of Montreal, who had just finished a term as national president of the Young Christian Workers. He was joined in Ottawa in 1966 by Rev. John Carley of Montreal, as national chaplain of the office. Their mandate was to promote and support lay apostolate initiatives.

Only two Catholic Action movements ever had much success in English dioceses: the Young Christian Workers and the Christian Family Movement. A high point of activity for the CCC's English lay apostolate office was the 1968-1970 effort to form a national pastoral council. After the failure at the end of 1970 to launch such a council immediately, the laity office was one of those designated to continue the effort, but nothing came of it. The office was phased out in the 1973 reorganization of the secretariat.

No French Catholic Action office was established at the CCC secretariat. However, in 1964, the CCC agreed to integrate into its budget the operating costs of the Montreal secretariat of Action catholique canadienne.

This arrangement ended after three years. Then, late in 1968, the French sector commission launched a major study of the participation of laity in the Church and the future of Catholic Action. When this study – the Dumont Commission – completed its work, its recommendations were directed mainly to the Quebec bishops and not the CCC. Meanwhile, from 1967 to 1973, the CCC subsidized fifteen specialized Catholic Action movements. This was one of the financial burdens that led to the CCC's quarter-million-dollar deficit in the early 1970s. With the end of these subsidies in 1973, therefore, neither French nor English sectors of Catholic Action had a CCC office or its equivalent. However, when the Pastoral Team was organized in 1974, one staff member was designated to be responsible for matters relating to the lay apostolate. The CCCB continued to have an episcopal commission for lay questions, designated after 1990 as the commission for relations with associations of priests, religious and laity across the country.

IX. DEVELOPMENT AND PEACE

For many Canadian Church members, the Canadian Catholic Organization for Development and Peace (CCODP) has been this country's most successful instance of collaboration between bishops and laity.

Development and Peace – to use the term by which most people came to know CCODP – began at a time of great effervescence in Canadian Church life. It was a time, too, of high public awareness of poverty in Canada and the world. The bishops had just returned from Vatican II, which ended in December 1965 with acceptance of the *Constitution on the Church in the Modern World* as one of its final acts. It pledged the Church to solidarity with "the grief and anguish of the men of our time, especially of those who are poor or afflicted in any way."[166] The bishops and CCC staff were trying to spread ideas from the Council to clergy, religious and lay groups across the country. As a result of four years of Council encounters with fellow pastors from around the globe, the bishops had a heightened awareness of the problems of the developing nations. In Canada, ecumenical collaboration was increasing. Within a few months it would give rise to two highly visible projects: the Christian Pavilion at Montreal's Expo '67 and the 1968 Poverty Conference, also in Montreal. In addition, as the CCC was completing its process for launching Development and Peace, Pope Paul VI published his powerful encyclical *On the Development of Peoples*.

Jesuit Father Gordon George, who became English general secretary of the CCC just as Vatican II ended, had a meeting early in 1966 with Archbishop Philip Pocock of Toronto. George urged that the Canadian Church should have an organization with the specific mission of motivating Canadian Catholics to give more aid to the poor in developing countries. They agreed that to get the question to the agenda of the next CCC meeting, Pocock would write a letter asking for discussion of an aid fund.[167]

If George was expecting to get Pocock's May 6, 1966, letter, he and Charles Mathieu, French general secretary, were surprised when the day's mail also brought an almost identical letter dated May 5 from Cardinal Paul-Émile Léger of Montreal. Both letters noted the success of an "Aid to India Fund" that the Canadian bishops had launched in response to Paul VI's appeal after his visit to India. Pocock asked that the next CCC board meeting discuss the feasibility of a "Canadian Fund for the Relief of Hunger."[168] Léger suggested that the twenty-five-year-old Montreal diocesan anti-poverty organization known as Gold Cross be transformed into a national interdiocesan project.[169]

Prompted by the two letters, the general secretaries set up a process for study of the proposed fund. On July 15, 1966, fourteen men met with George and Mathieu in Ottawa "with a view to preparing some suggestions for the consideration of the Hierarchy regarding the possible establishment of some kind of permanent foreign aid institution under the aegis of the Catholic Church in Canada."[170] They agreed that there should be such a national Catholic organization. Its three aims should be public education on the responsibilities of Canadians to the less wealthy, emergency relief, and aid to development programs. It should provide a high degree of lay involvement and relate to other Churches and to public programs. However, even with information about similar initiatives elsewhere in the Church,[171] the meeting could not decide whether to transform Gold Cross or start something new, what to call it ("Canadaide" was suggested), how to involve laity, and whether two organizations might serve best –one for education and the other for development aid and relief. The meeting ended with the naming of a committee to prepare a report and set up another consultation in September if the general secretaries deemed it useful.[172]

Soon afterwards, George received a letter from Robert M. Bedolfe on behalf of a group that called itself the Toronto Laymen's Committee on World Poverty. Bedolfe wrote of a July 28 meeting at the Catholic

Information Centre in Toronto that had brought together representatives of labour, management and various Catholic organizations. They had unanimously agreed to write to the CCC to urge a Canada-wide weekend conference to study world poverty "and search out the best means for setting up a Canadian Catholic agency." Bedolfe and R. Helling of Windsor were present when the CCC group reconvened on September 19 in Ottawa.[173]

During the October 1966 CCC plenary meeting, twenty-seven bishops attended an "optional day" session to discuss the proposed new aid organization. The topic arose on the plenary agenda as a proposal for a "National Fund to Help Developing Countries." On a motion by Bishop Albert Sanschagrin apostolic administrator of Amos, seconded by Archbishop Martin M. Johnson of Vancouver, the meeting agreed unanimously that a "national relief fund" be set up. The president was authorized to set up a committee to launch the fund as soon as possible. Laity were to be consulted and involved from the beginning.[174]

Archbishop Joseph-Aurèle Plourde of Ottawa, who was chairman of this committee, gave a progress report to the March 1967 CCC board meeting. The meeting unanimously accepted a proposed constitution for the "National Fund to Help Developing Countries." The committee was authorized to proceed to incorporation. Plourde reported to the CCC plenary meeting a month later that agreement had been reached on a procedure for electing the nineteen lay members of the first board of governors. They would be the petitioners for incorporation. As for the two episcopal members, the English sector had elected Archbishop Pocock, and the French, Plourde himself.[175]

As of the June 9, 1967, meeting of the CCC board, the new organization was on its own. It was now officially called Canadaide, Plourde told the board. The work of the committee he had headed was finished. The minutes record that he "spoke enthusiastically" of the previous day's meeting of the governors of the new organization. Its executive committee, he reported, set up procedures for finding an executive director and an assistant, and had decided that the first campaign for funds would take place during Lent 1968. Plourde reported that the CCC had spent $2,000 to launch the organization. On a motion by Bishop Georges L. Pelletier of Trois-Rivières and Archbishop Anthony Jordan of Edmonton, the board unanimously approved the amount be considered a grant. Board members also "took note of a cheque for $1,000 from the cathedral parish of

Edmundston, New Brunswick, the first recorded donation to this 'National Fund.'[176] The eventual adoption of the name Canadian Catholic Organization for Development and Peace (CCODP) was a decision of the governors of the new organization.

The two bishops named by the bishops' conference to the CCODP board have always been active members. Their annual report is a standing item on the agenda of each plenary meeting of the bishops. The conference has issued major statements in support of CCODP on the occasion of its establishment and on its tenth, twentieth and twenty-fifth anniversaries. Although launched and supported by the "centre," CCODP, which is lay directed, is clearly distinct from the bishop-centred Caritas organizations that are its partners in many parts of the world. Moreover, the conference's messages for CCODP's anniversaries show that the wish of the Canadian bishops is that CCODP extend its roots ever deeper and farther in the dioceses and parishes. The bishops want CCODP to become a concern of all the laity, the means by which local Church members, consciously and actively, care for and share with the poorest of their sisters and brothers.

X. CANADIAN PASTORAL COUNCIL

If Development and Peace is an example of successful co-operation by the bishops with lay people, the attempt to set up a Canadian pastoral council is an effort that failed. Yet, in the end, perhaps it was not a willingness to co-operate that was lacking. Perhaps the model being tested was not appropriate, or maybe it was simply premature or fell victim to an inauspicious moment in history.

As Archbishop Joseph-Aurèle Plourde later recalled, the project began when, "in 1967, a committee of eight bishops was formed to study the role of the Conference of Canadian bishops in the light of Vatican II. This study led us to the following interrogation: has the time come for establishing a national organization, representing all the People of God in Canada, whose goal would be to work in close liaison with the Bishops to foster evangelic life and renewal of the Church in Canada?"[177]

When they returned from Vatican II, the bishops took no time for introspection about their own organization. They set about dealing with the immediate renewal agenda – liturgy, ecumenism, social action, mission activity, catechetics and other fields. As new pastoral programs were implemented, new offices were added at the CCC secretariat or existing ones were expanded. But with the growth came a question: Where would it end? Early in 1967, the CCC decided to take stock.[178] During the following months, the idea developed that, along with the bishops' organization, there should be another national organization "made up of laymen, priests, religious and bishops, for the purpose of assisting the bishops in carrying out their pastoral duties at the national level."[179] At the September 1968 CCC plenary meeting, therefore, the nature and role committee was given the new task of studying the feasibility of a Canadian Pastoral Council (CPC).

At the next plenary, in April 1969, the committee chaired by Plourde was ready to suggest the immediate setting up of a provisional CPC. It was agreed that the proposed body would be composed of four members (one priest, three laity) from each of the Atlantic and Western regions; fourteen (four priests, ten laity) from Quebec; and six (two priests, four laity) from Ontario. The Canadian Religious Conference, which grouped the major superiors of religious orders, would have three female and three male representatives. The CCC designated its five representatives: William Power (Atlantic), Anthony Jordan (West), Gérard-Marie Coderre (Quebec), Emmett Carter (Ontario) and the CCC president or his representative.[180]

The first meeting of the forty-one representatives took place November 21-23, 1969, in a retreat house in an Ottawa suburb. The idea that shaped the project, Plourde stressed, was co-responsibility at the national level in the Canadian Church. "As this is not possible unless an appropriate organization be constituted, they [the bishops] want you to tell them if the time has come to set up such an organization and, if so, to determine its nature and its objectives."[181]

The weekend's bilingual discussions focused on four questions: What do you think of the present way of deciding on matters of concern to the whole people of God in Canada? What do you think of the present way of establishing pastoral priorities in Canada? Do you think that the desire to participate is sufficiently strong to warrant the establishment of a national mechanism for participation? If you favour the establishment of a national mechanism for participation, what do you think would be the best form for it to take in the present situation?

Three responses emerged from the small groups. One minority favoured the immediate creation of a provisional Canadian Pastoral Council (CPC). Another opposed any CPC but urged better use of existing structures to promote co-responsibility in the Church. The majority voted that the group should continue as a steering committee with the ultimate aim of establishing a CPC. They committed themselves to meet once a year for three years, with shared responsibilities for financing their research and meetings – the CCC providing office services and the committee raising travel and meeting expenses. They constituted an eleven-member executive committee.[182] Three people were later designated as the "core executive": Archbishop Plourde; Jean-Marie Robin (a layman from the city of Laval, Quebec); and Toronto Redemptorist Rev. Edward Boyce.

The eleven members of the executive committee met in Montreal in February 1970 and decided that the second meeting of the entire study committee should be held in Toronto on the next Thanksgiving weekend, October 9-12.[183] During the spring and early summer, preparations for the October meeting in Toronto went ahead. In August, difficulties began to appear. Plourde, who had agreed to serve on the CPC core executive when he was still CCC vice-president, found that his new duties as the CCC's president left him insufficient time for the CPC. He asked that Bishop Emmett Carter replace him on the CPC core executive. Boyce also left, and was replaced on the core executive by Sister Marie-Berthe Dorais of the Montreal Grey Nuns. Then, just before the Toronto meeting, Robin had to miss meetings of the core group, reducing it to Carter and Dorais.

Attendance was down as the second study committee meeting opened on Friday evening, October 9. Even some executive members were absent. Carter told the group that he thought some progress should be made or else some indication given to the CCC that the project was not viable at that time. He found the absence of so many delegates disheartening and felt that the seriousness of the situation should be drawn to the members' attention.[184]

Momentous events in Canada that same weekend cast a shadow over the gathering. The October FLQ crisis was at its peak. As CPC delegates sat in session on the Saturday, kidnappers in Montreal seized Quebec Labour Minister Pierre Laporte, who was found murdered a few days later.

A varied program for the weekend was intended to help members discern the needs of the Church and how a Canadian Pastoral Council might respond to them. By Saturday afternoon, the meeting had a sense through reports from the small groups that opinion was as divided as it had been the previous November. For some, the existing committee should become a provisional CPC at once. Others favoured delaying a new CPC but making better use of existing Church structures.

On Saturday night, Carter and Dorais, as the core executive, met with other executive members. A resolution prepared by the core group was discussed. It proposed that "a body be set up immediately under the title of an experimental CPC for a period not exceeding two years." Those who had participated in the process so far would be invited to continue as members. Provision would be made for adding new members "to obtain the widest and most representative participation." The present executive would be asked to remain in office. As Carter later reported to the CCC board, he thought at the time "that there was a pretty good consensus about the future of the CPC, although many of us were worried about the mechanics and the possible expenditures to cover implementation of our resolution."[185]

As the executive was meeting, members became aware that another resolution was in the making, for which André Desmartis, a lay representative of the Archdiocese of Quebec, became the spokesperson. He was invited to the executive meeting to explore a possible compromise. His proposal had a preamble setting out six considerations. It noted that difficulties in establishing and operating diocesan pastoral councils were being met and that the CPC committee had run into problems functioning. Yet everyone wanted wider participation of priests, religious and laity in the Church's pastoral action, and felt that closer communication with the hierarchy should be assured. The bishops' conference, it also noted, already had well-organized offices directed by well-qualified staff. Therefore, said the main motion, the establishment of a CPC should be abandoned or delayed. Instead, the existing CCC departments should encourage or develop mechanisms of participation that would "integrate the laity, religious and priests at all levels of decisions in the pastoral order and in subsequent action." The motion foresaw bishops being directly involved through CCC commissions and departments. Besides, ad hoc committees would be created if necessary for specific problems. Moreover, the motion proposed the formation of an "animating team" composed of the staff of the CCC Internal Relations department (the offices for laity, religious and clergy) and delegates from the four Canadian pastoral regions. This team would have two goals – to promote participation of priests, religious and laity in the work of CCC bodies and to promote similar participation in the four regions and in individual dioceses. Finally, the motion suggested that early in 1971 the CCC convene a congress to share information about progress made, outline projects for the coming year, and "project in a definite way the image of the Church in Canada which is formed of bishops, priests, religious and laity, working together in the different fields of a joint pastoral plan." It also proposed one or several such meetings during the coming year in each of the four regions, and a serious effort to develop diocesan pastoral councils.[186]

Given the divergence between the executive's motion and that of Desmartis, it was decided that both would be presented to the Sunday morning session. Debate on the two motions continued during the afternoon. The discussion was interrupted at one point so members could hear a scheduled talk by Quebec Dominican priest and theologian Rev. Bernard Lambert on the theology of co-responsibility and how various models of a CPC could bring it to reality. He noted that a real need had emerged in the Church across the country to express co-responsibility in a new national body – or in several of them. Several forms of participation at the national level already existed. But, in his view, a new, full-fledged Canadian Pastoral Council was premature. What would such a council really be, how would it work, what would it do? He preferred the idea of male and female religious associating more intimately with the laity in the work of existing CCC bodies, whether commissions or offices. In a few years, he maintained, the most suitable form for a CPC might emerge, though not as part of the CCC, which would be contrary to the nature of both a bishops' conference and a pastoral council. He had tried to present all sides of the question, he stressed, but clearly his analysis gave most support to those who opposed the immediate formation of a provisional CPC.[187]

Discussion during the remainder of Sunday afternoon failed to produce a proposition that could resolve the two views. In another effort to do so, the executive met again Sunday evening with Quebec delegates. A detailed compromise resolution was worked out. It proposed "that the establishment of a Canadian Pastoral Council be pursued within the structure of the Canadian Catholic Conference." Detailed procedures for doing so were suggested in the second part of the motion.[188]

The Monday morning session discussed this proposal. When it came time to vote, there was almost unanimous agreement with the nine parts of the motion setting out possible procedures for dealing with the CCC, the four regions and the dioceses. However, the main proposition – to proceed *within* the CCC – was approved by only thirteen of the twenty-three who voted. The thirteen who voted in favour were French and English; the ten who opposed it were almost all English.

Carter was particularly disappointed that some anglophone members of the executive and other delegates had failed to support the compromise. He was committed to the idea of a CPC apart from the CCC. Yet he would have seen no difficulty, he later reported, with the idea of pursuing the CPC within the CCC structure had the vote for that plan been decisive. "Their vote of thirteen to ten leaves the bishops in a most embarrassing position," he said. "It would have been hard enough to integrate the operation as suggested in the resolution. What enthusiasm could they now expect from the bishops when it was almost a fifty-fifty vote, split, moreover, almost totally along language lines?"[189]

One anglophone lay member among the ten who opposed the compromise later explained her vote. "An invitation had been given by the Bishops to the people of Canada to share in a collegial way in the life of the Church," she wrote. "It would seem that we have said No to this invitation. To me, the hesitation to accept the opportunity to at least consider how we could effectively function as full status members of the Church constitutes an unsureness which could be translated into a 'No, we are not ready. We still want to be sheltered from the consequences of our actions by continuing to exist under present hierarchial structures.'" Also, she interpreted the compromise motion as a return to a minority position rejected at the November 1969 meeting.[190]

A francophone priest delegate, in turn, recognized that the executive's motion reflected the views of a good part of the anglophone participants. They saw the proposed CPC as a way to help the bishops and as a privileged opportunity for laity to take part and make their views known. Without rejecting the idea of a CPC, he added, the francophones thought it too soon to go ahead, even experimentally. A deeper study was needed of the role and attributes of such a body and of its relations with the CCC. Equally, the few diocesan pastoral councils were recent and still not evaluated. Before creating new structures, the existing ones at national, regional and diocesan levels should be known better and used more. This position explained the motion, voted thirteen to ten, to continue the study and development of a CPC within the CCC's structure, reaching out to other levels through flexible and simple mechanisms.[191]

Ten days before the CCC board was to study Carter's report on the CPC meeting, Bishop Power of Antigonish wrote to Archbishop Plourde. Power asked that the board consider setting up a small committee similar to the Dumont Commission.[192] He noted that "in the French Canadian expression of the Church there is a longer tradition of Catholic organizations geared to the apostolate and to relationships with the hierarchy," particularly through Catholic Action. "The same relationship on as wide a scope has not existed in the English-speaking expression of the Church." Secondly, he noted, the Dumont Commission "has by the nature of our times become an enquiry into the whole Church in the French Canadian expression. This has afforded...an opportunity for a very wide participation by many people and organizations in the life of the Church." If such a process were established to explore the situation of the English expression of the Church in Canada, Power explained, "I think that it could stir up a considerable amount of interest and satisfy, for the time being, the need for some participation by the laity on the national scene. Were this done we would still be providing a constructive outlet for these aspirations, and buy the time necessary to bring the whole Church together on a national level once the Dumont report has been submitted."[193]

The minutes of the board's December 3-4, 1970, meeting show that Power chaired the discussion about the CPC. There was nothing in the minutes about his letter to Plourde or the committee Power had suggested to explore Church life in English Canada. The board recorded that "the Study Committee for the formation of a Canadian Pastoral Council was seriously divided in its recommendations to the CCC" and that many members of the steering committee "wished to abandon, at least temporarily, the idea of a CPC." The board, it added, "considers it would be unwise to integrate the CPC into the CCC." The board entrusted further study of the CPC to the CCC's internal relations department and recommended "that a continuing study, first at the regional level and subsequently by a combined group of regional representatives, be made of the feasibility, purpose and structure of a CPC."[194]

When the CCC secretariat informed CPC members about the board's decision, it was interpreted as agreeing with the CPC's October motion. "When this [board] motion is compared with the final text of the proposals presented to the Bishops of Canada by the Members of the Study Committee, everyone will certainly be most encouraged in continuing the study," the letter said. "The pursuance of the establishment of a Canadian Pastoral Council within the structure of the Canadian Catholic Conference according to the norms or procedures suggested in the CPC motion has also become the desire of the Bishops." Hope was expressed that CPC executive members and CCC personnel would be able to meet early in the new year.[195] However, no such meeting was ever convened. The idea of a Canadian Pastoral Council simply faded away.

Sixteen years later, 150 lay representatives from every diocese joined the bishops for two days of study and discussion to prepare for the 1987 Synod of Bishops on the laity. Both laity and bishops were enthusiastic as the study days ended. It was a session such as a meeting of "a CPC within the structure of the CCCB" might have been – but nobody in 1986 referred to what had failed to happen in 1970.

XI. SOCIAL COMMUNICATIONS

Concern about the communications media began early in the life of the CCCB. The World War that was ending as the conference was launched had profound effects on all parts of Canada. Industrialized, urbanized, and diversified by new waves of refugees and immigrants, the country did not return to pre-war lifestyles with the end of hostilities. Nowhere was this more evident than in Quebec. Gone was the largely uniform rural scene, where parish life and especially the parish pulpit had been a main definer of what people thought and did. Instead, there was pluralism, spread in large part by the press, cinema and radio, over which the Church had no direct control. In this rapidly evolving cultural context, the archbishop of Ottawa established a press and cinema service in 1946. It was attached the next year to the Catholic Centre of Ottawa University and began publishing moral ratings for books and films.

A commission for press, radio and cinema was one of the first services organized by the new CCC. It recommended to the 1948 plenary meeting that the secretariat should have a centre for sending out news about the Catholic Church in Canada and gathering Catholic news from elsewhere. A motion to that effect by Archbishop William Duke of Vancouver and Archbishop Joseph Charbonneau of Montreal was approved. Use of existing agencies, such as the University of Ottawa's Catholic Centre, was to be studied.[196] Eventually, the CCC Information Service, English and French, answered this early concern. Publication of a daily French news bulletin began early in 1953; its English counterpart began in December 1955. The French service was suspended in April 1966, and the English service thirteen months later.[197] A public relations/information office was organized for each sector after 1967.

At the 1950 CCC meeting, the press, radio and cinema commission reported its concern about the negative influence of these three media. It recommended increased use of the Legion of Decency or some similar organization.[198] Even more specifically, the commission recommended in

1953 that it was time to establish a Canadian Legion of Decency. It suggested that the services of the Ottawa Catholic Centre be enlisted to promote the work of the Legion.

By 1956, a number of dioceses had centres inspired by the one in Ottawa. In order to co-ordinate their efforts, the CCC founded a national French-sector Catholic centre for cinema, radio and television (CCCRT). Located in Montreal, it had three aims: to teach about the morality of films and broadcasts, to form critical consciences in listeners and viewers, and to collaborate with producers to make the new media become instruments of grassroots education. After 1961, it was called the National Catholic Office for Broadcasting Media (Office catholique national des techniques de diffusion or OCNTD), and in 1969 it was again renamed the Office for Social Communications (OCS). When the CCC was restructured in 1973-74, the OCS was given a new status – no longer as a CCC office, but as an independent service, funded in part by the CCC for services rendered to francophone dioceses.[199]

The English sector's National Catholic Communications Centre (NCCC) in Toronto was founded in 1959. The Montreal centre had been established to serve existing diocesan centres, but the English centre grew out of the media apostolate of the Paulist Fathers in Toronto. Rev. Frank Stone led the efforts to win support from bishops for the Paulists' plan to have their Toronto centre serve all anglophone dioceses. Stone directed the NCCC from 1959 until its status as a national CCC office ended with the restructuring of the CCC in 1973-74.

The four sessions of Vatican II were high points of activity and collaboration for the two information services and the two national media centres. Personnel from all four were in Rome to assist Canadian media representatives and to send their own direct reports about the Council to media outlets in Canada.[200]

In the CCCB's internal structure, there continue to be English- and French-sector episcopal commissions for social communications. The French-sector commission's work is largely defined by the continuing projects of the Office for Social Communications in Montreal. The English-sector commission, in contrast, has no similar centre, despite several attempts since 1974 to establish an alternative national Catholic service for anglophone media and dioceses.

XII. FAMILY

Although the CCCB has published some thirty major statements about family life, it has had a family office for only six of its fifty years. Opened in June 1967, the Family Life Bureau was phased out during the 1973-74 restructuring of the conference. During the early 1950s, Rev. Francis Marrocco, then director of the English social affairs office, organized a committee at St. Patrick's College in Ottawa for research on family questions. His successors continued to raise the question of a family project within the CCC. The possibility was discussed in the 1959-60 annual report of the social affairs office for the French sector. The need for research on family questions was admitted, but preference was expressed for helping some university set up a centre where the CCC could sponsor specific family studies.[201]

The idea of a CCC family office took on urgency when it became clear early in 1966 that Parliament would review the civil law on contraception, divorce and abortion. The Family Life Bureau (FLB) was set up and given a five-part mandate by the October 1966 CCC plenary meeting.[202]

The bureau's first major project centred on the debate in Parliament about divorce law changes. It also began to gather information about the kinds of family life and sex education programs being developed and promoted by provincial education departments across Canada. Then, just prior to the Winnipeg discussion of *Humanae Vitae* – Paul VI's 1968 papal encyclical on the regulation of births and related aspects of family life – the bureau prepared and published the booklet *Contraception, Divorce, Abortion.*[203] It presented the bishops' statements to Parliament on these matters and added discussion questions for possible use by small study groups.

After the promotion of contraception was decriminalized in 1969, the Family Life Bureau began monitoring the new public family planning programs, especially that of Health and Welfare Canada. Evidence showed that the Family Planning Federation of Canada was the only private-sector organization with which federal officials were working to define the department's program. Advocates of natural family planning, including the Quebec-centred couples' movement, SERENA, were being systematically excluded. Through overtures to Health Minister John Munro, the CCC's Family Life bureau and SERENA were given places on a thirteen-member planning committee for the national conference on family planning early in 1972, and the bureau's director was invited to present a paper there. The majority view at this conference tended to define family planning as primarily a question of the medical means of birth prevention, including sterilization and abortion. A minority view was registered, however, particularly by SERENA couples who advanced a broad definition for family planning as "including all that is involved in each couple trying conscientiously to plan and control the life chances of the family of their choice."[204] During the national conference, when Munro announced the first federal funding for family planning, a small grant to SERENA indicated that the monopoly of the Family Planning Federation had been broken.

Research on family planning trends showed that in the United States, the birth control debate was escalating into efforts to win support for government population control policies. The CCC Family Life Bureau developed a proposal during 1971 for early Church involvement in the defining of a Canadian policy on population. The November 1971 CCC board meeting approved plans for "a seminar on population policy for Canada."[205] The thirty-five participants in the June 5-9, 1972, seminar came from government, universities and the Church.[206] The seminar examined five factors – economic policy, social organization, technology, social values and population numbers – as the key elements in a comprehensive population policy. It explored how change in each of the five factors can affect the other four. As one result of the seminar, the CCC had a sophisticated social change model for assessing how the federal government went about developing a Canadian policy for the United Nations 1974 World Population Conference.[207] The same analytical framework was used later by the Inter-Church Population Project (ICPOP).

New family policies and programs for the Church itself were the Family Life Bureau's fifth major research concern. The bureau's early study of family life and sex education programs concluded that "society seems to be involved in setting up new ways of handling the cultural process of giving family life/sex information and values to a new generation. Whereas formerly these things were 'more caught than taught,' now a 'direct education' process is being developed." What would be the Church's role in such education programs, the report asked.[208] One of the main ways the CCC pursued this research was through the special family committee set up after *Humanae Vitae* was released. Neither the Family Life Bureau nor the special family committee developed detailed educational programs. They tried to make known what their research revealed about needs being identified and about local pastoral efforts to meet them. The bureau's 1970 "Activities Report" summed up: "Most urgently needed for the future, therefore, are adequate diocesan resources for family life programs. The main work will be done at the local level."[209] The April 1973 plenary retained the family as a major study theme. It gave pastoral priority to family life issues and emphasized dialogue as the preferred program method.[210] The Family Life Bureau was then phased out and some of its research and program work was transferred to the new Pastoral Team.

XIII. PASTORAL TEAM

The CCC's Pastoral Team operated as a "research and development" unit from 1973-74 until 1990. It began with the restructuring of the secretariat after the 1972 evaluation study, and phased out as part of the restructuring following the 1986-90 study by the Task Force on CCCB Future Directions.

Its membership – six bishops and six members of the CCCB's professional staff (including priests, religious and lay men and women) – was based on a specific vision of Church members working together and sharing responsibilities. As part of their response to the pastoral questions surrounding the 1968 encyclical *Humanae Vitae*, the bishops had pledged themselves to co-operate with other Church members in the search for solutions. The special family committee established as part of the CCC's follow-up to its Winnipeg statement brought together bishops, priests, religious and laity in a new kind of working unit. In 1969-70, there had been an attempt to organize a national pastoral council that would unite bishops, priests, religious and laity in structured collaboration. The Pastoral Team was another example of a such a model.

There were some changes over the seventeen years in how the bishops were selected to the team. However, all were members or chairmen of one of the national episcopal commissions. They were elected by the plenary to be members of a given commission and of the CCC board, as well as of the Pastoral Team. Thus, it was foreseen, the bishops would bring detailed knowledge of their commission's work to the team's study and they would be well-informed advocates of team proposals when these came before the board.

The original description of the six staff members called for them to be "a bilingual, multi-disciplined, polyvalent team" – that is, three anglophones and three francophones, having among them a variety of professional skills and being capable of working on a wide range of pastoral problems. One of the three English members of the new team was made responsible for the CCC's desk for ecumenism after the Toronto ecumenism office was discontinued. Similarly, one of the francophone team members took on part of the work formerly done by the French-sector offices for religious education and clergy relations. Two other team members, it was specified at the outset, would be theologians, and two would have social science backgrounds.[211]

During its seventeen years, the Pastoral Team had a hand in virtually every question on the CCCB agenda. The board and executive could refer any question that did not seem ready for a decision to the Pastoral Team for further study. The general secretaries, who supervised the work of the staff team, could call on its members to help prepare agenda items for consideration by the executive, board or plenary. Team bishops could propose that questions from their commissions be studied by the team. The six staff members could also suggest items from their areas of competence and concern.

In addition, the Pastoral Team undertook to make the theme "Growth in Faith in and through the Family" a major pastoral orientation for itself and for the conference. The idea developed as a follow-up to the 1977 Synod on catechetics and as a preparation for the 1980 Synod on the family. The main outcome of the project was a series of booklets on Marriage and Family (1980) and on Responsible Parenthood (1983). The local response, as measured by sales of books to dioceses across the country, did not meet preliminary estimates. This was one of the CCCB projects that showed the difficulty of mounting a single national pastoral animation program as a priority for every diocese.

Over time, some important structural weaknesses of the team became evident. With the participation of the two general secretaries and two public relations directors, the team had sixteen members, a larger than optimum number for a discussion group. Also, the staff of several important CCCB offices, including missions, social affairs, liturgy and religious education, were not team members. They could be invited to attend or could ask to do so. However, the fact that they were not usually present meant that the team did not effectively play the co-ordinating role that was one of the main purposes originally assigned to it. Therefore, the Pastoral Team came to an end during a major evaluation review, just as it began with a similar review. The Task Force on CCCB Future Directions proposed, in effect, that the six team bishops become a new "Program and Priorities Committee" for the conference. The staff team, reduced by attrition to four members from six during the late 1980s, became a professional resource unit available to the general secretaries for research and planning assignments.

XIV. RESTRUCTURING THE CCCB

In the middle of Vatican II, the CCC board made a decision that gave a dynamic orientation to the CCC secretariat. It is recorded in a February 14, 1964, declaration of the CCC board that reflects the bishops' enthusiasm after Vatican II's first two sessions. "It is incumbent on the Episcopacy of our country to bring to reality the fruits of the present Council and to lead the Canadian Church in the renewal so much desired by John XXIII and the Sovereign Pontiff gloriously reigning [Paul VI]," the statement began. "To accomplish this great pastoral mission actively and efficaciously," it added, "the Episcopacy needs a dynamic and top-quality general secretariat, oriented towards study and research, equipped to give specialized and competent services promptly, able to discern social changes, to observe and analyze all problems of interest to the Church, whether in Canada as a whole, in the English and French sectors, or in the numerous regions and provinces of our vast country."[212] The years after 1964 brought many changes to the CCCB's secretariat, but its general mandate was never changed.

A key detail of the 1964 statement mandated the general secretaries "to undertake without delay, and in a systematic way, an evaluation of the entire CCC operation." This evaluation was undertaken by the two general secretaries, Rev. Gordon George and Rev. Charles Mathieu. The latter was the main author of their voluminous report.

The most important proposals of the report, everyone involved agreed, were those that democratized the conference. Photographs of plenary meetings taken over the years record one of the key changes. Originally, members faced a "table of honour" at which the cardinals and leading archbishops sat with conference officers in formidable array. A scowl from a cardinal could kill a motion before it was even seconded. With the changes, only the elected president and vice-president face an assembly in which all other members sit as equals. As well, all members became eligible for election. The president and other officers were elected by the assembly. Parliamentary rules of order were adopted for notices of motion, debates and voting. Moreover, all these rights, limitations and procedures are specified in formal regulations, which are completed by a code of procedures for public interventions in the name of the CCCB.

A crucial development, already mentioned in the account of liturgical changes, had to do with the use of the mail for consultations and indicative votes. Processes were expedited in this way. Even on major questions, work could continue in the long intervals between plenary meetings, to be ready for discussion and formal voting at a plenary. Also, through the circulation of questions, followed by summaries of initial reactions, members could be kept informed and given opportunities for participation they likely could not enjoy if study and reactions were limited to formal meetings.

Growth Problems

As each new CCC service and office was conceived, it was justifiable in itself. The cumulative effect of growth had some negative effects, however. In his April 1967 report, Treasurer Alexander Carter noted that in four years, the CCC's operating costs had gone from $177,000 to $1.1 million.[213] Already, in January 1967, the general secretaries warned that the CCC was living beyond its means.[214] Four years later, they noted that the 1971 fiscal year ended with a deficit of nearly $212,000.[215] Another consideration also concerned the bishops. During Vatican II, warnings had been heard that the offices of bishops' conferences would become dominating bureaucracies, limiting the freedom of bishops in their own dioceses. Was that happening as the CCC offices grew in number and size? For both practical financial reasons and more theoretical considerations, therefore, the CCC launched its 1967 study of the nature and role of the conference. One conclusion, reported to the 1968 plenary, was that the CCC should define itself clearly as the association of the bishops – not a more general "Church headquarters." Out of this conclusion, the idea developed that some CCC projects might be taken over by a Canadian Pastoral Council. This did not occur. However, the idea of cutting back on CCC operations carried over into a second evaluation by the general secretaries, which was undertaken by Charles Mathieu and Everett MacNeil in 1972.

Along with the prospect that a pastoral council might take some burdens from the CCC, the idea developed that the national conference, for pastoral and financial reasons, should deal only with national and international concerns. Diocesan, provincial and regional issues, it was argued, should be taken up at other levels. In September 1971, the Assembly of Quebec Bishops (Assemblée des évêques du Québec or AÉQ) voted in favour of regionalization – that is, that the bishops of the Atlantic, Quebec, Ontario and Western regions should develop their own offices with the capacity to deal with issues that were not clearly national or international.

Regionalization meant somewhat different things to the bishops of each of the four designated regions. The Quebec bishops had been meeting regularly for more than a century. Indeed, their meetings had led to the idea of forming a national conference as a mechanism for regular meetings of all the bishops in Canada. Not long after the CCC secretariat was set up in Ottawa, the Quebec bishops converted their informal one-person secretariat into a formal office in Montreal. During the 1960s, the AÉQ had to face major challenges, trying to integrate into Church life the changes arising almost simultaneously from Quebec's "quiet" social revolution and from Vatican II. The AÉQ offices grew accordingly, with specialized staff in a number of pastoral fields. The Ontario bishops also had to deal with pastoral concerns in just one civil province. Their secretariat in Toronto has remained smaller than the AÉQ's, however. In sharp contrast, the Western and Atlantic regional bishops' conferences each cover four provinces, with the West in addition including the two territories. Education, health, welfare and other provincial matters of the kind that occupy the Quebec and Ontario regions hardly ever arise on the agendas of the Western and Atlantic conferences. The bishops of each province have to deal directly with such issues in their provincial capitals, and also meet with regional confreres over remaining issues of common regional interest. Consequently, the Western and Atlantic regions have limited their secretariats to the person designated to be their secretary.

The AÉQ's 1971 call for stronger efforts to develop the four regional conferences therefore challenged the other bishops in several ways. In each of the three other regions, the bishops had to decide what regional and provincial pastoral tasks they should undertake and what kind and size of secretariat they needed for their foreseeable tasks. For the CCC, the prospect of perhaps handing over some work to a national pastoral council and some to the four regions was attractive. This kind of budget reduction looked good against the large deficit of the early 1970s. Besides, was this development not an application to the Church itself of the principle of subsidiarity, doing at the higher level only what could not be done at a lower one? However, was there a point beyond which the CCC could not cut and still remain effective to deal with national and international issues? Where might the CCC and the regional conferences end up if the political movement for Quebec independence gained ground? As well, did not the CCC have to maintain a fairly high level of resources to serve the bishops of the Western and Atlantic regions, who preferred calling on the CCC to setting up their own regional pastoral services?

The general secretaries' *Evaluation-1972* report affirmed both a strong CCC and the principle of regionalization advanced by the Quebec bishops. From then on, every CCC undertaking had to face a basic question: Was it national or regional? The mandates of national commissions and offices no longer extended to active animation efforts in dioceses across the country, as during the first years after Vatican II. Some critics of this cutback identify it with a slowing up of the process of integrating the renewal of Vatican II into parishes and dioceses. The concept of regional animation developed instead, though it was not equally realized in all four pastoral regions, especially at the beginning. In turn, as a positive development, the increased emphasis at the CCC on national and international questions was reflected in projects undertaken with the national offices of other Churches, in work on international human rights issues and in relations with other bishops' conferences.

The rapid post-Council growth of the CCC ended with the 1973-74 restructuring. The Toronto offices for ecumenism and communications were closed, as were the Montreal offices for health and welfare and clergy. The Ottawa offices for clergy, family, laity and francophone religious education were eliminated and their mandates were absorbed into the new Pastoral Team. The Montreal offices for communications and ecumenism were made independent, with limited CCC service contracts. The CCC's core operation, however, not only survived but emerged perhaps better placed for other changes still to come.

Questioning went beyond the methodological issues involved in trying to establish criteria for deciding when an issue was diocesan, regional, national or international. The Pastoral Team in the mid-1970s launched a theological study that attempted to relate to the conference the traditional definition of a bishop as teacher, priest and ruler. During 1976 and 1977, successive plenary meetings agreed that the conference should give priority to the first of these roles: prophecy. In response, the social action commission, for one, related its many statements to this prophetic role. The Code of Canon Law promulgated in 1983 gave conferences a large role in Church governance as well. Then, during the 1985 extraordinary Synod of Bishops, questions resurfaced about collegiality and subsidiarity and about the theological status and teaching authority of conferences.

In 1986, therefore, the CCCB mandated the "Task Force on CCCB Future Directions" to undertake yet another study. Several reasons were cited for the new self-examination: change of the CCCB itself and the need for new priorities and policies for the future; questions about collegiality and subsidiarity raised during the 1985 Synod; developing relations with lay and other groups in the Church; the requirements of expanding ecumenical relations; the unequal development of regionalization (minimal in the West and Atlantic regions); growing international relations with other conferences; questions about the functioning of CCCB bodies, including the Pastoral Team; and perennial questions about what programs to undertake or maintain, and how to finance them.

Many of the most important suggestions of the Task Force can be grouped under the heading of collegiality. The plenary meeting was redesigned in an effort to make it more clearly a gathering of episcopal "college" members. Instead of a fall, weekday hotel business meeting, it became a weekend seminary retreat session late in the summer, so that fraternity could be increased without loss of efficiency. The plenary became the place for deciding priorities and programs and related budgets. The aim was to give all bishops a chance to direct the work of commissions and offices, to overcome the complaints of some that they had little or no part in things that were done or said in their name. To develop a sense of "ownership" of the conference by every one of its members became an explicit aim. The Pastoral Team was discontinued on the grounds that it did not serve the purpose of co-ordinating conference projects and avoiding gaps and overlaps in pastoral programs. As an alternative, the bishops heading the six national episcopal commissions were designated as the programs and priorities committee. The mandate given them was to propose priorities to the plenary for debate by all members. The general secretaries' role, too, was defined clearly as one of pastoral animation. As a further way to emphasize the immediate responsibility of each CCCB member, the idea of a fundraising campaign to generate an independent operating fund was abandoned. The CCCB would continue to operate year by year on revenues from a diocesan levy. Each plenary meeting would face the challenge of choosing the next year's program priorities and providing the funds to finance them.

The most important result of the Task Force's 1986-90 evaluation may have been the adoption of a reformulated statement on the nature and role of the CCCB (see Appendix 1). The conference, it said, "is the collegial assembly of the Canadian hierarchy. Its purpose is to enable the bishops, united with the Pope, to discharge their collective pastoral office with and for other members of the People of God in the mission confided to the whole Church. This involves working with all men and women to evangelize contemporary culture and to build a society of justice and love called for by Jesus Christ. It also involves the promotion of unity among Christian Churches and of understanding with other religions." Overall, the statement tried to position the CCCB to move into the future.

1 FIRST BISHOP. Venerable François de Montmorency-Laval, bishop of Quebec (1658-1688), was responsible for a territory that included the Mississippi Valley and extended to the Pacific. (From a portrait by Brother Luc Pinxit. Reproduced with permission of the Archdiocese of Montreal.)

2 FIRST PRESIDENT. Cardinal Jean-Marie-Rodrigue Villeneuve, O.M.I., archbishop of Quebec, president of the Canadian Catholic Conference (CCC), 1943-1947. As of January 1, 1977, the Conference was called the Canadian Conference of Catholic Bishops (CCCB). (Photo: Roger Bédard, Photographie commerciale)

3 FIRST GENERAL SECRETARY. Msgr. Paul Bernier was first general secretary of the new Canadian episcopal conference, to some extent modelled on the U.S. National Catholic Welfare Conference (eventually the United States Catholic Conference and National Conference of Catholic Bishops). Msgr. Bernier (right) is with Msgr. Michael J. Ready, NCWC general secretary, during a 1944 visit to Washington, D.C. (Photo: Catholic News Service)

4 FOUNDING MEETING. When the bishops of Canada assembled in Quebec City, October 12-13, 1943, for their fourth quinquennial meeting, they agreed to establish a national episcopal conference. At a subsequent meeting, September 26-28, 1945, the Canadian bishops chose the original name of the episcopal conference and drafted its first constitution. (Photo: J.E. Livernois, courtesy of the Archdiocese of Quebec)

5 CELEBRATING END OF WAR. Archbishops Joseph A. O'Sullivan of Kingston (left) and James C. McGuigan of Toronto prepare to join a September 27, 1945, thanksgiving Mass for victory and peace in Quebec City, attended by representatives of the federal, provincial and municipal governments. (Photo: Moderne Enr.)

6 BRIDGING 50 YEARS. Two members of the Canadian episcopal conference in 1993 had been present when it was established 50 years earlier in Quebec City: Marie-Joseph Lemieux, O.P., later archbishop of Ottawa (left), and Camille-André Leblanc (right), bishop of Bathurst.

7 ECUMENICAL FIRST. Seven Canadian Churches, on December 22, 1964, announced their intention to build a Christian pavilion at the 1967 World's Fair in Montreal. The joint venture was heralded as a world first in bearing common Christian witness. Left to right: Dr. Earl Treusch, Lutheran Church; Rev. Emrys Jenkins for the Federation of Baptist Churches; Montreal's Anglican Bishop Kenneth Maguire; Cardinal Léger, archbishop of Montreal; United Church Moderator E.M. Howse; Dr. Ritchie Bell for the Presbyterians; Bishop Timothy Rodostolou, Greek Orthodox bishop of Canada and Alaska.

8 PRE-COUNCIL TOUR. Shortly before the Second Vatican Council opened, October 11, 1962, representatives of the world press were invited on a tour of the papal summer residence at Castel Gandolfo. Bernard Daly is second from the left. (Photo: © Giordani, Foto Attualita)

9 VATICAN II. Shown during the first session of the Second Vatican Council are (front row, left) Cardinal James C. McGuigan, archbishop of Toronto, seated beside Cardinal Gregory Peter XV Agaganian, patriarch of the Catholic Armenians. (Photo: © S. Appetiti)

10 CANADIAN MEDIA. During the second session of Vatican II, September 29 to December 4, 1963, Bishop Gérard-Marie Coderre, chairman of the CCC social communications commission, called an informal meeting of Canadian members of the media. Back row, left to right: Gérard Lemieux, Radio-Canada; Bernard Daly, CCC information service; Yvon Desrosiers, CCC social communications office; Réjean Plamondon, CCC information service; Msgr. Lucien Foucreault, secretary to Bishop Coderre. Front row: Marcel Adam, *La Presse*; Bishop Coderre; Father Émile Legault, CSC, Montreal newspaper and radio commentator. Seated at left, Mrs. Lemieux. (Photo: Service Foto Express)

11 POPE VISITS CANADIAN COLLEGE. During the fourth and final session of Vatican II, September 14 to December 8, 1965, Paul VI visited the Canadian College in Rome. Surrounding the Pope, left to right: Cardinal Maurice Roy, archbishop of Quebec; Maurice Baudoux, archbishop of Saint Boniface; Antoine Hacault, auxiliary bishop of Saint Boniface; George B. Flahiff, archbishop of Winnipeg, then CCC president; and Cardinal Paul-Émile Léger, archbishop of Montreal. (Photo: © Felici)

12 SYNOD. Members of the Canadian team at the first Extraordinary General Assembly of the Synod of Bishops, 1969. Left to right: Alexander Carter, bishop of Sault Ste. Marie; Cardinal Maurice Roy, archbishop of Quebec; Maxim Hermaniuk, C.Ss.R., archeparch of Winnipeg and metropolitan of Ukrainian Catholics in Canada; and Msgr. Charles Mathieu, CCC general secretary and member of the secretariat for the Synod. (Photo: © Felici)

13 PAUL VI WITH CCC PRESIDENT. Conference presidents, with the vice president and a general secretary, make an annual visit to Rome. Shown during one of these as 1973-1975 CCC president is Archbishop Jean-Marie Fortier with Paul VI. On an earlier visit, CCC president William Power with Fortier as vice president told the Pope that he was "doing a good job," a remark that extremely moved Paul VI. (Photo: © Giordani, Foto Attualita).

14 PREPARATIONS FOR 1974 SYNOD. Participants at a CCC preparatory meeting for the 1974 Synod on evangelization. Left to right: Romeo Maione; Jacques Grand'Maison; Everett MacNeil (then CCC general secretary); Emmett Carter, then bishop of London; Remi De Roo, bishop of Victoria; Sister Suzanne Bertrand, Canadian Religious Conference; Bernard Hubert, bishop of St-Jean-Longueuil; Jean-Marie Fortier, archbishop of Sherbrooke; Maxim Hermaniuk, archeparch of Winnipeg; Bernard Daly; Bob Laplante; Tim Ryan; Louis-de-Gonzague Langevin, bishop of Saint-Hyacinthe; Henri Légaré, archbishop of Grouard-McLennan; William Marrevee; William Power, bishop of Antigonish; Marcel Dumais; Huguette Isabelle; Guy Poisson; Annette Arbique; Krystyna Szymanski. (Photo: Paul Hamel)

15 PAPAL VISIT TO CANADA. During his 1984 Canadian visit, the bishops of Canada met on September 20 with Pope John Paul II at the Sisters of Charity mother house in Ottawa. Immediately beside the Pope are John Sherlock, bishop of London, then CCCB president (left), and Jean-Guy Hamelin, bishop of Rouyn-Noranda, CCCB vice president (right). (Photo: © Photo Features Ltd.)

16 ENTHUSIASTIC WELCOME. This September 16 scene of the Pope's 1984 visit is from Winnipeg. Gallup estimated that 10 per cent of Canadian adults, that is two million people, lined the streets of Canadian cities to see the Pope, while 63 per cent of all Canadians watched television coverage of the papal trip. (Photo: © Concacan Inc., 1984)

17 RETURN TO ROME. When the CCCB chartered an airplane for the Pope's return flight to Rome on September 20, representatives of the thirteen host dioceses and of the CCCB staff were offered some of the extra seats for a one-way flight to Rome with the Pope. Shown here at the airport in Rome with the Pope are Pierrette Warwick and Marie-France Bédard (right). Bernard Daly is in the background (centre). (Photo: © Felici)

18 FORT SIMPSON. Because bad weather prevented the Pope from meeting with Native people in the Canadian North during his 1984 visit, a second Canadian visit was scheduled for Fort Simpson, September 20, 1987. There John Paul II also had a private meeting with leaders of national associations for Canadian native peoples: George Erasmus, Assembly of First Nations; James Sinclair, Metis Council of Canada; Louis Brière, Native Council of Canada; and Rhoda Inuksuk, Inuit Tapirisat of Canada.

19 LOCAL DISPUTE. When the CCC held its September 1974 Plenary Meeting in Quebec City, a local parish was involved in a labour dispute. Jean-Guy Hamelin, director of what was then the CCC social action office, and Bernard Hubert, bishop of Saint-Jean-Longueuil, agreed to meet with demonstrators. Signs in French read "Do not oppress the little ones" and "Injustice exploits the Church."

20 SOCIAL AFFAIRS COMMISSION. At the end of December 1982 and well into the new year, the CCCB social affairs commission was the focus of national attention with its statement *Ethical Reflections on the Economic Crisis*. Shown here at a January 1983 meeting of what was then the department of social affairs and laity (left to right): Peter Sutton, archbishop of Keewatin-The Pas; Raymond Roy, bishop of Saint Paul; Adolphe Proulx, then bishop of Gatineau-Hull, now deceased; and John O'Mara, then bishop of Thunder Bay.

21 CANADIAN COUNCIL OF CHURCHES. Following a number of years of negotiations, the Canadian Conference of Catholic Bishops in 1986 joined the Canadian Council of Churches as an associate member. Shown here at the April signing of the formal agreement are (left to right): Anglican Primate Ted Scott, then Council president; Edith Shore, associate general secretary of the Council; Rev. Don Anderson, general secretary of the Council; and Bernard Hubert, bishop of Saint-Jean-Longueuil, then CCCB president. (Photo: © Photo Features Ltd.)

22 ABORTION PROTEST. The CCCB has been insistent that a law which offers some protection for the unborn child is better than no law, and that Catholic members of Parliament can vote for such legislation. However, not all pro-life groups and individuals agree. About 100 Catholics protested in front of the CCCB offices in Ottawa in February 1990. (Photo: Michel Tessier, *Le Droit*)

23 NOBEL PEACE PRIZE. Rigoberta Menchu, winner of that year's Nobel Peace Prize, visited the CCCB in November 1992, during a trip to Canada organized by the Canadian Catholic Organization for Development and Peace. The Guatemalan visitor is shown meeting Msgr. James Weisgerber, CCCB English general secretary. In the background are Marcel Gervais, archbishop of Ottawa and then CCCB president (centre), and Father Alexandre Taché, OMI, then CCCB French general secretary (right). (Photo: © Concacan Inc., 1992)

24 50TH ANNIVERSARY. A eucharistic celebration in honour of the 50th anniversary of the CCCB was held in Ottawa's cathedral during the 1993 Plenary Meeting. The service, in English and French, official languages of the conference, included music in Latin and Greek, the traditional languages of the Church. The Gospel was proclaimed in Ukrainian, the largest Eastern rite in Canada. Six rites are represented in the CCCB: Armenian, Maronite, Melkite, Slovak, Ukrainian, and Latin. (Photo: Joyce Harpell © Concacan Inc., 1993)

25 PAPAL REPRESENTATIVE. Archbishop Carlo Curis, Papal Nuncio to Canada, reads a message of "joy and gratitude" from John Paul II (see Appendix 2). (Photo: Joyce Harpell © Concacan Inc., 1993)

26 FESTIVE MEAL. The 50th anniversary celebration brought together some 250 bishops and current and former staff, with their spouses, for a festive meal. Left to right: Sister Donna Geernaert, SC, CCCB ecumenical officer; Aloysius Ambrozic, archbishop of Toronto; and Frederick B. Henry, then auxiliary bishop of London. (Photo: Joyce Harpell © Concacan Inc., 1993)

27 OTHER GUESTS at the 50th anniversary celebration. Left to right: André Vallée, bishop of the Military Ordinariate of Canada, and Msgr. Dennis Murphy, former general secretaries; Msgr. James Weisgerber, current general secretary; Everett MacNeil and (with back to camera) William Ryan, also former general secretaries.

28 CCCB OFFICES. The main offices of the Canadian Conference of Catholic Bishops, at the corner of Guigues Street and Parent Avenue, Ottawa. (Photo: Joyce Harpell © Concacan Inc., 1993)

CHAPTER FIVE

Tough Issues

I. CONTRACEPTION, DIVORCE AND ABORTION

Abortion, contraception and divorce are the issues over which the Canadian bishops have faced the most anger from Church members. These issues touch both the private domain of individual conscience and the public forum of civil law. On both fronts – freedom of conscience and the rule of law – the bishops have been criticized by some for being too unbending and attacked by others for being too lenient. Some of the latter have even accused CCCB members of being "unfaithful to the Pope, the Church and to every Canadian Bishop who went before them."[216] The CCCB's official statements have presented the Church's traditional teaching on these issues. On each topic, that teaching can be summarized in a few sentences. True, some think the traditional teaching should be modified, but that opinion has not been the reason for most of the disagreement and protests. Rather, the quarrels have been about how traditional teachings should apply in specific situations regarding Canadian civil laws.

Just after Vatican II ended in December 1965, the Canadian Parliament began to debate changes in the civil laws regarding abortion, contraception and divorce. Changes were being proposed, that is, in civil laws that for years had harmonized with and seemed to reinforce and even to enforce traditional Church teaching. Many disagreed with how the bishops handled these challenges. In effect, the discontent and protest arose around how the bishops tried to apply Vatican II teaching regarding the Church's role in the modern world and, especially, regarding the mission of the Church's lay members to evangelize that world.

Of course, for many in the Church and outside of it, the storm really broke over Pope Paul VI's 1968 encyclical, *Humanae Vitae*. For the CCCB, however, the struggle to formulate pastoral policy on such issues for today's world was already fully engaged when *Humanae Vitae* was published.

Contraception

Contraception was the first of the major issues to come up for public debate. Early in 1966, Parliament began the process to amend Article 150 of the Criminal Code, which made it a crime to give information or to sell or distribute materials for any method of birth prevention or of contraception. A parliamentary committee began hearings on the matter and invited the Catholic bishops to appear and present their views.

On September 9, 1966, the CCC issued two statements on the subject. One was a pastoral letter "to all the Catholic Faithful," the other a statement to the Commons committee. Each text set out in similar terms why the bishops did not intend to oppose changes in Article 150. The pastoral letter dealt with the civil law through a summary of post-Council teaching on family life. The statement to the committee reviewed Council teaching about the Church in the modern world, a world in which issues like the future of Article 150 had to be resolved.

Considered together, the two texts revealed much about what the Canadian bishops thought about Vatican II. "Many of the new challenges we face today in the Church and in the world flow from the active spirit of renewal which marked the progress and outcome of the Council," the pastoral letter said. "We ourselves were caught up and moved by the spirit. We have come back with a lively desire to make real and effective in the Canadian Church those fresh insights and initiatives which, under the guidance of the Holy Spirit, found their way into the Council documents." To approach complex problems in the true spirit of Vatican II means, in practice, "bearing in mind and using where applicable the Council guidelines on ecumenism, on religious liberty, on the lay apostolate, on the pastoral role of bishops, and especially on the Church in the world today."[217]

The Council, the bishops explained to the parliamentary committee, had "given all of us deeper insights into the nature of the Church, the relationship of her official teaching authority to her other members and of all of them to the political community." It illustrated these insights by quoting extensively from *Pastoral Constitution on the Church in the Modern World*, as well as the *Dogmatic Constitution on the Church* and the *Decree on the Apostolate of the Laity*. The text commented on the citations to explain their relevance for Church members who, as citizens or legislators, were faced with issues like proposed changes to Article 150. In addition, the brief included, as an appendix, the entire text of Chapter 4 of Part II of the *Pastoral Constitution on the Church in the Modern World*. Entitled "The Political Community," that chapter dealt with modern public life, the nature and purpose of the political community, participation by all in public life, and the political community and the Church.

The brief to Parliament noted the Council's teaching in *The Church in the Modern World* that "within the political community Christians act '...in their own name as citizens.' Their actions, to be sure, should be guided by a well formed Christian conscience since '...even in secular affairs there is no human activity which can be withdrawn from God's dominion.' But the fact remains that their decisions and actions in the political sphere must be their own. Their rights and duties do not flow from the fact that they belong to the Church." From the Council's *Dogmatic Constitution of the Church*, the brief highlighted the teaching that "because the very plan of salvation demands it, the faithful should learn to distinguish carefully between those rights and duties which are theirs as members of the Church, and those which they have as members of society. Let them strive to harmonize the two, remembering that in every temporal affair they must be guided by a Christian conscience." In the *Decree on the Apostolate of the Laity*, the brief continued, "laity are told that they must take on the renewal of the temporal order as their own special obligation." The brief then summed up the bishops' understanding of these Council teachings:

> The Christian legislator then has a Christian conscience and if it is truly formed it will be thoroughly imbued with Christian principles. But it remains *his or her* conscience. The Church may play a major role in the formation of that conscience through her teachings on the social order and the moral aspects of the political order. But these teachings do not properly extend to the technical areas of social or

> political questions. It will be up to the legislator to apply the principles to the concrete and often complicated realities of social and political life and to find a way to make these principles operative for the common good. They should not stand idly by waiting for the Church to tell them what to do in the political order. The ultimate responsible conclusions are their own as they fulfil the task they have along with other legislators. That task is the promotion of the common good through the provision of wise and just laws.... The Christian legislator must make his or her own decision. The norm of action of a legislator is not primarily the good of any religious group but the good of society. Religious and moral values are certainly of great importance for good government. But these values enter into political decisions only in so far as they affect the common good. Members of Parliament are charged with a temporal task. They may, and in fact often will, vote in line with what the Church forbids or approves because what the Church forbids or approves may be closely connected with the common good. Their standard always lies in this question: is it for or against the common good?[218]

Regarding Article 150, the bishops noted, as summed up in their pastoral statement, that even the teaching of natural family planning was "quite likely a criminal offence according to the present law." A "large number of honest Canadians sincerely believe that this law violates their rights of conscience." Besides, the law was not being enforced and "cannot be enforced without creating greater evils than it might prevent." In their parliamentary brief they supported others who had called for safeguards built into the law against irresponsible sales and advertising. A change in the law, the bishops warned, could open the way to government-backed birth regulation programs. In the name of privacy and freedom, acceptance of contraception should never become a condition for financial help to the needy. Finally, they urged the government to monitor the effects of any change in the law on individuals, families and the common good. Given safeguards and protection, they did not think it their duty to oppose appropriate changes in the law and "could easily envisage an active co-operation and even leadership on the part of lay Catholics to change a law which under present conditions they might well judge to be harmful to public order and the common good."

Divorce

On April 6, 1967, the bishops presented another statement to the Special Joint Committee of the Senate and House of Commons on Divorce. They emphasized that the principles outlined seven months earlier in their brief on contraception were essential to a precise understanding of their views about divorce; so the earlier statement was included as an appendix – with, again, the text of Chapter 4 of Part II of *The Church in the Modern World.*

The CCC brief on divorce had three main parts: on Church teaching about marriage; on proposed changes in Canada's divorce legislation; and on programs to strengthen family life.

A change in Canada's civil law about divorce would not change Church teaching about the indissolubility of a valid marriage, legal separations or civil divorce without remarriage, the bishops affirmed. They noted allegations that the existing law encouraged perjury and collusion, if not adultery itself. They said that they would not oppose changes that were "truly directed to advancing the common good of civil society." However, they continued, "we cannot overemphasize that an indiscriminate broadening of the grounds for divorce is not the solution to the problem of unhappy marriages." They added: "An eventual revision of the divorce law makes sense only if it is part of a wide, positive policy for strengthening family values and particularly for ensuring the serious motivation and proper preparation of couples intending to marry." They therefore urged public support for family research, marriage education and programs to strengthen family values. Especially, they urged that reconciliation efforts be built into the procedures of divorce courts.[219]

The parliamentary committee received nearly 1,600 pages of statements, briefs and personal testimonies about divorce. The mid-summer report of its conclusions ran to ninety-nine pages and ended with a draft *Divorce (Extension of Grounds) Act.* A copy was sent to every bishop by the CCC secretariat. The CCC's president, Archbishop Louis Lévesque, wrote to CCC members to propose that they meet their local members of Parliament and of the Senate "for an informal discussion of the shortcomings of the proposed legislation." The draft act, Lévesque said, "conspicuously overlooks and omits taking into account recommendations made in the Brief of the CCC, no less than in those of other religious and social welfare bodies, namely that a mere extension of grounds for divorce would not be for the benefit of Canadian family life, unless there is included in such legislation procedures for reconciliation, and the safeguarding of family life." He noted that "the Board at its August 11 meeting also encouraged a continuing communication with other Churches and organizations through the Family Life Bureau to present as broad a front as possible in obtaining more satisfactory legislation."[220]

The collaboration with other Churches, referred to in Lévesque's letter, focused on a study of the 1,600 pages of submissions that the joint committee on divorce had received. An interchurch group that included the staff of the CCC's Family Life Bureau summarized its analysis in a "Statement to the Minister of Justice about the Proposals to Reform the Divorce Laws." Members of the group met with Justice Minister Pierre Trudeau on November 8, 1967, to present their conclusions.

Divorce and the reform of divorce laws often had been presented as subjects that deeply divided Canadians, the statement noted. However, analysis of what Canadians actually told the joint committee showed that there was broad agreement "on the need for legislative reforms that will provide more adequate social means to deal with marital troubles." It was agreed that the law on divorce – "a last recourse" – should be reformed. Canadians, however, also shared the view that lifelong marriage is the ideal, and that there should be adequate preparation for it, with public support. The brief said that even the best of marriages sometimes need counselling services, which should have public funding. Reconciliation efforts, it said, are often effective and should be part "of any legal proceedings dealing with faltering or broken marriages." The brief ended with the affirmation that "it is the duty of the state to strengthen marriage and family life. It should be the declared intention of the federal government, as an example and incentive to those in other levels of responsibility, to apply itself earnestly to progressive, positive updating of all laws and social programs affecting marriage and the family." [221]

The brief was one of the first major interchurch social interventions after Vatican II. The novelty of Anglican, Roman Catholic, Lutheran, Mennonite, Presbyterian and United Church representatives making a joint presentation impressed Trudeau and officials from the justice department. There never was any indication, however, that the Church proposals were taken seriously. Trudeau was not expressing just a personal view when he said later, on another topic, that the state had no business in the nation's bedrooms. The 1967 divorce debate showed that most MPs and senators, Catholics included, saw no need for the state to enact laws to establish a comprehensive social framework to support marriage and family life, as advocated by the bishops' conference and other Church bodies.

Later Divorce Statements

After 1967, the question of divorce came up for public discussion on several occasions and the bishops' conference contributed statements. In January 1977, the CCCB board submitted a brief to the Minister of Justice on the *Family Law Report* of the Law Reform Commission of Canada. The brief welcomed and supported some sections of the report, but criticized it for being more a "divorce report" than a family law report. It argued that "good laws should be normative and should educate us about our values. They ought to support our fundamental institutions. They should assist us to be just in our relationships." In particular, "measures strengthening family values," they suggested, "should be the priority of legislators; measures that will appropriately terminate marriages which offer no hope of reconciliation are of less importance." The brief specifically opposed the report's recommendation that "marriage breakdown" should become the sole legal basis for divorce. In opposition to this concept, the brief reiterated the CCC's 1967 statement that "We cannot over-emphasize that an indiscriminate broadening of the grounds for divorce is not the solution to the problem of unhappy marriages. Such legislation undoubtedly would contribute to the destruction of the essential values on which our society is built."[222]

Eight years later, the bishops' conference renewed many of the same arguments in its brief regarding Bill C-47. The bill had been brought forward in the context of a review of divorce developments since passage of the 1968 act. "We cannot accept," the bishops said, "any reform proposals that would seem to regard marriage as no more than a private contract between two individuals that could be dissolved at will. Marriage is...an eminently social event and undertaking.... There is a serious public interest in the perpetuation and reinforcement of the institution of marriage. Neither at the beginning of marriage nor at its end can the state be simply 'gatekeeper.'" The bishops urged parliamentarians "to resist further attempts to privatize marriage and its dissolution. Instead we ask you to use the shortcomings of the present divorce procedures as an opportunity for government to strengthen family life in Canada and to take the time needed to design divorce procedures that will emphasize conciliation, reconciliation and personal renewal."[223]

Abortion

The CCCB's involvement in the debate about Canada's abortion law can be divided into two phases. The first, from 1967 to 1988, was the period of the law introduced in 1967 when Pierre Trudeau was justice minister and enacted in 1969 after he became Prime Minister. It said that abortion was a criminal offence except in a case certified by a hospital committee to be a threat to life or health. The second phase began with the January 1988 Supreme Court decision that this law was unconstitutional. This phase ended with the defeat in the Senate three years later of a new abortion law proposed by the Mulroney government, which the CCCB called "seriously flawed" but better than no law at all.

During each of these two phases, the CCCB was involved on two levels. On one level, the bishops tried to respond to the need to present Church teaching in a way that would both challenge and assist Catholic (and other) legislators and also clarify and shape public opinion. At the same time, on a second level, the bishops were being confronted by public reproach and anger from some Church members who considered what the bishops said to be both inadequate and incorrect. The latter quarrel within the Church was never about the morality of abortion as such. It was about Canada's civil law on abortion and, in particular, about how the post-Vatican II Church should go about trying to shape temporal affairs according to the plan of God.

On this latter point, the bishops tried to make their position clear well before their first 1968 statement about Canada's abortion law. They detailed it in their 1966 pastoral letter to Church members as debate began on the Criminal Code section outlawing contraceptives. The bishops said that to approach such complex problems in the true spirit of Vatican II means one must take into account the new perception of the Church in the modern world.[224]

When asked by Parliament in 1967 for a statement on abortion and the civil law, the CCC set up a drafting committee. It consulted theologians, doctors, sociologists, lawyers and married couples. A draft text was then sent to all bishops, some of whom consulted local groups before they replied. The final meeting of the drafting committee was scheduled for December 20 in Ottawa. The day before this meeting, the Commons health and welfare committee unexpectedly published an "interim" report. At their December 20 drafting session, therefore, the bishops tried to incorporate references to the Commons report. The very next day, however, the government published a bill of amendments to the Criminal Code, including new sections on abortion. After the Christmas holiday, the CCC executive had a complex situation to reassess. The December 20 drafting session had, of course, taken no account of the draft bill tabled on December 21. The CCC's expected meeting with the Commons committee had been set for January 23. There was insufficient time before that date to reconvene the drafting committee, revise the text to include references to the bill and circulate French and English copies for approval by CCC members. Besides, the question had moved from how to advise a parliamentary committee to how to respond pastorally to draft legislation. The decision was made to postpone the committee appearance until March 5. The work of the CCC drafting committee was rewritten to take the form of a general pastoral statement, published on February 7, 1968.[225]

Starting with that statement, the bishops' conference would issue more than twenty briefs, statements and formal letters, as well as a number of press releases and telex messages, all about abortion. The first seven of these came during the years following the government's first move to legalize abortion. The continuing public debate took on a note of urgency, if not frenzy, however, when on January 28, 1988, the Supreme Court, in the Morgentaler case, struck down the Trudeau government's therapeutic abortion law as unconstitutional. In the next three-and-a-half years, the CCCB intervened sixteen times. No other topic occupied the CCCB as much during that period. Yet, at the end of it, through the actions of Parliament and of the courts, and because of a strange alliance between those for and against abortion, Canada was left with no law at all to prevent or even regulate the arbitrary ending of unborn human life.

For the bishops' first pastoral statement in 1968, the context was provided by the interim report of the Commons health and welfare committee and the government's draft bill. The committee recommended that therapeutic abortion be allowed where a pregnancy would endanger the mother's life or health; in its draft bill, the government wrote this concept into law. The CCC pastoral statement made a number of major points in response. The Vatican Council had repeated the Church's teaching that, from conception, life must be guarded with the greatest care, "while abortion and infanticide are unspeakable crimes." This teaching, the bishops said, echoes the commandment "Thou shalt not kill," and the great law of Christian love. Scientific findings, they added, "lead us to look upon the whole development that begins with conception as the slow, complex maturing process of a distinct individual...." Some people represented a broadening of the law as progress, but "progress in civilization," the bishops insisted, "consists in the increasingly clear recognition of the dignity, sacredness and absolute inviolability of the human person." The bishops criticized the proposed amendment, therefore:

as a too simple solution to a serious and complex problem. We have in mind a completely different approach. Respect for human life at all stages of development should be fostered through education and through laws that teach respect for life. A serious study of the frequency of illicit abortions and of means to eliminate them should be undertaken. Medical research should be encouraged. Real efforts should be made to provide mothers in distress with the medical and psychiatric care they need. There should be a more humane understanding of unwed mothers and their children and we should provide them with real help. Greater effort must go into care of those afflicted by mental illness. More adequate social and family policies should be planned and developed with all seriousness and real generosity. The state must devote itself to a program of this kind. For our part, we call on the Catholic people to become active leaders and ardent collaborators in this common undertaking. This is the way to real social progress and true freedom. For us only one approach is worthy of mankind, of civilization and of Canada's spiritual mission in the world. That approach calls for creative imagination, not the all-too-easy imitation of other countries. It calls for ever-increasing respect for all human life, including the defenceless and most dependent.[226]

This first CCC pastoral message on abortion set the tone for all subsequent ones. Each of the various statements by the bishops discussed some of the personal and social conditions that may make pregnancy seem insupportable. They spelled out repeatedly the many fronts on which efforts must be made to oppose abortion. "To be involved in the task of making this a society hospitable to life is a foremost requirement of social justice," they said in 1973. "That is why we must take most seriously the rebuke that those who oppose abortion care too little about the special problems of mothers and the burdens of rearing children after they are born. If respect for life seems to end with birth, our perceptions and values are truncated and incomplete. The call of Christ, that we should bear one another's burdens, demands that we reach out in practical ways to share all the burdens of parenthood. The indicated aid and support will include working to change economic and social realities in the direction of justice and respect for life. From doing this we must not flinch."[227]

Male attitudes and behaviour are to be included among the social conditions that need change, the bishops said in 1986. "In every case of distressful and unwanted pregnancy," they noted, "the man must accept his responsibility and not leave the woman alone to face the difficulties. Moreover, male attitudes and actions are at the heart of the problems of related forms of violence, such as battered women, incest, rape, prostitution and pornography. Those who teach respect for life cannot remain silent about these matters if our communities are to grow in respect for every human life."[228]

At the end of this series of pastoral messages on abortion, up to 1991, an analyst noted that "the bishops have articulated the rights of the unborn as an issue of justice for the most vulnerable in our society – those literally without a voice. They have affirmed that these rights are integral to a vision of a just and good society.... In effect, the bishops have presented a profoundly countercultural position that contains an inherent critique of capitalism and consumerism. This biblically founded vision has been integrally linked to economic and social changes that would commit all of us to sharing the cost and responsibility for raising children in this society."[229]

After the Supreme Court's 1988 decision on abortion, the CCCB interventions focused on calls for a new law. The broader justice issues were always kept in mind, however. "In the process of working for new legislation," Archbishop James Hayes, the CCCB's president, said on the day the law was struck down, "all Christians must also apply themselves to the continuing pastoral work of evangelizing the modern culture regarding God-given values and rights of every human life, and the need to safeguard and respect that life in all circumstances."[230] The issue, he stressed in an April 1988 pastoral statement, is not the rights of a woman versus the rights of the unborn. It would be more appropriate to say "that the issue is whether the wants and needs of the women and men of the present will be allowed to predominate over the basic needs of the women and men of future generations. The society which accepts abortion as a solution to present problems (whether personal or social) is also a society which abuses its children, lays waste the environment, risks nuclear war and implements economic policies in which the immediate benefits of some now will be dearly paid for by many in the future. All of us are tempted to live as if there were no tomorrow. Persons who are still in the process of coming to birth are a real reminder to us of the fact that, for some, the future is just beginning. These beginners are holdouts for humanity, our humanity."[231]

Public events set the stage for each subsequent CCCB initiative regarding the abortion law. In May 1988, the government tried to test three legislative options but had to withdraw them in the face of opposition in Parliament. A month later, it tabled a similar three-option legislative plan.

In a round of voting on July 28, the government's options and several amendments all were defeated. The summer of 1989 brought the Paul Dodds and Chantale Daigle cases before the courts; the CCCB did not get involved. In November, the government introduced Bill C-43, which made abortion a crime except if a doctor ruled that a pregnancy threatened a woman's life or health. The CCCB presented a brief when parliamentary hearings were held in January 1990. The Commons passed Bill C-43 in May. It was defeated in the Senate at the end of January 1991, however, and Canada was left with no civil law on abortion.

In various ways, during all these events, the CCCB made four main points. First, the bishops urged that abortion be made subject to law and not be left as only a private matter. Second, they favoured placing an abortion law in the Criminal Code and not in some administrative statute. Third, they specifically opposed the "gestational" approach as a basis for an abortion law because that involved declaring some aspects of human life to be outside the law. Finally, they spoke often of what would be involved in living with the "best possible" rather than the "perfect" law.

These four points and other aspects of the CCCB's position were reflected when the bishops participated in the parliamentary hearings on Bill C-43 early in 1990. Bishop Robert Lebel headed the CCCB delegation presenting a brief on January 31. It noted that the most frequently cited causes of abortion are poverty, rape, incest, family violence and the inequality of women. Abortion, however, is a false solution because "it does not and cannot address the underlying causes.... Governments at all levels must introduce policies and programs which are truly hospitable to life.... These measures cannot be realized, however, without the educational efforts required to motivate such social change." Governmental reforms, the brief added, "must be accompanied by social changes throughout society. Communities must be more responsive to families and women in need. Adoption needs to be promoted as a solution to an unwanted pregnancy but with greater compassion for the agony of giving up a child. Educational, cultural and other institutions, including the Catholic Church, must be more active in promoting the equality of women and respect for them as persons. Some male attitudes and behaviours have to change radically if there is to be an end to violence against women, more co-responsibility in parenting, and more respectful interpersonal relationships."

In the government's bill, the bishops saw three positive elements at the level of principle: the gestational approach was abandoned; the requirement of grounds affirmed that abortion was not just a matter of private choice, and the use of criminal law gave a "powerful message." However, the bill was seriously flawed because in practice it would not sufficiently protect the unborn. The CCCB therefore outlined five areas for amendments: a more restrictive definition of health; procedures for accountability; informed consent requirements, perhaps including a legislated waiting period and mandatory counselling; differentiated sanctions for abortionists and the pregnant women involved; and a conscience clause for health care workers. The brief also discussed Vatican II's teaching on pluralism in society. It concluded with an appeal to legislators to "draft a law that will protect the unborn child to the maximum degree possible."

"It is understood, however," the brief concluded, "that as bishops it is not our role to suggest in detail the best possible legislative solution. As we wrote to your predecessors in 1966, Christian legislators must make their own decisions...." The brief then discussed some aspects of debate going on within the Church on this matter. It noted:

> During the difficult debate of the last two years around legislative options, some have said that Catholics can support only a law which completely accords with Church teaching. This opinion may have been occasioned by failure to distinguish between the moral law and the civil law or to appreciate the special problems of balancing conflicting claims in a pluralistic society.
>
> While Catholics may not dissent from the Church teaching that abortion is morally wrong, they may differ as to the most effective approach for achieving legal protection of the unborn child. In selecting particular approaches, Catholics are guided by their consciences, informed by Church teaching from which certain general principles can be drawn.
>
> In particular, Catholics may not favour abortion or any proposal which seeks to weaken existing legal protection of the unborn child. Nor may they advocate that there be no legal protection. However, when it is the only available or feasible option, support may be given to legislation which attempts, if only imperfectly, to restore protection or strengthen existing protection and to express publicly their opposition to abortion.
>
> Questions as to feasibility and whether the legislation improves or weakens the legal position of the unborn child, are always matters of prudential judgment where certitude is not possible.

> In a country as diversified as ours, in matters of religion and ideology, Catholic politicians must assess the legal and political realities they face and work for the law which will provide the maximum possible protection for unborn children.

The brief's final word was that "no civil law will alter our moral teaching on abortion or affect our commitment to a comprehensive and respectful attitude to life at all stages."[232]

The CCCB's stand on Bill C-43 was met by angry protest from a number of anti-abortion groups. About thirty of their members picketed the CCCB's headquarters in Ottawa on February 21. They carried a large banner that said "Canadian Catholic Bishops Support Abortion." With many smaller placards[233] and in comments to media representatives who gathered,[234] they accused the bishops of failing to present the Church's teaching.[235]

The bishops, for their part, continued to press their basic positions. They intervened three times: when Bill C-43 was reported by the committee without any amendments, before it was passed by the Commons, and before it was defeated by the Senate. The day after the Senate vote Bishop Lebel, as CCCB president, reiterated the CCCB's call for legislation "that will provide effective protection for the life of the unborn." He added: "The right to life is clearly the primary human right. It should not, however, be approached in isolation from other complementary rights such as the right to work, the right to food, the right to shelter and the right to equality. It is our intention to encourage within the Catholic community the development of a comprehensive pro-life ethic that will demonstrate a common concern for the protection of human life and the promotion of human dignity."

Lebel announced that the CCCB had prepared materials on abortion and nine complementary life issues for use by parish, student and other discussion groups. He concluded: "We call upon governments at all levels, as well as all our Christian communities, to address the social and economic factors that have been identified as contributing to abortion. We renew our support for the efforts of those who offer immediate and practical assistance to women and families faced with difficult or unexpected pregnancies and for those who are working to transform social attitudes and structures to make them truly hospitable to life. For our part, we shall continue to educate about the value and dignity of human life and to promote respect and protection of all human life at all stages of development."[236]

At the end of this summary of the CCCB's involvement in a quarter-century of public debate about a Canadian abortion law, questions remain.

What did the Vatican think? Did the Canadian bishops, as some allege, use one standard for their position on laws regarding abortion, contraception and divorce and another for issues involving economic and political issues? Why did the bishops' teaching not have more apparent impact?

In a 1992 interview for this book, Archbishop James Hayes, CCCB president from 1987 to 1989, recalled "the understanding, appreciation and support that was offered, in an official way, by the Holy See to the Canadian hierarchy for their efforts." The office to which he specifically referred was the Vatican Secretariat of State, where Hayes found support from both Cardinal Agostino Casaroli and the deputy for general affairs, Archbishop Edward L. Cassidy. When Hayes was most under attack by some Canadian Catholics on account of the CCCB's position, he went to see Cassidy, who supported the Canadian bishops "not only for what they were trying to do but the methods they were using to try to do it," Hayes recalled.[237]

In his book *Catholics against the Church*, Michael W. Cuneo theorizes that the CCCB used "the principle of Canadian church-state separation" to keep a certain distance on questions like abortion but not when they spoke on economic and similar matters.[238] Such a double-standard theory is not backed by the evidence. The bishops based all their post-Vatican II social interventions on the same broad cluster of Council principles (noted, for example, in their 1966 pastoral letter on a contraception law). Moreover, CCCB officers deny recourse to "the principle of Canadian church-state separation" or to any double standard in their approach to such varied issues as laws on abortion, refugees, unemployment insurance or native rights. "You can't speak of church-state separation in Canada," said Bishop Alexander Carter, conference president from 1967 to 1969. "The Churches – not just Catholics – do exercise influence on government, but our influence is spiritual. We can tell our people what we think they should do in conscience, but we don't want political control. We don't want a police state and we don't want the Church to be the police or tell the police what to do."[239] Whether on abortion or unemployment or any other social issue that they have discussed, the bishops have been trying to make two main points: that moral values apply in secular affairs and that lay Church members have primary responsibility for applying them.

What, then, of the bishops' influence in the abortion law debate? In Canada, as has been suggested for Ireland, it seems that in the popular culture, abortion has been shifted from the fifth commandment ("Thou shalt not kill") to the sixth ("Thou shalt not commit adultery"). "Abortion has become a sexual 'right' (or a sexual sin), along with divorce and contraception: it does not belong, as it should, with murder, manslaughter, death on the roads, assassination, capital punishment, the mass killings of war, or the mass deaths of plague and famine," Irish writer Sean MacReamoinn has observed.[240] The statements of the Canadian bishops about abortion law during a quarter-century show they are convinced that not just one law but the entire culture is to be transformed. The tools they offer for social change are Vatican II concepts that relate in particular to the mission of the laity – ideas that, it seems evident, still are not grasped or lived in a way to bring about the hoped-for civilization of love and justice.

II. 'HUMANAE VITAE' DEBATE: A CASE STUDY

No conference plenary meeting was ever taken up by a single issue the way the *Humanae Vitae* debate dominated the September 1968 assembly in Winnipeg.

A different agenda was being planned during the spring and early summer of that year. The bishops agreed to go to the Manitoba capital to join in celebrating the 150th anniversary of the founding of the Church in St. Boniface. An important report by a committee on the nature and role of the conference, the CCC's first post-Vatican II assessment, was scheduled for discussion. There was to be a vote on the restoration of the permanent diaconate. Letters to the United Nations and the Canadian government were being prepared by the social action commission to protest human rights violations in the war in Vietnam, the Nigeria-Biafra civil war and the invasion of Czechoslovakia. The Family Life Bureau had been directed to prepare a study session on family life and CCC members had been canvassed about their concerns and interests in that area. The regular reports of other offices and commissions awaited attention.

However, it all became secondary in an instant when the Apostolic Delegate joined members of the CCC executive at the end of their regular summer meeting, near Ottawa at the lakeside chalet of Archbishop Joseph-Aurèle Plourde, then CCC vice-president. It was not unusual that Archbishop Emanuele Clarizio should join them for a social evening after their day's work. What made it unforgettable was that they had no inkling Pope Paul VI had finished work on an encyclical on human life until Clarizio opened his briefcase and handed out copies. The executive members did not need the July headlines around the world to tell them they had a major topic for September 21-27 in Winnipeg.

An early summer postal strike across Canada delayed distribution of the document. While individual CCC members refrained from major public comments, plans were made for a collegial discussion during the plenary meeting, and the Conference monitored reactions of Canadian Church members. In August, a questionnaire was sent to the bishops. What part of the encyclical did they consider most urgent as a discussion topic? What procedures did they think would be most effective for aiding the discussion? As CCC president, Alexander Carter also informed them that "Since the content of Humanae Vitae touches on the areas of theology, religious education and social doctrine, I am appealing in a particular way to the episcopal members of these three commissions, under the leadership of the Theology Commission, to prepare the framework for fruitful debate and decisions."[241]

The summer consultations also provided a list of four priest theologians who were invited to work with the bishops. They were Rev. Joseph Bisztyo of the diocese of Saskatoon, Sulpician Father Édouard Gagnon of Montreal and two Jesuits, Rev. Édouard Hamel of Quebec and Rome, and Rev. Edward Sheridan of Toronto.[242]

Commission members, theologians and staff met for the first time on Saturday afternoon, September 21, in Winnipeg.[243] Besides deciding on working roles and procedures, the first meeting invited two priests, Rev. Ora McManus of Edmonton and Rev. Leonard Murphy of Winnipeg, to present the results of a survey conducted among priests of western Canada. Many priests reported that they were torn between faithfulness to the magisterium and the duty to follow a prudently formed conscience and asked the bishops to address this issue. McManus was invited to remain in Winnipeg as a consultant.

The report of the western priests' survey was only one item in a flood of reactions that poured into the CCC offices after publication of the encyclical. Letters and telegrams continued to arrive at the hotel during the week. Lay groups in Toronto, Ottawa and Vancouver purchased space in local daily papers, inviting reactions. They reported up to ninety per cent saying the encyclical had not settled the issue for them. From several Toronto parishes, thirty-five telegrams declared "whole hearted support for the Pope" and "complete assent." Another eight expressed good wishes to the CCC and the hope that "conscientious choice" would be respected. No attempt was made to collect or count similar messages that individual bishops may have received.[244]

The bishops, theologians and staff met for a second time on Saturday evening. Discussions centred on an outline for a pastoral statement that Bishop De Roo had sketched after discussions with laity and priests in his diocese.[245] The commission also agreed to read a text submitted by Hamel, and various other papers, in time for a Sunday morning meeting.[246]

At that meeting, the commission agreed that Hamel's text was good, but not pastoral enough. Bisztyo proposed a five-part outline touching on collegiality with the Pope, solidarity with the people, the role of conscience, formation of conscience, and pastoral aspects. De Roo, Hamel, Sheridan and Bernard Daly were named as a drafting committee, with three consultants: Joseph Bisztyo, Édouard Gagnon and Louis Chabot, the CCC's French public relations director. That meeting concluded as a brainstorming session to explore ideas for a draft text for the discussion groups on Monday morning. The commission met again on Sunday afternoon to hear a report from a special meeting in Montreal of La société canadienne de théologie. It was presented by Sulpician theologian Rev. André Naud of Montreal. Like McManus the previous day, Naud was invited to remain in Winnipeg as a consultant.

On Sunday evening, the drafting committee and the invited theologians met to work on the draft text. The first draft was in English. Charles Saint-Onge worked all night to translate it and have a French text ready for the Monday morning group discussions. That night, and for the next four nights, English and French secretaries also worked until very late or very early to type and make copies of the successive texts. Every CCC member received English or French versions of every draft and all comments made about them.

For their first working session Monday morning, the bishops divided into small discussion groups. Members of the CCC professional staff were assigned to each group, to share their expertise and to serve as note-takers. The four invited theologians also participated. Each group discussed the draft from the theology commission that had been completed overnight. On the basis of comments from all groups, the drafting committee was asked to prepare a second draft for Tuesday morning's plenary session. On Monday afternoon, the bishops began work on other items of the week's agenda.

For Tuesday morning's plenary discussion, important ground rules were clarified. Just three years after the end of Vatican II, all the bishops were familiar with the way conciliar texts had been prepared for study and voting. In general, Vatican II procedures were followed for the *Humanae*

Vitae discussion in Winnipeg. A simple majority vote would approve a text as a basis for discussion. Two-thirds plus one would be required for final acceptance. President Alexander Carter also ruled that no detailed minutes would be kept during the actual debate, to provide maximum freedom for each member to express his views.[247] On this basis, the Tuesday morning session accepted the drafting committee's second text as a basis for discussion. At the end of that session, members were invited to submit their written comments and suggestions later in the day.

When the theology commission met on Tuesday afternoon to review the written comments, it decided that the drafting process needed to be completely changed. There was no time for the theologians to review the written comments and make suggestions to the drafting committee before the theology commission had a chance to study what the bishops proposed. Instead, the bishops of the commission took over as the drafting committee. Bishop Emmett Carter was invited that evening to assist them in the drafting. The theologians from then on became a "reaction committee."

Following Tuesday afternoon's procedural changes and to meet other commitments, Bisztyo, Gagnon and Hamel decided to leave for home. For the rest of the week, Sheridan, McManus, Naud and R. Laflamme of Quebec (named by Cardinal Roy to replace Hamel), with Daly and Saint-Onge as secretaries, formed the reaction committee.

The third draft of the week and the first written by the bishops was distributed to the members at Wednesday's plenary. Once again, after some discussion, they were asked to submit written comments and suggestions. The text was discussed again at Thursday morning's session. The bishops also received English and French copies of the views of the reaction committee on the third draft.

At the Thursday afternoon session, the text was discussed in detail and accepted in substance. The theology commission was instructed to begin incorporating revisions into another draft. This was examined at a special plenary called for ten o'clock that night. At that session, paragraphs revised by the commission were examined. Since there was no time to prepare printed copies, De Roo and André Ouellette, commission co-chairmen, took turns reading the English and French versions of the proposed changes. The revisions were incorporated into a fourth draft, which the staff had ready in both languages for distribution to the bishops as they entered their Friday morning session.

At this session, the bishops examined the fourth draft, paragraph by paragraph. As each page was completed, in French and English, the secretaries made any indicated changes and began printing the final version. At the conclusion of the detailed examination and with each paragraph approved, a formal vote was taken on the whole document. All bishops present agreed, except for four who formally abstained. There were no opposing votes.[248] The completed text was made public immediately at a press conference.

Reactions

Besides debate about what the statement said regarding freedom of conscience, public criticism of the bishops focused on the contention that, overall, the bishops had not supported the Pope. Twenty-four years after the event, the bishops who led the process at Winnipeg described their intentions in the very words they used at the time. Their challenge, they insist, was not to support the Pope but to counsel Canadian Catholics.[249]

"Our statement was purely pastoral," Alexander Carter wrote after the Winnipeg meeting. "It did not, nor did it pretend to, deal with the teaching of *Humanae Vitae*. As chief Pastors of the Canadian Catholics we had to try to apply the principles of theology to the real moral crisis which exists in this complex area of belief and practice. We did not repudiate the teaching of the Holy Father – I can hardly visualize a Canadian hierarchy doing that. Neither did we attempt to ignore a fact that stares us in the face. This teaching is neither accepted by nor acceptable to a large number of otherwise excellent Catholics just as loyal to the Church and the Holy Father as we are. We have spoken to them with love and understanding. This is how we conceived our role." He and many other bishops felt, he added, that

> this whole matter has been incredibly complicated by the procedure chosen by His Holiness. With all the respect and love that I have for him, I feel that we Bishops have just got to have decency and honesty to let him know our concern. Major matters affecting the conscience, the intimate life of our people, call for more previous pastoral consultation and a wide range of theological opinion. The Pope as well as the Bishops promulgated a teaching on collegiality. If there was one time since the Council when a collegial exercise was obviously needed surely this was it. Had it been used, even if the same conclusions were reached, the whole tone and appearance of *Humanae Vitae* could have been expressed in contemporary terms intelligible to the people. That

> this was not done will remain one of my most profound regrets and a source of disquiet. It will, I fear, prove to have done irreparable harm to the authority and credibility of the magisterium.[250]

The same point was discussed in a letter by Bishop Emmett Carter. He was reacting to a press report, which he called factually incorrect, about debate at the Winnipeg meeting regarding support for the Pope's teaching. "Debate was engaged upon the matter," he wrote, "and a number of us presented to the bishops the position that we could not and should not take up a stance of either approval or disapproval of the teaching of the Holy Father. We pointed out that we had not been asked to collaborate in the preparation of this Encyclical; that the Encyclical is now a fact and had to be treated as the Magisterium of the Church and therefore a priori to be accepted. If we were going to say that we agreed with the teaching of the Encyclical we would have to open the door to a possible statement that we disagreed and we felt it was much more prudent for the Canadian Bishops simply to accept the teaching of the Holy Father without statement of our approval or disapproval which had not been requested."[251]

In the absence of detailed minutes, another glimpse into the discussion is provided by a statement Alexander Carter was authorized to make by the first CCC board meeting after the Winnipeg plenary. It was partly in response to press speculation, he noted, and went on to emphasize that

> ...there was no cloak-and-dagger atmosphere, there were no camps, and there was no tension of any proportion. Hard work and honest disagreement in abundance until an acceptable formula was found. But no confrontations and no "taking-to-the-floor" of positions and no "block" separations. These are the simple facts. Even here it is not our intention to make any attempt to write a record. But we must note that on the various votes taken concerning the substance of this document, votes which were based upon the various sections, each was unanimous with the exception of one vote in which there were six dissenting voices against approximately seventy in favour. There was one close vote, a matter of a majority of one, and that concerned a procedural matter allowing the Drafting Committee to use its discretion about the retention or the removal of the words "In his teaching" in Article 2 of the Declaration. The interesting part of this matter is that the Drafting Committee found it possible to retain the words and when the formula was presented it was unanimously approved by the Assembly.
>
> Consequently, we repeat that the backstairs divisions and the dramatic "appeals to the floor" so dear to the mind of the seeker for the spectacular were not there. In this connection it was very different from many of the dramatic struggles that took place in Vatican II. We could

> sum up our positions by saying that there was a constant basic unity in the Theological Commission; we achieved unity – not without some small difficulty – between ourselves and our consultors; the Bishops themselves arrived at a consensus that was about as close to being unanimous as can be achieved in this world.[252]

Papal Reaction

Alexander Carter, as conference president, asked Cardinal Maurice Roy, who was going to Rome, to deliver copies of the Winnipeg statement to Pope Paul VI. In a letter to Roy, Cardinal Amleto Cicognani, Vatican Secretary of State, assured him that the Pope thanked him heartily for his October 8 letter with the English and French texts. The Roman cardinal asked for copies, when they were ready, of the follow-up statement mentioned in paragraph 24 of the Winnipeg statement.[253] On his return to Quebec, Roy informed Carter that in his audience with Paul VI, he had insisted that the Canadian bishops had wished to express a pastoral concern of the kind the Pope himself had shown at the end of his encyclical. Also, they had wanted to avoid being brusque with priests and people who were doubtful and confused. Roy added that he thought the Pope had not yet read the text, for he had made no comment except to say that after agonizing over what to decide, he could now face calmly the difficulties the encyclical might cause, being sure he had said the only thing he could say.[254]

The CCC president also received two identical letters from Archbishop Emanuele Clarizio. In English and French, they informed Carter that the apostolic delegation had promptly sent the Holy See a copy of the Winnipeg statement. "Now I am happy to notify Your Excellency," Clarizio wrote, "that His Eminence, Amleto Cardinal Cicognani, Secretary of State to His Holiness, has just communicated that the Holy Father, Pope Paul VI has taken cognisance of the document with satisfaction."[255]

CCC Follow-up

When the CCC board members met in Ottawa in November for their first meeting after Winnipeg, they unanimously agreed in principle that a special committee of bishops be set up. It would work with a team of CCC office directors to develop a multi-media follow-up to the Winnipeg statement. It would begin the dialogue mentioned in the statement, draw up pastoral directives and set down a program of family life education, the board proposed. The theology commission was to form the core of this committee.[256] Bishop André Ouellette, chairman of the French theology commission, reported some hesitation about the idea of getting to work immediately on another doctrinal text. An education plan begun at the local level seemed a better starting point. The December CCC executive committee meeting asked Bishop Pelletier to meet with the French commission members.[258] Ouellette wrote to Alexander Carter to report that they preferred to start by finding out what was being done in the dioceses. He outlined elements of a suitable questionnaire. It would also gather names of persons who might collaborate with the CCC.[258] Ouellette met in January of 1969 with Bishop Paul Reding of Hamilton, new president of the English theology commission, to finalize the questionnaire.[259]

The two theology committees decided in February to set up a Special Family Committee, which would bring together bishops, priests, religious and laity in dialogue, as recommended in the Winnipeg statement.[260] They also decided not to prepare another statement. The planned project of the Special Family Committee, they concluded, was to reply to what the Winnipeg statement said about the CCC's future intention. More action would serve better than more words. During its March 4-7 meeting, the board decided to insist that the theology commission prepare a draft statement for study at the April plenary meeting. The Special Family Committee met in Ottawa on March 27-28 and proposed four motions that the theology commission could present to the plenary. Then, during the plenary week, the theology commissions met[261] and prepared a short statement to deal especially with some interpretations being given to the Winnipeg statement. As they proposed, the text issued by the plenary on April 18 combined the Special Family Committee's four recommendations and the theology commission's text.

The first of the four resolutions accepted by the plenary urged the CCC to give "utmost support" for marriage preparation programs – "short of recommending that they be compulsory for Church marriages." The CCC also was urged to initiate a study of the theology of marriage and to support family life education in the school as a supplement to parental efforts and with particular stress on preparation of teachers for such courses. The possibility of an "apostolate to new parents" was also recommended. A study in Quebec City had shown how drastically the birth of a first child changed the lives of new parents. It suggested that this was an important time for Church and society to reach out to young adults.

The text added that the bishops remained fully committed to their Winnipeg statement and wanted to insist that it be properly interpreted. Their teaching on freedom of conscience and the role of the Church's teaching authority had been reflected inaccurately by some. A Catholic, they reiterated, "is not free to form his conscience without consideration of the teaching of the *magisterium*" – in this case, the Pope's encyclical. "It is false and dangerous to maintain that because this encyclical has not demanded 'the absolute assent of faith,' any Catholic may put it aside as if it had never appeared. On the contrary, such teaching in some ways imposes a great burden of responsibility on the individual conscience." The plenary concluded with the proposal that, to avoid further distortion of the Christian attitude to the transmission of life, "we believe that this whole question will best be studied and situated in the larger context of the formation of responsible conscience in general."[262] The recommendation that the study on the formation of conscience be initiated as soon as possible was fulfilled four years later.

III. CONSTITUTIONAL QUESTIONS

Debate among Canadians about their country's federal constitution has had an important effect on the CCCB. This is evident from the conference's statements and also from its decision not to speak on some occasions.

During the entire post-Vatican II period of the conference, some aspect of the federal constitution has been a preoccupation of Canadians. The approach of the 1967 centenary of Confederation raised the question of how the CCC would observe the occasion. Preparations for celebrating the event had a high public profile. A world's fair was coming to Montreal during the year. Although it was not specifically arranged to mark the centenary, it had the air of a national fete. There were, moreover, plenty of Confederation celebrations planned and no national body could avoid questions about how it would mark the event.

The question touched the CCC at several levels. For example, it affected a plan by the staff of the social action office to organize a joint bilingual session of the Social Life Conference and the Semaines Sociales. These two big annual teaching events had been held separately but on the same theme annually since 1953. At the suggestion of the staff, a joint session in 1967 was approved. However, at a February 1966 meeting of the English section of the social action commission, difficulties were reported. The staff members, John Shea, William Ryan and Jean-Guy Hamelin, were making little progress in arranging the event. Unlike the Social Life Conference, the Semaines sociales was not a conference project. It had an independent corporation headed by a Jesuit, Rev. Richard Arès. The proposal for a joint session aroused "no evident enthusiasm" among the directors of the Semaines, Shea and Ryan told the commission. "The dominant reason for their hesitation was doubtless their anxiety lest such a joint conference in 1967 be interpreted as a witness to the success of the Canadian Confederation and as such do much harm to the Church in the eyes of many French Canadians. For them, such a conference must be associated with Expo '67 and as totally dissociated with the birthday of Confederation as possible." The report to the commission thus summarized a reality that would grow in importance for the conference.[263]

Even as the plan for a bilingual social life conference was collapsing, other conference members and staff were at work on an even more difficult project. In April 1965, the board began considering the publication of a pastoral letter for 1967 and, at the beginning of 1966, work on it had begun.[264] At the October 1966 plenary the crucial decisions about its content had to be made. The documents sent to CCC members reveal some of the difficulties. Montreal theologian André Naud, then in charge of research at Cardinal Léger's secretariat, was the main writer of the text. By the time of that meeting, his French text had gone through six or seven drafts. Each bishop received a copy of Naud's outline of the difficulties of writing such a text. The Catholic Church incorporated "the Canadian problem," he wrote. Its members included those who were comfortable with Confederation and those who did not want to celebrate it. Groups of the St.-Jean-Baptiste Society in Quebec had announced their opposition and other groups would be sure to oppose any celebration. Naud saw a need for a pastoral letter on the "problem," but with no note of celebration or thanksgiving for Confederation as such.[265]

Conference members involved in the process look back on the 1967 Confederation statement, approved by the April 7, 1967, plenary, as their most difficult and most successful message. As Naud recommended, it addressed "the problem" and avoided disappointing those of various opinions about Confederation. "The chief malady of Canadian society," it said, "consists in the deep discontent felt by a growing number of French Canadians at the difficulties which their community must face in its attempts at growth, and in the uneasiness which the claims of the French-speaking group arouse in other parts of the country.... It is beyond dispute that the French-speaking group of Quebec has a right to existence, to normal development in all spheres of life, to civil and political institutions suited to their genius and peculiar needs, and to that autonomy without which their existence and prosperity would enjoy no good guarantee. But at the same time, one must not forget that the legitimate aspirations of Quebec may be justly fulfilled only when there is full respect for the greater common good, and for the inviolable rights of others."[266]

As noted above in the review of CCCB social teachings, the April 21, 1972, plenary affirmed Quebec's right to political self-determination. "We affirm that all options which respect the human person and the human community are a matter of free choice on the individual as well as the community level," the 1972 text said.

Eight years later, the question of whether to speak in the midst of yet another constitutional debate would convulse the CCCB. At issue was the passage of a Canadian Bill of Rights in the context of the repatriation of the constitution. Asked a dozen years later what the conference's greatest failure was during its fifty years, some bishops would say that for them it was the CCCB's failure to present its views to the parliamentary committee studying the Canadian Bill of Rights.

The problem was not uncertainty about what to say about the Bill of Rights. A November 1980 board meeting directed the executive of the conference to say three things: that the government should consult Canadians more thoroughly; that the CCCB was taking no position for or against entrenchment of a charter of rights in the Canadian constitution; and that if the government went ahead with plans for a charter, the conference wanted to discuss denominational schools, abortion, guarantees of fundamental freedoms, anti-discrimination provisions, native rights, minority language rights, and Canada's official languages.[267]

The executive ran into difficulty because the charter question arose as part of the Trudeau government's decision to repatriate the constitution without Quebec's participation. When the executive began to implement the board's direction about the charter, it found it impossible to separate this project from the issue of unilateral repatriation.

To follow up its mandate from the board, the executive circulated to CCCB members a draft brief to the parliamentary committee. One of the comments received was from the executive of the Assembly of Quebec Bishops. It recorded the opposition of the Quebec bishops to the brief as then written. Among the five objections listed, the key one was "the fact that the text makes no comment on the unilateral procedure used by the government"[268] to repatriate the constitution.

There is no detailed record of the debate in the January 1981 executive committee meeting. The committee reported only that "in view of the impossibility of producing a brief which would have respected the mandate confided to it by the Board, the Executive decided not to make a presentation to the Special Committee."[269] Bishop Bernard Hubert spoke for the Quebec bishops as a member of the CCCB executive. He said in a later interview that, in his view, the disagreement involved a double veto. The Quebec bishops insisted that a common brief of the CCCB should include a statement that unilateral repatriation of the constitution without the accord of the province of Quebec was unacceptable. The Quebec bishops issued a statement to this effect on January 29, 1981.[270] The Quebec opposition to the brief on that ground came up against the unwillingness of some anglophone bishops to speak out against unilateral repatriation, Hubert explained.[271]

One result of the difficulties of this event was that during many years, the voice of the CCCB was silent on the political difficulties faced by the people served by conference members.[272] It would be ten years before the CCCB attempted to write another statement about Canadian constitutional problems. The silence was broken by the board's June 1992 statement on the 125th anniversary of Confederation.

IV. SEXUAL ABUSE

Inglorious evidence of sins of sexual abuse by some Canadian priests and religious brothers gave rise, among other things, to one of the most important collegial actions undertaken by the Canadian bishops. The Conference as a whole sought appropriate ways to help both victims and offenders.

During the 1980s, more and more evidence came to light across Canada of incidents of sexual abuse against children, especially young boys. Charges were laid, here and there, against men of varied backgrounds: Boy Scout leaders, doctors, fathers, husbands, police officers, social workers and teachers. The greatest publicity was accorded, not unexpectedly, to cases where the abuse had been committed by a priest or teaching brother. Shock and scandal were scarcely adequate words to describe the feelings experienced by Church members and others as guilty pleas, convictions and jail sentences left no doubt that the charges were true.

The first responsibility for dealing with the accused and the victims rested with the local bishop, when a diocesan priest was involved, or with the religious superior, when the accused was a member of a religious community. To help local Church authorities, the CCCB circulated general guidelines early in 1987. They specified the requirements of Canada's child protection and criminal laws, and of Church law, and suggested some initial pastoral responses in the event of an accusation.

Two years later, wider and deeper aspects of the problem had become evident. During the 1989 October plenary meeting of the CCCB, several bishops asked the conference for help in studying what to do after priests from their dioceses had served their sentences. The conference moved to share the pastoral burden of trying to respond to all aspects of the problem. The ensuing discussion led to a project examining long-range prevention, continuing pastoral care for victims and their families, and the treatment of abusers and their future. A media release about the project expressed "deep concern and sympathy for victims" and for the members of dioceses suffering through current cases. A special effort would be made, it added, to enlist the help of all members of the Church in establishing new pastoral policies. "The problems go beyond what we bishops can resolve on our own," the conference president, Bishop Robert Lebel, stressed. "We will be calling on all Church members to help us understand these problems more fully, and to plan how the whole Church can respond in the future."

Three members of the CCCB's permanent council, a parish priest and three lay professionals were named to the ad hoc committee that directed the project.[273] Four work groups were formed to study the specific aspects of the committee's mandate. More than thirty resource persons, including several victims of sexual abuse, were named to these groups. In addition, members of the CCCB's professional staff were involved. The results of the committee's work were presented to Church members and the public in two stages. First to appear, in March 1992, was *Breach of Trust, Breach of Faith: Child Sexual Abuse in Church and Society*, a 64-page booklet intended for use in parish and other discussion groups. Prepared by CCCB staff under the committee's direction, it contained educational and discussion materials aimed at helping to eliminate the sexual abuse of children in Church and society. Topics covered in the material for five proposed study sessions were sexual abuse of children in the Church; dynamics of child sexual abuse; factors in Church and society that may contribute to child sexual abuse; personal and community responsibility in child sexual abuse cases; and preventing child sexual abuse. Each booklet had pull-out pages on which study groups could propose recommendations for action to their local bishop and the CCCB. The committee said in an introduction that "The materials in the booklet don't provide all of the answers, or even pose all of the questions. Greater study and debate are necessary. It is hoped that the conclusions and recommendations of the study groups will advance the understanding of what needs to be done."[274]

The committee's main report was published in June 1992. Summarizing more than two years of work by committee members and the four work groups, it was entitled *From Pain to Hope*. It made fifty recommendations: five addressed to the Catholics of Canada; eighteen to the Canadian Catholic bishops; ten to those responsible for priestly formation; ten to those responsible for priests in a diocese; and seven to the CCCB itself.

One of the recommendations to the CCCB referred to the allegations that native children had been abused in the former residential schools directed by members of Catholic religious orders. When revelations of these charges received wide public attention in the latter part of 1990, it was clear that they fell outside the mandate on which the ad hoc committee was already at work. At a special meeting in Saskatoon early in 1991, therefore, a Steering Committee on Residential Schools was planned. Named to it were a bishop, several native people, and representatives of the religious communities of men and women whose members had been involved in the former schools.[275] One of the recommendations of the CCCB ad hoc committee called on the bishops' conference to continue to co-operate with the Canadian Religious Conference "in working towards healing as initiated with the native peoples."

The CCCB was also asked to prepare and implement a code of professional ethics for clergy and pastoral agents. It should, the committee added, explore ways of participating in a telephone service designed to help troubled youth. The CCCB should also collect suggestions coming from groups using the CCCB's discussion materials and provide the best follow-up possible. It should have competent authorities undertake to update the official guidelines for the formation of future priests. It should call for "immediate and continuing research in the social sciences regarding the complex reality of human sexuality (both heterosexual and homosexual), the sexuality of celibates, and the issues linked to the deviant expression of sexuality." It noted on this recommendation that, according to some researchers, it is urgent to establish a scientific basis on which clear guidelines can be made for the treatment of sexually dysfunctional priests.

A seventh recommendation to the CCCB urged the conference to "support and foster the present involvement of the diocesan Churches of Canada in their efforts to emphasize baptismal priesthood and promote an ecclesial communion in which the ministerial priesthood serves the priesthood of all the faithful." An explanation by the committee clarified the background and purpose of the proposal. Throughout the country, the committee said, "we see a progressive transformation in the way certain diocesan structures function, e.g.: greater accent on the partnership of women and men; clearer expressions of the ministries of priests and pastoral agents; diocesan synods; etc." The committee recognized, it added,

> that there is a direct connection between a certain model of Church life and the deviations we deplore in the behaviour of some of the Church's ministers. We do not claim this relationship is one of cause and effect but suggest, based on certain studies, particularly the Winter Commission, that a model of Church life in which priests live their ministry as if it were an undebatable power, provides a more favourable environment for committing and continuing acts of child sexual abuse (see Winter Commission, Vol. 1, pp. 137-138). However, rather than belatedly putting hypothetical blame on outdated social structures that still exist, we ask the CCCB to support and promote all that is being done to implement the true spirit of the Second Vatican Council. Indeed, it is through fidelity to their own vocation of renewal and conversion that our diocesan churches will indirectly become less vulnerable to possible deviations by some of its ministers.[276]

At a special meeting, the CCCB executive committee formally received the ad hoc committee's report. It referred to the CCCB's permanent council the seven recommendations addressed specifically to the conference. The executive also added a recommendation of its own: "That the Conference set up some kind of internal mechanism for monitoring reaction to and implementation of the report." At its August 1992 plenary meeting, the CCCB formally accepted the report and thereby approved the processes for implementation of the recommendations for which the conference itself was responsible.[277]

CHAPTER SIX

Relations with the Holy See

I. PAPAL REPRESENTATIVE IN CANADA

A main link in relations between the CCCB and the Holy See is provided by the papal legate in Ottawa. The post was established as an apostolic delegation by Pope Leo XIII on August 3, 1899. It became an apostolic nunciature on October 16, 1969, under Paul VI, after the Canadian government established diplomatic relations with the Holy See.

The records of the conference meetings show an evolution in the role of the papal representative. Before 1943, he was a promoter of the formation of the Canadian conference. In the first meetings after the conference was set up, he was usually present at the opening session of the plenary, which he addressed formally, presenting a list of information items, suggestions or requests from various offices of the Vatican curia. For example, the minutes of the CCC's 1953 plenary show that as the meeting opened, the Apostolic Delegate brought to the attention of the bishops thirteen requests or information items from various Vatican offices.

Since Vatican II, the delegate (formally referred to as pro-nuncio between 1969 and 1993, and now nuncio) has been invited to enter the plenary meeting at a specified time. He is greeted by the president, gives an address, is thanked by the vice-president, and leaves. During the week of a plenary meeting, the nuncio is usually the guest of the CCCB at a luncheon with members of the executive or board, and all conference members are guests of the nuncio at an evening reception. Of course, there also are ad hoc meetings with conference officers whenever the CCCB or the nuncio wishes, and regular exchanges of correspondence.

As a fully accredited ambassador from the Holy See to Canada, the nuncio has responsibilities that do not involve the CCCB. As the Pope's personal representative among Catholics in the country, he may deal with a diocese or some group or organization on matters that do not interest the conference. There remain many questions calling for direct relations between the nuncio and the conference. For example, just as the nuncio is personally responsible for sending to Rome the names for appointment of a new bishop, so he is the first to know of a nomination and informs CCCB members. Also, it is usually through his office that major papal or other Vatican statements are released to the bishops and the Canadian public – although often not before the media in Rome announce the news. While all this involves regular exchanges, it is evident, nevertheless, that the CCCB is not fully aware of all that the nuncio thinks or does.

As noted in the introduction to this book, research for it had to be confined to the CCCB's archives. On the matter of relations between the papal representative and the CCCB, therefore, the CCCB's files may not contain all that could be reported if files of the nunciature and Vatican were examined. Moreover, no minutes are kept when CCCB officials on occasion meet the nuncio about a matter of mutual interest.

In general, CCCB files and the personal recollections of conference officials reveal only amicable relations with the papal representatives who have served in Ottawa over the years. One documented incident of serious disagreement will be examined in some detail here because of what it shows about unity and mutual support among the Canadian bishops. That is, the CCC acted in a collegial manner, in solidarity with the individual members involved.

The matter began when Archbishop Emanuele Clarizio was invited as usual to address the bishops' April 1969 plenary meeting. Immediately after the meeting, Bishop Alexander Carter, then CCC president, informed the Apostolic Delegate that he had "greatly surprised all the bishops and upset some of them"[278] by some things he had said at the plenary. The CCC's response was described in Carter's letter. The board of the conference called a special meeting to read and discuss Clarizio's text. The meeting directed Carter to write immediately to Pope Paul VI to assure him of the loyalty of the Canadian bishops and to describe the incident with Clarizio.[279] Carter was also directed to ask Clarizio for additional explanations and examples, if possible, of the incidents he had mentioned in his address. The board's decisions were then confirmed by a majority vote of the plenary meeting.

Carter's April 25 letter to the Pope was taken to Paul VI by Cardinals George Flahiff and Maurice Roy, who were travelling to Rome on other business at the time. Carter told the Pope that as usual the Apostolic Delegate had been invited to the CCC meeting. "To our surprise," Carter wrote, "the Delegate expressed here and there in his talk several complaints that seemed to question the behaviour and actions of some members of the Canadian Episcopate. We were particularly astonished because we had never foreseen such an eventuality. At least we could not have expected it on the basis of the previous official dealings between Archbishop Clarizio or his predecessors and the general assembly of the Canadian bishops." Giving no further details about what Clarizio had said, Carter told the Pope that the CCC was in communication with the delegate. The CCC thought "some explanation and some examples are needed to remove the present ambiguity." The main reason for the letter to the Pope, Carter added, "is to make sure that nothing in this present misunderstanding adds to your anxiety."

Carter's long letter to Clarizio the same day cited the parts of Clarizio's talk that had surprised and upset CCC members. A copy of the CCC letter to Paul VI was enclosed. "We are ready to receive and study seriously any explanations you wish to give us, and, should the need arise, we are ready to undertake the necessary remedies," Carter said. He noted that the letter to the Pope "passes no judgment on anything or anyone. It merely relates the facts and reassures the Holy Father of the deep and sincere sentiments of the Canadian Episcopate."[280]

Carter asked Clarizio for "some enlightenment and some facts" about the latter's remark to the plenary that an unspecified number of unnamed Canadian bishops used "words of veneration and submission" when in Rome in front of the Pope and members of the curia, but have "an opposite attitude" when at home in Canada. Clarizio had added: "From my very first days in Canada I noticed that for some it was thought stylish to demonstrate opposition to what Rome said, and to do the contrary of what Rome requested. Speaking to me in private: courtesy and unity of thought; but reunited as a group, sometimes only a few minutes later: opposition, sarcasm and even ridicule. I admire the great majority of the Bishops: dignified, well-intentioned and loyal to the Holy Father and to the Holy See. But at times these Bishops are overshadowed by some who are organized to realize set programs."[281]

Clarizio's May 6 reply to Carter said he thought a meeting with some CCC representatives would be preferable to putting more details in writing.[282] The June 5-6 CCC board meeting studied Clarizio's invitation for a group of CCC members to meet with him. There is no record of that meeting, which apparently settled the affair.[283] The final words exchanged were not put in writing. Archbishop Clarizio returned to Rome to another assignment about a year later. In the end, the main point on the public record is that the bishops stood united among themselves, and in solidarity with the Pope, in the face of criticism that had been directed ambiguously against only a few of them.

II. MARRIAGE TRIBUNALS

In a personal interview for this book, retired Ottawa Archbishop Plourde, a former conference president, said that in his view the most difficult dealings between the Canadian conference and the Vatican had to do with the country's marriage tribunals.

Seven regional tribunals[284] to deal with marriage nullity cases began operations at the beginning of 1947. The Canadian bishops asked the Holy See to found them. The aim was to overcome difficulties of the diocesan courts and so assure the administration of justice regarding marriage cases.[285] To protect the rights of each party in a marriage dispute and to be certain that Church teaching about the indissolubility of marriage was fully respected, each original judgment had to be appealed for thorough restudy. A system of rotating appeals was therefore begun, whereby cases from one tribunal would be studied in appeal by another.[286] Because of the stress placed by appeals on the regional tribunals, the CCC requested and obtained a February 1971 indult from the Vatican allowing for a single appeal tribunal for the whole of Canada. However, because agreement could not be reached about where to locate this court or how to staff and finance it, the permission to found it was left in abeyance for a time.[287] Meanwhile an eighth tribunal, in Edmonton, had been added.[288]

The Holy See published some new norms for tribunal procedures in 1971. In November 1974, some adaptations requested by the Canadian bishops were granted.[289]

An exchange at the CCC board meeting in January 1975 showed the cause of some tension with Rome about the tribunals. Earlier, the Apostolic Pro-Nuncio in Ottawa had informed the bishops about the contents of letters from the Vatican, sent to him but not to the CCC, about application of the 1974 norms in Canada. The board members wanted the Vatican to be more even-handed and direct in its dealings with them. Canadian bishops and canon lawyers had been comparing the Vatican decisions regarding Canadian tribunals to what was being granted in the United States, Australia or similar situations. "The members of the board clearly indicated," minutes say, "that it would be preferable and avoid much confusion if the Holy See were to grant to all Episcopal Conferences equal privileges and restrictions." The board also asked its president, Archbishop Jean-Marie Fortier, to "express concern at the fact that there has been no direct communication with the Canadian Catholic Conference."[290]

It was at this time that Rev. Guy Poisson succeeded Rev. Charles Mathieu as French-sector general secretary for the conference. One of the tasks that Poisson faced in his new office involved the regional tribunals. Under one of the new procedures that had been agreed upon between Rome and the conference, decisions on marriage cases were to be sent to the conference by the regional tribunals for review. As a canon lawyer himself, Poisson was prepared to deal with the matters of fact and law involved, but not with the massive amount of work that was necessary to read or get other canonists to read hundreds of cases. One suggested solution for this problem was especially resisted by Poisson. It would have meant agreeing to verify only every tenth or fifteenth regional decision. Fearing that this could result in an error or oversight that could discredit the Canadian tribunals, Poisson refused to go along with it. He held out for the establishment of a full-fledged national appeal tribunal as the proper way to review the work of regional courts.[291]

During their September 1983 plenary meeting, the bishops decided to set up one bilingual appeal tribunal for all of Canada.[292] The circumstances that had delayed the step in 1971 no longer prevailed. The Vatican's approval, for a three-year trial period, came two months later, on November 23.[293] On January 25, 1984, the CCCB formally established the

Canadian Appeal Tribunal, and it began operating the following April in Ottawa, headed by Monsignor André Desrochers as judicial vicar.

The new tribunal was equipped with a computerized system to record data on the cases received so the facts could be analyzed rapidly. For any questions of law, Ottawa was well located for recruiting canon lawyers to serve as judges. The tribunal's report for 1985 showed 3,400 cases received, with just 120 cases still under study at year end. A later report showed that the caseload in 1991 had totalled 4,700, or forty-six per cent more than in 1985. Yet the tribunal's total income had risen only from $480,000 to $498,000 over the six-year period, as the per-case cost had been lowered from $150 to $106.[294]

A new round of tension with Vatican officials began when the tribunal's first experimental three-year approval period ended. On January 31, 1987, a six-month extension was granted. When that ended, approval was extended for another six months. Archbishop James Hayes, the CCCB's president, summarized these steps in a letter to Cardinal Agostino Casaroli, Vatican Secretary of State, and told him the Canadian bishops were annoyed by the Vatican's successive postponements of definitive approval for the tribunal. The appeal tribunal fully satisfied the Canadian bishops. The experiment had quickly proven conclusive, as far as anyone in Canada was concerned. The doubts raised by the Vatican's recurring delays of final approval were prejudicial to the Church in Canada, said Hayes. They were beginning to create a climate of unhealthy ambiguity. They made it difficult to get canonists to serve, created insecurity for secretarial staff, and reduced the appeal tribunal's moral authority in dealing with first-instance courts, he added. While not questioning the Vatican's role in the matter, the CCCB hoped their tribunal soon would be established without restrictions, Hayes concluded.[295]

Through the Apostolic Pro-Nuncio, in a March 4, 1988, letter, word came from Cardinal Aurelio Sabattani that there was another extension, this time for nine months, until the end of October 1988. The delays had been needed to give Vatican experts more time "for the study of the problem by the light of the abundant documentation sent there. This study is not yet finished," the letter said.[296] A second letter from the pro-nuncio, dated October 24, 1988, simply announced that provisional approval of the tribunal had been granted for another three years. It was still not definitive. With the decree of prolongation came a long Vatican letter raising questions about the tribunal, to which the CCCB was asked to reply.[297]

The CCCB took its time about answering. The canon law commission was asked to study the Vatican's questions. It proposed in March 1989 that a draft reply be prepared and sent to all Canadian bishops for their information and approval. Then the matter was placed on the agenda of the 1991 CCCB plenary meeting. All members were asked to comment on the draft reply and to vote on a request for approval of the appeal tribunal. One reason for this involved procedure was to satisfy a Vatican remark that an earlier request had come from the sixteen-member CCCB permanent council and not the entire conference membership. The 1991 plenary voted unanimously to request definitive approval of the tribunal. The CCCB's letter, also approved by the plenary, was sent by Archbishop Marcel Gervais.

One of the Vatican questions had to do with how the tribunal could handle the 3,960 cases reported for 1986. The CCCB replied that, besides being able to recruit extra canonists, the use of data processing equipment enabled the tribunal to focus attention on judicial issues, "leaving the more material aspects of the cases to be handled through the use of technology."

Questioning the grounds on which the Canadian tribunal based its decrees, the Vatican had written that "one could suspect that the Tribunal's jurisprudence does not fully conform with John Paul II's doctrine." This "implied condemnation of their tribunals" could not be accepted by the CCCB, the conference letter said. That remark in the Vatican letter "might imply that the Tribunal personnel is not loyal to the Church and its teaching. We do not consider this to be justified by the facts," the CCCB reply insisted. It added that, "at this time, it is the opinion of the Canadian Conference of Catholic Bishops that the personnel of the Canadian tribunals merits and needs its unqualified support and the Conference intends to do what it can to offer it."

The reply also noted that some of the cases questioned by the Vatican were those from lower courts. The bishops were trying to make sure there were no irregularities at that level. Meanwhile, any that did occur could not be held against the appeal tribunal which, as the Vatican itself insisted, had no administrative authority to police the first-instance courts.

The final issue was what the Vatican letter had called "a surprising fact" – that the conference had rejected the previous system of four regional tribunals, which seemed to the Vatican to have "many advantages." In contrast, the single appeal tribunal "is accessible to the parties only with great difficulties, both because of great geographical distances, and because it requires a large number of judges and employees." The letter urged all diocesan bishops to seek adequate solutions "without excluding the possibility of establishing several tribunals of the second instance."

The CCCB reply pointed out that under the previous system, courts often were as distant from their appeal centre as they now were from the one Ottawa appeal tribunal. Moreover, the Vatican had given one appeal tribunal in Australia competence also for New Zealand and other Pacific islands, "at far greater distances from the place of the court than are the Canadian first instance tribunals." For the CCCB, therefore, "it would be unreasonable and impractical to revert to the former system. The bishops have expressed their full support of the present system which, having experienced its growing pains, is now running quite smoothly to the satisfaction of all directly concerned." Hence the unanimous 1991 vote for its definitive establishment – a matter still not settled when this text was written.[298]

III. NOMINATION OF BISHOPS

Another aspect of Church life about which the Canadian bishops did not achieve ready satisfaction was the process for listing names of priests as possible candidates to become bishops. The heart of the problem has been how to adapt universal Roman norms for a country as large, varied and culturally complex as Canada.

The norms in question were published by the Vatican in March 1972 after consulting the various episcopal conferences. In the fall of that year, the CCC began the required study of how these general norms could be applied in this country. The study moved by slow stages. Three years later, in October 1975, the proposals were sent back to Rome.

The Roman norms directed the bishops of each ecclesiastical "province," at the invitation of their archbishop, to meet regularly and draw up lists of priests in their area who could be candidates for the episcopacy. These lists make their way to the Vatican through the office of the Apostolic Nuncio in Ottawa. The president of the bishops' conference is to receive a copy of each list, for possible comments. In this way, standing lists are to be kept up to date, as a starting point for the process detailed in Canon 377, by which a short list (a "terna") is prepared for the Pope's final decision when a vacancy does occur.

The CCC's 1975 proposals began with the idea of a special fourteen-member committee of bishops who would have a central role in the regular list-making process. It would consist of the conference's president and vice-president, and three bishops elected in each of the four pastoral regions: Atlantic, Quebec, Ontario, and the West. For dioceses in each region, the list-making committee would consist of five bishops: the conference president and vice-president, and the three bishops from that region. If special circumstances required it, all fourteen committee members might be involved. The CCC proposed that the committee be involved with the Apostolic Nuncio in consultations about candidates before actual nominations were made. They also wanted the short list going to Rome in the event of a vacancy to be co-signed by the Apostolic Nuncio and the conference's president. They further proposed that, because of the culture and size of Canada, the meetings to update the standing lists be convened every second year, that candidates have competence in both English and French, and that there be greater opportunity for pre-nomination consultations, including with the laity. These suggestions were sent to Rome by Archbishop Jean-Marie Fortier as CCC president.[299]

Three years later, Archbishop Gilles Ouellet was president and felt it necessary to remind archbishops of the process by which, "for the good of the Church in Canada, the CCCB has constantly been concerned in cooperating with the Holy Father in the choice of the best possible candidates for the Episcopacy." Ouellet recalled that earlier efforts to approach the Holy See in order to adapt the Vatican norms to the Canadian situation "did not meet with complete success." As for the list-making committee that the CCCB has proposed, "it must be acknowledged," he said, "that this committee has functioned only sporadically and that it should be evaluated before proceeding further."[300] That evaluation, aimed at increasing Canadian participation in the list-making and nominating processes through adjustment of the Vatican norms, was still proceeding at the end of the period covered by this book.

IV. ANNUAL CCCB VISIT TO ROME

Since 1970, the conference has delegated its president and vice-president, with one general secretary, to go to Rome each year for a formal visit with the Pope and the Vatican dicasteries or curial offices. Each visit's agenda is prepared by the executive committee. Conference members are consulted for suggestions about topics to be discussed. The list of topics is sent in advance to the Vatican and a schedule is set up for meetings with the offices concerned.

When the bishops were canvassed for topics before a visit by Bishop William Power as CCC president, Edmonton's Archbishop Joseph MacNeil suggested, "Tell the Pope he's doing a fine job." Later, exchanging greetings with Paul VI, Power opened the conversation in English by repeating just what MacNeil had said: "Holy Father, the Canadian bishops think you are doing a good job." Archbishop Jean-Marie Fortier, who was CCC vice-president, recalls that Paul VI seemed confused by the remark, so Fortier repeated in French, "Vous faites un bon boulot." It was evident immediately that it was not Power's use of English but the sentiment he had expressed that so surprised the Pope and seemed to leave him uncertain about how to react. Fortier later recalled the incident to a senior Vatican official, who said, "You know, that probably was the first time anyone said that to the Pope."[301]

The CCCB officers report that they always come away from their meeting with the Pope buoyed up and encouraged. Their mood is not always so when they leave other Vatican offices, however. Power recalls that he once went to the Congregation for Bishops to ask that the secrecy rule for new bishops be changed. The Canadian bishops wanted to make it possible for a priest to consult someone after being asked to become a bishop. The cardinal who was head of the congregation at the time suggested to Power that in such a situation a priest should ask another to hear his confession, proceed in such a way that the seal of confession would apply and then change the topic and ask for advice about becoming a bishop. Thus, the priest who was consulted would be bound to secrecy. "In other words, to abuse the sacrament rather than change a rule," Power recalls disapprovingly.[302]

Similarly, Archbishop Gilles Ouellet, going one time to the Congregation for the Doctrine of the Faith, was challenged, even before being seated, about a recipe for eucharistic bread that had been published in an issue of the CCCB's *National Bulletin on Liturgy*. Calling it in Italian a "cake" recipe, the official pulled down various reference books as he argued that Mass said with such bread would be neither licit nor valid. He suggested that the stipend offerings for such Masses might have to be returned to their donors. At the end of the argument, Ouellet promised only that he would raise the Vatican's concern at the next CCCB board meeting. Leaving the office, Ouellet told his companions that he was reminded that Galileo must have walked down the same stairs saying, as legend has it, "Even so, it moves." Said Ouellet: "I don't care what they say, it's still bread!" Later, the CCCB board did discuss the matter, decided to do nothing about it, and nothing more was heard of it.

After his 1990 visit to Rome, at a time when the CCCB was being severely criticized by some in Canada for its handling of the abortion law debate, Bishop Robert Lebel issued a rare public statement about the purpose and overall spirit of the visit he had just made to Rome as CCCB president. In a press release, he said:

> We go there to exchange views about various topics that come up in the everyday life of the Conference and at meetings of our Permanent Council and, especially, our Plenary Meeting. Of course, this could always be done by mail. The most important aspect of our visit to Rome is, then, its meaning: We see it as a sign of solidarity and communion with the Holy Father and the persons who assist him in his ministry of unity.
>
> Our link with the Pope and the Holy See is very important to us; it is one of the Canadian Bishops' chief and constant concerns. We have organized our Conference as the means by which we live episcopal collegiality in this country. This collegiality would not be authentic, however, if it did not join us to the person who is head of the Apostolic College in its full reality. The College of Bishops doesn't exist without its head, the successor of Peter in the Church of Rome.
>
> Sometimes we hear or read that some individuals or groups have doubts about what kind of relations we have with Rome, and about our solidarity with the Pope and his guidelines and teachings. We are hurt by these suspicions and accusations; they are unfounded, unjust and defamatory.
>
> We accept the fact that some say they disagree with our positions. In the Church there is a kind of freedom that is legitimate, on matters that do not touch our faith directly. But we do not accept that, in order to reinforce their criticism or condemnation of us, some people try to set us against the Pope.
>
> In such a case, our teachings are caricatured, cited out of context or falsely interpreted; or else, the Pope's teachings are interpreted with a rigidity that they do not really have. The Pope's worst enemies may be those who defend the autocratic and intolerant image they have of him and attribute to him their own approach. Do they follow him in his social teachings? Do they share his teachings on the merciful Father, on Christ, the Holy Spirit, the Virgin Mary?
>
> In Rome, when we met those who work closely with the Holy Father, we were praised for our solidarity with the Holy See and for the correctness and richness of our teaching. Several times, without us seeking it, we were assured at the highest levels that the Canadian Bishops have a good reputation in Rome. The message that we read in these

remarks is that they were meant to offset the worries we might have about those who denounce us to Rome in an effort to curry favour there at our expense.

While in Rome, we also had a spirited and relaxed conversation with the Holy Father. He knows that we stand with him on his position on Humanae Vitae, on his clear moral teaching on abortion, on the need always to refer to the basic teachings of our faith. We make our own the rich teachings of his Encyclicals and Apostolic Exhortations on dogmatic questions and social issues.

This is what we want to say to Rome by our annual visit. We raise questions with the Pope's collaborators; we discuss questions, giving our own views; we share information about the life of the Canadian churches. Our exchanges are sometimes lively and always frank. They listen to us with interest. They study our reports carefully. We can say that what is going on in Canada is well known in Rome. Truth, frankness, solidarity, communion: These are the words which best describe our relations with Rome, especially as lived during our ad limina visits and the annual visits of the CCCB President and Vice-President.[303]

CHAPTER SEVEN

Special Events

I. POPE'S VISITS

There is no record of how many times the Pope was invited to visit Canada before John Paul II arrived in 1984. Paul VI was invited when the CCCB president and vice-president, Emmett Carter and Gilles Ouellet, were in Rome in 1976.[304] Probably several such occasions went unrecorded. The first invitation to John Paul II was on the occasion of his 1979 visit to the United Nations and the eastern United States.[305] It was declined on the grounds that the planned visit could not be further prolonged.

The June 1980 meeting of the CCCB board considered extending another invitation. For Edmonton's Archbishop Joseph MacNeil, the personal highlight of his term as CCCB president was John Paul II's decision to come to Canada. During their October 1981 visit with the Pope and other Vatican officials, MacNeil and Archbishop Henri Légaré learned that a formal invitation would meet with a favourable response. The executive committee began to make plans at their December 2-3, 1981, meeting.[306] The October 25-28, 1982, plenary meeting, in turn, agreed to give the four-member executive committee authority to decide all aspects of the visit for which the CCCB would be responsible. The bishops in each of the four regions were asked to agree on the places the Pope might visit within their region. Each host diocese was responsible for its own program. Ottawa-Hull was on the list – not as host diocese, but as the national capital where the Pope would meet all the bishops, the diplomatic corps and government officials, and end his visit. The list at that early stage also mentioned an unspecified "northern diocese" as a possible visit site.

By the end of March 1983, the executive committee had a general plan. An objective for the visit had been decided: "In accordance with general and specific themes to be determined by the CCCB, to provide an extraordinary opportunity for the preaching of the Gospel particularly as it applies to Canada in the '80s." The structure, under the CCCB executive, would include a large national committee to help formulate general policy proposals. At the CCCB headquarters, the general secretaries would act as co-ordinators of "desks" for pastoral planning, liturgy, logistics and travel, media/public relations, finance and government participation. The directors of these desks would be aided by groups of advisers.[307]

During their April 1983 visit to Rome, the CCCB president and vice-president, Archbishop Légaré and Bishop Paul Reding of Hamilton, received official confirmation that the Pope would come to Canada in 1984 for a ten-day visit, from September 9 to 19. They had taken a map to Rome showing the host dioceses chosen by the regions, from St. John's, Newfoundland, to Vancouver and back to Ottawa. They had the assurance that the federal government would be responsible for protocol, security and transport for the papal party, as well as press accreditation and facilities. All the bishops were informed[308] and the news was made public on May 4.

From the beginning of planning, the CCCB emphasized that the visit would be pastoral in spirit and content. The pastoral planning desk was therefore considered to be the most important one. Through an extensive consultation, a national theme was chosen: Celebrate Our Faith. Similarly, a major theme was chosen for each host diocese. Choices were guided by the plan that the Pope's various talks during the visit should form a unified body of teachings. Theme suggestions were submitted to the Pope, who approved them except for one word.[309]

The CCCB co-ordinated all that was required for the Pope to carry out the planned program – what he would do each day, where he would sleep, what he would eat, how he would travel (popemobile, limousine, helicopter) and who would meet him upon arrival and bid him farewell.

The host dioceses had their wishes on these matters, and the Vatican and federal and provincial governments had theirs. Sufficient rest for the Pope was a concern, as was his safety and that of the crowds. Overall, the main concern was to maintain a pastoral atmosphere. The CCCB secretariat had to negotiate hundreds of three-party agreements aimed at harmonizing diocesan, Vatican and governmental interests.

The CCCB's liturgy desk was responsible for determining the Holy See's ceremonial requirements, communicating these to the host dioceses and seeing to it that final diocesan plans were acceptable. It was also responsible for preparing and publishing the necessary liturgical books and other materials. Each altar the Pope approached had to have on it the texts he would need, in English or in French, and often in other languages, for the liturgy that was planned.

The minutes of the September 12-16, 1983, CCCB plenary meeting record the difficulty of the debate dealing with the city where the Pope would begin his visit. When Légaré and Reding went to Rome in April 1983, part of the material they gave Vatican officials was a map of Canada. It showed distances and travel times between the proposed host dioceses. On the basis of this map it was calculated, and agreed, that nine days would be required. The map was not released by the CCCB as the official itinerary, but media in St. John's obtained a copy of it and announced their city as the starting point. The diocesan committee planning the St. John's visit held the same view, of course. This was challenged by those who argued that the visit had to begin at Quebec City, Canada's first diocese. The CCCB executive committee, reduced to three members by Reding's illness, voted for Quebec City as the starting point and then asked the September plenary meeting to discuss the matter and vote on it. The executive committee cited both religious and historical reasons for choosing Quebec City, "the first diocese governing almost all of North America and Mexico and where now lie the remains of the first bishop." The plenary voted sixty-seven to ten, with two abstentions, to support the executive's decision.[310]

Native Event

When public speculation began about a possible papal visit, native leaders took a special interest. John Paul II's statements in support of aboriginal peoples in Brazil and elsewhere were well known to Canadian native people. They organized several delegations to Rome to lobby Vatican officials and to seek to persuade the Pope to meet with native people while in Canada. Partly because of such pressure, early CCCB plans for the visit mentioned "a northern diocese" as a possible stop on the tour, but there was no mention of this in the nine-day schedule announced in May 1983.

The CCCB executive committee decided that any meeting with native people would be the responsibility of the CCCB itself and not that of any one diocese. Then, native leaders were asked to agree among themselves and propose one site. In the end, it was a personal wish of the Pope that made the difference. He let it be known that, along with everything else being planned, he wanted to meet the native people and to have some private time in the mountains. Bishop John Sherlock, by then CCCB president, later spelled out to Bishop Omer Robidoux of Churchill-Hudson Bay how the issue was settled:

> It was the Native peoples themselves, in a lengthy and tense meeting with Msgr. (Dennis) Murphy and myself, who finally agreed upon Fort Simpson as the site. This decision was reached after a large number of alternatives in southern and northern Canada were discarded as inappropriate locations for meetings with Native peoples and their leaders. It is worth noting that the (nine-day) itinerary which Bishop (Jean-Guy) Hamelin and I took to Rome in January (of 1984) would only with difficulty have permitted any visit to the North at all. The time available in the itinerary and the unwillingness of other regions to yield time would have made it most difficult. It was during our personal meeting with the Holy Father that we learned of his intense desire to go to the Canadian North and were able to convince him of the necessity of an additional day if he were to go North and at the same time have a full half day of rest in this very lengthy trip.[311]

So the Pope added one day to his 1984 Canadian visit, but in the end bad weather prevented him from going to either Fort Simpson or the mountains. He spent his half-day holiday in Elk Island National Park near Edmonton and completed his visit to Fort Simpson in 1987.

Each host diocese and the Fort Simpson committee proposed a local program. The CCCB's role was mainly to ensure that local plans could be accomplished in the time available and within Vatican and government guidelines. The CCCB was more directly involved, however, in the process of preparing the Pope's texts. The pastoral planning group, having overseen the selection of themes, gathered theme materials and local Church information to be sent to the Pope's staff. A summary in the form of a draft text was included. In mid-summer, Bishops Sherlock and Hamelin went to

Rome to work directly with the Pope's staff. Jesuit Father Bill Ryan and Sulpician Father Guy Poisson went along for detailed work on the English and French versions of the text. They found that John Paul II was doing more of the writing than they had expected, especially for his homilies. The Vatican then sent the final versions to the CCCB just before the visit began on September 9. The package contained only one text, French or English, for each homily and talk. The CCCB had to have every text in both languages. Even as the Pope was being greeted in Quebec City, his texts for later in the visit were still being translated in Ottawa.[312]

Wherever the Pope went during the visit, he was filmed by the CBC's host broadcaster team. Much of this coverage was broadcast by the CBC and other networks, and was watched for hours by millions of people. For most Canadians, their strongest impression of the visit came from watching it on television.[313] In all, more than 7,000 applications for media accreditation for the visit were received by the CCCB. The government task force handled this aspect of the visit. There had to be complex rules and lists of events – such as the visit to Bishop Laval's tomb in Quebec City – at which only a limited number of reporters and writers could be present. The Pope's texts had to be copied and distributed. As well, a media plane was organized to accompany the papal plane across the country for a core group of international and national media representatives who paid for the service.

Only one short event was dedicated exclusively to the Canadian bishops. That was their meeting and luncheon with the Pope at noon on his last day of the 1984 Canadian tour. They met in the lofty chapel of the motherhouse of the Sisters of Charity in Ottawa's historic Lower Town district and had the luncheon in an adjacent hall.

To help the Pope prepare his address to the bishops, and to outline the points that the bishops wished to discuss with him, the executive committee sent him a paper expressing the major concerns of the various CCCB episcopal commissions. The social action commission noted that it was particularly inspired by the teaching of the 1971 Synod of Bishops that "action on behalf of justice...(is) a constitutive dimension of the preaching of the Gospel." It noted efforts being made to find "new ways and means to make our pastoral efforts for social justice more and more effective" and told of Canadian efforts to build links of solidarity with the diocesan churches in Latin America and elsewhere. The canon law commission noted two continuing concerns: to receive news of Vatican decisions before the media published them and to overcome delays in decisions concerning the laicization of priests. Some ambiguities felt by priests and laity about changing roles in the Church were discussed by the commission on ministries and the apostolate. The missions commission reported growing interest in the lay missionary apostolate and experimental efforts to inculturate divine revelation into the traditional Amerindian culture and religion. The ecumenism commission concentrated on Canada's Anglican-Roman Catholic dialogue and the work of the liaison committee of the Canadian Council of Churches, the CCCB and the Canadian Jewish Congress. The theology commission noted its efforts to clarify the best ways for bishops to teach the faith and to overcome the split between the Gospel and contemporary culture. Efforts to equip pastoral workers and laity to use the modern media were reported by the two social communications commissions. Similarly, the sector commissions for Christian education discussed the formation of catechists and research in adult education. The liturgy commissions dealt with progress and problems in implementing Vatican II's reforms. It noted the commissions' particular interest "in the precise role of the bishop in directing and promoting liturgical adaptation and inculturation." The Pope had received all these points in advance in writing and many of them were raised by the bishops during their dialogue with him.[314]

For his part, John Paul II stressed to his brother bishops that preaching the Gospel was a bishop's first task. "All the ethical reflections and the questions which we can and must raise as pastors...are subordinated to the proclamation of salvation in Jesus Christ." In the homilies during his visit, he said, he had "tried to place the faithful face to face with this Revelation from on high, to lead them to contemplate the glory of God...." He said that he knew of the CCCB documents on such topics as justice, the dignity of man and woman, work, aid, charity, social love and solidarity with the poor, and of the efforts to respond to new questions posed by the sciences and technology. "I understand and approve this preoccupation. You wish to avoid a break between Christian teaching and life, between the Gospel and culture, between faith and justice." He said he knew the bishops had tried to improve the legislation touching broken homes, separations and divorce. "You know," he added, "that abortion is very widespread. And many have recourse to contraceptive means...." Among the causes of these things, he listed a generalized tendency to hedonism, a forgetting of God and "without a doubt an ignorance of the theology of the body." On these points, he concluded, "Sex education, the preparation of young people for marriage and support of family life should be top priorities here." He stressed the bishop's role in leading people to prayer and personal conversion. "There have been truly commendable efforts to point out the communal aspects of Penance," he noted, but this "must never lead to abandoning the personal act of the penitent and personal absolution." He stressed that the pastoral care of vocations requires close work with families and with youth. Laity, he added, can take up new ministries to assist priests and also have "the apostolate that is their very own" to carry into "the fabric of society the principles of social doctrine which your documents emphasize."

Besides its ecumenical accomplishments, he noted Canada's "extraordinary" wealth in cultural and linguistic traditions. Given Canadian conditions, he said, "I am convinced that the Church has the task of promoting mutual acceptance, esteem and recognition, of promoting the fuller participation of everyone in the life of society, in helping all to overcome all forms of chauvinism or exaggerated nationalistic sentiment." He noted that the Canadian bishops were aware that their responsibilities extended to other countries. Church members should be helped to open their eyes, hearts and hands to a concern for less favoured countries. As well, the spiritual needs of others should increase their missionary spirit. The Pope appealed for special concern for those deprived of freedom of conscience and of religion. He thanked the Canadian bishops "for all you have done and will do" to participate in the mission of the universal Church, in communion with the Pope and in collaboration with the departments of the Holy See.[315]

* * *

For the costs arising from the 1984 papal visit, four major accounts can be mentioned. Besides what the federal government paid for security, transportation and related responsibilities and the CBC's costs as host broadcaster, the Church had two major sets of bills to cover: the costs in each host diocese and the expenses of the national secretariat. Early in 1983, the CCCB executive committee asked the bishops to support a June 12 national collection for visit expenses.[316] It realized just over $2 million, of which the host dioceses retained $820,000. A second collection was later approved for June 17 the next year. From it, the host dioceses retained all that they collected; what was raised in the other dioceses went to the CCCB.[317] A study by Touche Ross & Partners after the visit put the total cost incurred by the host dioceses at $23 million. Their net costs, after taking into account various revenues, were $13.5 million. After a discussion at the 1984 October plenary, the CCCB board decided that these net costs would be paid regionally and that there would not be a third national collection. It was decided at the same time that any national surplus should be shared on a per capita basis among the host dioceses after $200,000 had been shared with Winnipeg-St. Boniface, "given the exceptional costs incurred by these dioceses."[318] The final audited CCCB statement for visit finances to the end of 1986 showed just over $3.3 million received and $2.8 million spent at the national level, with a revenue balance of $483,000.[319]

* * *

The Pope's visit to Fort Simpson on September 20, 1987, was treated by the CCCB as a completion of the one event that had to be dropped from his program three years earlier. For the Pope and for the native leaders who had kept pressing, it was the fulfillment of his promise to return. Speculation and rumours increased after his visit to the western and central United States was announced for late summer 1987.[320] Finally, on June 18, a press release confirmed that he would return to Fort Simpson on September 20, the day after the end of his U.S. visit in Detroit.[321] The plan was straightforward. His return flight from Detroit to Rome would be by a polar route and would land in Edmonton. The Pope would stay overnight in the same Grey Nuns' convent used during his 1984 visit to Edmonton. A smaller plane chartered by the CCCB would take him the next day to Fort Simpson and back to Edmonton. All requirements for transport, logistics, security and the media were virtually the same as three years earlier, and some members of their 1984 teams were reassembled by the CCCB, federal government, RCMP and CBC. The Vatican personnel, too, was virtually unchanged.

Apart from the dramatic fact that the Pope was keeping his promise in this way, public attention probably focused most on what he had to say in his address after his private meeting with the native leaders and before the Mass. Native people had been heartened by the Pope's 1984 talk that had been prepared for delivery at Fort Simpson and read over radio from Yellowknife when his plane was unable to reach Fort Simpson. It reflected the situations of native people that had arisen from the policies of the Trudeau years. By 1987, Canada's native peoples had been dealing for three years with the differences of the Mulroney government's approach to native issues. For the Pope's 1987 talk, officials of the Assembly of First Nations worked with the CCCB to prepare the documentation to send to the Pope. It tried to convey what was unchanged and what was new in the lives of the peoples to whom he would be speaking.

During the week before the Pope's return, the CCCB received the texts of his talk and homily. They were translated as required[322] and prepared for distribution to journalists from the Fort Simpson media centre as the Pope began talking. People on the site or watching on television saw him rise from his meeting with the native leaders, take his text from the hands of his secretary, go to the microphone and begin reading. At a crucial point, what he read differed from the prepared text that had been distributed to journalists as the Pope had begun speaking. Media reports concluded that the conversation with the leaders had persuaded him to change his address on the spot. In fact, it had been changed the night before, on the plane from Detroit, at the suggestion of the CCCB.

When the texts for his talk and homily were received by the CCCB, among those who reviewed them were members of the social action office staff who had been working closely with native leaders. Tony Clarke, then co-director of this office, had noted that a difference between what the Pope said during his visit in 1984 and what had been prepared for Fort Simpson would make it seem that the Pope had weakened his support of native rights. Such an impression would be unfortunate for native people at that juncture in their discussions with the federal government, Clarke argued. Pressed for precision by André Vallée, who was co-ordinating the small CCCB secretariat, Clarke red-pencilled three proposed changes to page four of the prepared text. Archbishop James Hayes, the newly-elected CCCB president, and Rev. William Ryan, the CCCB's general secretary, agreed that the Pope should be asked to make the suggested changes. Hayes wrote a letter to the Pope to explain them. Several copies of an amended page four, in English and French, were attached to the letter. When he went to Detroit with two federal officials to join the Saturday evening flight to Edmonton, Bernard Daly, the CCCB's assistant co-ordinator for the visit, carried Hayes' letter and gave it to Cardinal Agostino Casaroli, Vatican Secretary of State, on the plane. Later that evening, on the bus following the papal limousine from the airport to the Grey Nuns' convent where the Pope would sleep that night, Joaquin Navarro-Valls, the head of the Vatican press office, informed Daly that there was a new page four for the next day's talk. Except for one detail, it was the page that had accompanied Hayes' letter.

Navarro-Valls also told Daly that the new page had been given to an assistant for distribution to the Vatican press group that was travelling with the Pope and spending the night in an Edmonton hotel. That would have meant that journalists travelling with the papal party would have the text hours before those waiting at Fort Simpson. Late-night negotiations between CCCB and Vatican officials were successful in keeping news of the change from all the working media until the Pope read his address, including the new page, at Fort Simpson.[323]

II. SYNODS

When Pope Paul VI announced the Synod of Bishops on September 15, 1965, he was launching a new Church institution that was dear to the heart of Archbishop Maxim Hermaniuk. Winnipeg's Ukrainian Metropolitan, as a member of Vatican II's preparatory commission for theology, had urged that the concept of collegiality be given prominence at the Council. Then, during its second session, he had outlined how that concept could be made real in the form of an "apostolic college," as Hermaniuk then called it. It would be a permanent body of representative bishops to meet periodically with the Pope on matters of Church governance. Others at Vatican II, including Archbishop Maurice Baudoux of St. Boniface, also spoke in favour of the idea.

In some ways, the Synod that was constituted by Paul VI was less than what these bishops wanted. It is not a deliberative body. Its defined task is only to inform and advise the Pope. He convokes it and decides what topics it will discuss. But those who wanted a deliberative body were encouraged by the provision that it "may also have deliberative power" when the Pope confers such power on it. In this way, it is a step towards a structure by which the world's bishops would regularly join the Pope in making pastoral decisions.

In efforts to make the Synod's operations more collegial and more responsive to the wishes of the bishops who attend, the Canadian delegation at each session has expressed concerns and made suggestions about Synod procedures. Canadian bishops want Synods to be occasions at which representatives of all the conferences may discuss and resolve pastoral questions with the Pope. Vatican II taught that the world's bishops form with the Pope a college having responsibilities for the welfare of the entire Church. The members of the CCCB want that theological concept turned into social reality at each Synod.

Consistent with its position that the Synod ought to become an effective instrument of collegiality, the CCCB has always prepared for a Synod and participated in it in a collegial manner. Preparation begins with a consultation of all CCCB members. They are asked what topic they wish to propose as the theme for the coming Synod. It is taken for granted that each bishop may consult other Church members before submitting his suggestion. Rome is informed of the major theme suggested by the CCCB in light of Canadian consultation. Once the Pope announces the topic he has selected and preparatory materials have been received from the Synod secretariat, the CCCB organizes another consultation. The bishops are asked for comments and suggestions about the preparatory materials, and about the best way to organize a pre-Synod study in Canada of the chosen theme. A third round of consultation a few months later calls for suggestions regarding what aspects of the chosen theme the Canadian delegates should raise at the Synod.

For each general Synod the CCCB, as a conference with more than one hundred members, may name four delegates. The four – two anglophone and two francophone bishops – are elected by a plenary at least a year before the announced Synod date. With resource persons invited according to the Synod topic, the four delegates become an ad hoc committee. The Ukrainian metropolitan, as *ex officio* Synod member, joins the committee that supervises the preparation of proposed Canadian interventions and their final selection at a CCCB plenary meeting closest to the Synod's opening. At the end of this process, the Canadian delegation – bishops and resource specialists (and one of the general secretaries as "team manager") – goes to a Synod with a set of draft interventions that are the products of wide consultation and of discussion and formal votes in a CCCB plenary meeting. Until they are delivered, however, it is understood that they are draft texts. The main reason for taking along resource persons is to give the Canadian delegation the capacity to adjust its interventions in light of ideas heard from other bishops at the Synod.[324]

The first general Synod was called in the fall of 1967. Even before it began, the CCC president, Bishop Alexander Carter, protested vigorously to Paul VI that information from the Synod secretariat gave the impression that the bishops attending would be doing so in a personal role, speaking from their particular individual competence rather than as the voice of the conference that they represented. The Canadian bishops, Carter told the Pope, "feel strongly that if the Synod does not prove to be representative of the Bishops of the world: a) Your own wishes...will be frustrated; b) there will be a general sense of disillusion on the part of priests and the informed Catholics throughout the world; c) the Ecumenical movement will suffer a severe reversal, especially though not exclusively, in relation to the Oriental Church." A similar protest was sent to Archbishop Rubin, Synod general secretary. Letters in reply from Cardinal Amleto Cigognani, Vatican Secretary of State, and from Ladislaus Rubin assured the CCC that delegates could indeed prepare and speak as conference representatives.[325]

The CCC plenary meeting of April 6-7, 1967, also urged full media coverage of the Synod, including advance publication of the agenda and daily press conferences in all languages. It also suggested that bishops be freed to release copies of their talks to the mass media. The Canadian delegation, it was also proposed, should appoint a secretary in Rome "who would guarantee that the Canadian news media receive adequate information on the Synod meetings."[326]

After the 1967 Synod, the Canadian delegates formally rated it "at least a moderate success." They recommended that, in future, conferences should be consulted in advance about the agenda; that it should be circulated many months in advance to allow for discussion of it; and that at the Synod commissions should be organized for sub-topics, provision made for immediate debate, and "much better" media arrangements made. (Now, conferences are consulted in advance and agendas are circulated.)

The first extraordinary Synod was called in 1969. Alexander Carter as CCC president was the one official Canadian delegate. Hermaniuk was again a member *ex officio*. The Pope named Cardinal Maurice Roy, then president of the Pontifical Council for Justice and Peace.[327] In preparation for the Synod, the CCC general secretary, Rev. Charles Mathieu, was invited to Rome for a March planning session with his counterparts from England, France, Italy and Spain, and also to work in the Synod secretariat during the Synod itself, particularly on the organization of the small discussion groups.[328]

Collegiality was the major topic of the 1969 Synod. The discussion was especially important at the time, for work was just beginning on the new Code of Canon Law. Collegiality would be one of the concepts defined in the Code (promulgated in 1983). When a draft Synod text was sent in advance to the conferences, the CCC commented that the idea of collegiality in it must be more fully developed. The Canadians also wanted it clearly stated that, while the Pope can reserve certain powers to himself, everything else outside these clearly defined areas should be understood as being within the jurisdiction of the local bishops and not faculties graciously conceded by the Holy Father or by a Roman department. As for Vatican departments, the CCC said, "we do not think of [their role] as being legislative, but executive: to take follow-up action on the decisions and directives of the Holy Father for questions which he has reserved to Himself and, otherwise, to be of service to the Bishops in the exercise of their functions."

About the Synod itself, the CCC wanted it made permanent (Paul VI later announced a permanent Synod secretariat). The Canadian suggestion was detailed:

> We suggest the *possibility* that the extraordinary Synod become the permanent Synod with the same members as today. It would meet two or three times a year. The Roman Curia would become as it were commissions of the Synod. They would only have executive responsibility. Important questions for the universal Church would be handled under the direction of the Holy Father. The Episcopal Conferences would take part in the preparation of the meetings. The general Synod would meet every five years.... These new arrangements would have the following advantages: the principal policies of the universal Church or of regions would be elaborated first at the local level. At a second level they would be worked on by the Conferences and the appropriate Roman departments. At a third stage, they would be discussed and accepted or rejected by the Synod under the direction of the Pope. It should be the normal means of elaborating the broad lines of policy and of decisions of the universal Church under the direction of the Pope. Major problems arising out of conflicts between Episcopal Conferences would also come before the Synod. The main point of view to be kept in mind is that of the hierarchical communion and collegial action of the Episcopate in all the important affairs of the universal Church. The permanent Synod would seem to be an appropriate instrument.[329]

These Canadian suggestions were followed by others two years later. As CCC president, Archbishop Joseph-Aurèle Plourde outlined the CCC view in a note to the Synod secretariat after the 1971 Synod. Theologically, he noted, the Synod "is the representative assembly by means of which the bishops, under the presidency of the Pope, exercise their responsibility of directing the periods between Councils. Therefore, the Synod is the mechanism that assures the continuity and the permanence of collegial government of the Church by the Council under the pontifical presidency. Consequently the Synod, which is actually consultative, should become deliberative or legislative; it should participate in the nature of the episcopal college itself which, at the time of a Council, is not consultative but constitutes the highest earthly authority in the Church.... The immediate entourage of the Pope should not any longer be the Curia, but the permanent Synod, representing the episcopal body. The various dicasteries should be the executive of the Pope and *of the Synod.* As a consequence, a permanent secretariat of the Synod should not in any way be regarded as one more dicastery." The note also gave detailed suggestions for organizing a permanent Synod secretariat.[330] The CCCB delegate made other suggestions for Synod procedures during the 1985 extraordinary Synod. After the 1987 Synod on the laity, a major critique was shared with a number of other conferences.

Most of these Canadian wishes for the Synod still are not realized. Canadian delegates often have returned from sessions very frustrated by Synod procedures. Even with its present limitations, however, Canadian Synod participants hail it as a great experience in collegiality. To be elected as a Synod delegate is "one of the greatest gifts the CCCB can give one of its members," in the view of past president Gilles Ouellet.[331]

Canadian Teaching at the Synod

The interventions of the Canadian bishops at the Synods form an important collection of Church teachings.[332] Unfortunately, few Catholics are aware that they exist. True, at one level, they are only the contributions of individual CCCB delegates to the debates at a collegial body that did not directly endorse what the Canadians said. At another level, however, because of the method used to prepare them, almost every Canadian intervention must be read as a summary of the views held at the time by nearly all Canadian bishops and a wide, informed cross-section of other Canadian Church members on the topic discussed. This collegial method was used for the ordinary general Synods on priestly ministry and justice in the world (1971); on evangelization (1974); on catechesis (1977); on the Christian family (1980); on reconciliation and penitence (1983); on the laity (1987); and on the formation of priests (1990); as well as for the second extraordinary Synod in 1985, which reviewed the results of Vatican II in the twenty years after its close. As well, analysis of papal statements summing up each Synod shows that many of the insights proposed by CCCB delegates entered into what the Pope wrote. Otherwise, regretfully, the Canadian Synod texts have been almost totally ignored once they were delivered. They await rediscovery, and there is space here only to recall that they exist.

CONCLUSION

The Canadian Conference of Catholic Bishops, as we have seen, defines itself as "the collegial assembly" of Canada's Roman Catholic bishops, having "a collective pastoral office with and for other members of the People of God in the mission confided to the whole Church." The key notions in this description – collegiality, communion and co-responsibility – are teachings of Vatican II. Can an assessment be made of where the CCCB stands on these matters? This general question can be divided into three further questions: How well has the CCCB as a collegial assembly of bishops incorporated Vatican II? What is revealed about the CCCB by the effect of Vatican II teachings on the lives of Church members and others, and on Canada's social policies? How does one assess the offices, programs and activities that carry the name of the conference?

Bishops' Conference and Vatican II

When asked what they think about their association, Canadian bishops, especially those who have been CCCB officers, tend to mention unity, participation and ownership as key considerations.[333] Unity is a self-evident idea. The question of participation explores whether bishops are active and involved in following the affairs of their conference and shaping its priorities, programs and projects. The question of ownership concerns whether CCCB members feel that the conference speaks for them, whether they know and agree with where it is heading and the positions it takes, and whether they are comfortable with its internal workings and public activities.

The shared view of English and French bishops and those of Eastern rites is that the CCCB has been for them an instrument of unity, of communion. Some of their comments are as follows:

- "It has formed the bishops of Canada into a closer bond, and enabled us to face national and international problems with a concerted effort, which we could never do without the conference."
- "The conference has created a fraternity."
- "The CCCB has put the churches [dioceses] of Canada together. In a difficult country, the Church has done the best job of putting people together – better than the politicians."
- "The conference has given a voice to the Canadian bishops. We can't operate now as in 1943, for example, when the bishops met, discussed and went home. It is painful when we can't speak with one voice, but even then we are not divided. Even when outside influences like the constitutional quarrel might have torn the CCCB apart, they didn't. That is more the result of supernatural forces than human skills."

Amid praises sung to unity, there also is recognition that unity is not complete. "There is a lot of unity, respect, affection among the bishops of Canada. The Holy Spirit holds us together. But a dualism, of expectations and vision, prevents us from going farther." An example of this dualism is then suggested. Some see the CCCB as unitary and are content to focus collegial activity there. For others, the principle of subsidiarity looms large. This leads to emphasis on the development in the four pastoral regions (Atlantic, Quebec, Ontario, and the West) of greater collegial capacity to handle at that level questions that clearly are not national or international. Finally, regarding unity of the bishops, it is noted that conference activities have aided bishops in their own dioceses rather than interfered with their work there: "The sense of collectivity engendered by the conference has actually strengthened the local bishops."

For participation, CCCB members do not give themselves as high a mark as they do for unity:

- "Although our conference is one of the best as far as I can see, we still did not manage to have all bishops really and truly participate in the work of the conference. Although the conference has tried very hard, there are still quite a few bishops who come to meetings, listen, but get very little involved in the work of the conference as a whole. The duty of all bishops as members would be to be involved in some way."

– "We need more participation."

If there is a perception that participation is a problem, it is located in the individual members more than in conference procedures:

– "The more democratic procedures brought into meetings is, I think, one of the CCCB's greatest accomplishments."
– "I am particularly proud of our structures of participation."

The question, then, is how much, or how well, are these structures used?

Concerns about ownership are more subtle than questions about participation. The latter can be measured by the number of meetings attended, the number of interventions made at meetings, the number of responses to consultations and questionnaires. However, a bishop's sense that the conference is not really his, that it does not belong to him, is noted more indirectly. Lack of a sense of ownership is clearly present if a bishop says the conference does not speak for him, or if he formally dissociates himself from some CCCB activities. Public instances of this kind have been rare. More often, a sense of unity and participation has prevailed. Still, concern about ownership was one of the reasons for launching the Task Force on CCCB Future Directions in 1986. Its major recommendations were reviewed earlier in this book. One of the purposes of these recommendations is to increase unity, participation and a sense of ownership. Evaluation of the effects of the recommendations will provide criteria for future assessments of the CCCB as a collegial assembly.

Within the CCCB itself, there can be further development of Vatican II teachings about bishops and the local churches, and therefore about the conference. The processes whereby each bishop personally internalizes the concepts of collegiality, co-responsibility and communion, and habitually acts in accord with them at the CCCB and in his own diocese, have not been completed. Further developments in this area will continue to reshape the CCCB. Canon law, for its part, clearly puts in the hands of conference members the means to adjust their conference's rules and procedures as their understanding of its collegial mission advances.

Already, some members hold that among the CCCB's major accomplishments was its "ability and willingness to change its structures as the need was discovered."[334]

CCCB and Vatican II in Church and Society

Whether one is pleased or dissatisfied with the post-Council Church in Canada, it is a Church largely shaped by the bishops' conference. Of course, each local church is influenced in a major way by the bishop who heads it. The teachings and directives of the Pope, of Vatican congregations and of international Church commissions have also been decisive in many aspects of Church life. However, it was the intention of Vatican II, specified in detail in the 1983 Code of Canon Law, that the bishops' conference in each country should have a central role in bringing Vatican II to life there and in continuing the Church's mission.

An account of how the CCCB has gone about this task fills the preceding pages. Along with what the conference has meant for its members, many bishops point to the implementation of Vatican II in Canada as the CCCB's greatest accomplishment. Manufactured products are rarely made entirely in one country these days; rather, they bear the mark of where they are assembled. Similarly, the mark "Assembled in Canada for Canadians" could be placed on most aspects of post-Council Church life in Canada. This is particularly true for today's liturgy, ecumenical activities, social affairs teachings and projects, religious education programs, missions activities and canon law applications. This assembling – drawing together elements from the experience of the Church at world, national, regional and local levels, and often creating new Canadian designs and arrangements – has been the work of the CCCB. All of this well illustrates the current theological assessment that "the power of the conference is not a power over the Church but in the Church."[335]

Several times, as noted throughout the book, the "Assembled in Canada" approach has involved decisions not to use European-style or Vatican-made models, at least not without some remodelling. For example, Canadians historically have contributed generously to the papal charities and pontifical mission collections. Yet, in this country, both these programs have been shaped distinctively at the insistence of the CCCB. Similarly, in the past, structures and programs that would have been imposed by Caritas Internationalis or the International Catholic Migration Commission were not adopted here. Instead, variations growing out of Canadian social realities were favoured. Again, when the Vatican was promoting the establishment of a Justice and Peace Commission in each country – and even though the much-revered Cardinal Maurice Roy of Quebec was head of the Pontifical Justice and Peace Commission – the CCCB chose to stick to a Canadian approach. What a bishop-led Canadian Justice and Peace Commission might have attempted was already being done by the lay-led Canadian Catholic Organization for Development and Peace and by the several CCCB-supported interchurch coalitions for research and action on social justice and human rights issues. What was involved in each of these cases was not disobedience or defiance towards Rome, but the CCCB's adaptation of proposed general models to the particular situations of this country.

If, at times, "Assembled in Canada" programs have been preferred, in another sense the CCCB has become increasingly open to and involved in international relations. Conference officers meet once each year with the executive committee of the U.S. bishops' conference. They also have an important meeting each year with a larger group at an inter-American meeting of bishops from Canada, the U.S. and Latin America. For these meetings, each of the three groups proposes topics for discussion. No formal decisions are taken and no minutes kept, but the Canadian participants regard the inter-American meetings as crucial for understanding the social challenges faced by the people in each area, their pastoral needs, and the responses being attempted in the local churches. Canadian bishops are also invited to meetings of European and African conferences of bishops. In his annual report to the 1992 plenary, Archbishop Marcel Gervais listed eight major international meetings that CCCB members had attended that year.

For some CCCB members, the conference's prophetic function over the years has been its most important accomplishment. "This is evident in the CCCB's social teachings, but not just there. There has been remarkable teaching on social, doctrinal and pastoral matters – about spiritual renewal, about suffering, about Jesus Christ, about the Christian family, about reconciliation.... At each Synod in Rome, the Canadian bishops are among the best prepared...." As noted earlier, the Canadian interventions at the Synods form an important, but almost entirely neglected, body of teachings.

Other bishops acknowledge that the CCCB's teaching efforts have not fully succeeded:

- "All that the conference has tried to say and tried to do has not been heard. We haven't been able to communicate, to share these good things."

– "We didn't succeed in follow-up to the Synods."

– "Our biggest failure was our failure to get through to people what we are doing. What's being done here hasn't permeated...."

The perception that the CCCB has failed to communicate raises questions about the means used and about the efforts made at various other levels of the Church. The chief method has been to issue statements, and sometimes to publicize them through press conferences or public appearances. Texts from the CCCB generally receive better coverage in the French media than in the English media. Coverage in either language has never amounted to a major adult education effort, however. The CCCB briefs to Parliament on contraception, divorce and abortion, for example, are detailed catechetical texts with broad, enduring teachings about the role of the laity in shaping temporal affairs according to God's plan. In general, however, they were read, and are remembered, only as not-too-successful lobbying efforts. Virtually every CCCB text – Labour Day messages, Synod interventions and the many others – contains abiding teaching that awaits study and use at the local level by adult educators, homilists, discussion group leaders, school teachers, catechists and parents. What the bishops have taught through conference statements has been largely neglected by those responsible for religious education programs intended for use at the local level, especially those for the faith education of adults.

During the Second Vatican Council, Bishop William Power spoke of the kind of formation he considered essential for the laity: "The apostolic formation of the laity," he said, "must necessarily take into account 'the secular character that is proper and particular to the laity.' These notions must plunge the layman more deeply and more actively into the realities of the temporal order." Only in this way, he said, can lay people be brought to the point where they can live their lives as laity and as Christians "in a responsible and autonomous fashion, even without the support of traditional Catholic institutions." Thus, a lay person "can become truly 'a witness and an instrument of the mission of the Church' and 'make the Church present and active in the heart of the temporal realities.'"[336] Cardinal George Flahiff outlined a similar pedagogy for Christian action in an intervention during the 1971 Synod on justice. Nearly thirty years after Power's remarks were made, some bishops identify the CCCB's greatest failure with the fact that "we did not succeed in involving the laity in the temporal order. We involved people in parish life; we gave courses for that. But we never had any courses to show them how to be witnesses in temporal affairs." Part of the CCCB's future agenda is foreshadowed in such a remark.

Two other aspects of conference life that some bishops regard as having been unsuccessful relate more to organizational responses than to teaching or prophecy. "Our failure to find a formula for national participation by the laity" is identified by some as one of the CCCB's main failures during its first fifty years. Others put a similar label on "our inability to communicate properly with women.... I think we were guilty of lack of awareness of how this was going to rise as a major problem in the Church today."

Conference Secretariat

During the Vatican II discussion about bishops' conferences, and occasionally since then, some fears were expressed that conference secretariats would become large bureaucracies with the power to manipulate or inhibit individual conference members in their work in their local Church. The CCCB challenged this risk directly. It opted in 1964 for "a dynamic and top-quality general secretariat, oriented towards study and research, equipped to give specialized and competent services promptly, able to discern social changes, to observe and analyze all problems of interest to the Church, whether in Canada as a whole, in the English or French sectors, or in the numerous regions and provinces of our vast country."[337]

In 1967-68, the conference re-examined its nature and role and defined itself more clearly as a bishops' institution. In 1972, in the face of a huge budget deficit and changes in the Canadian Church scene, especially the growing emphasis on the four pastoral regions, several post-Council offices were combined or eliminated. From 1986 to 1990, the Task Force on CCCB Future Directions once again rearranged the Ottawa secretariat, especially to enhance participation by CCCB members and increase their sense of ownership of their conference. However, none of these adjustments rescinded a word in the 1964 definition of the kind of secretariat the conference wanted for itself. It is unique among national institutions in having two general secretaries, one English and one French, each fully in charge, yet especially responsive to the needs of his own linguistic sector. On paper this arrangement is nonsensical, yet it has worked well in real life, "dynamic and top-quality," for fifty years.[338] With allowances for individual differences, the directors of individual offices and services have also had the qualities and skills required for the bilingual, bicultural secretariat that the bishops in 1964 thought necessary "to bring to reality the fruits of the present Council and to lead the Canadian Church in the renewal so much desired by John XXIII and the Sovereign Pontiff gloriously reigning."[339]

Several CCCB members would emphasize that the conference fulfills a major teaching function just by operating as it does:

- "In the light of Canadian history, the greatest accomplishment of the conference is to demonstrate that a truly bilingual, bicultural national institution can work, with mutual respect and with neither of the cultural groups sacrificing its integrity in any way."
- "The conference is a very good model for the country, a model of what regional respect is, and of what the overall Canadian reality is. I believe we have something that shows a sensitivity to regions, to cultural things, that could really help Canada understand itself. We have to live with the fact that ours is not a uniform conference, like that of France, England or Italy. We don't have that kind of uniformity in language, culture, historical background, because it's so different from one part of the country to another. But this, we believe as a conference, is inevitable; it is recognizing reality...."

Canadian theologian Jean-Marie Tillard, OP, has written that "the community of the disciples of Christ constituted itself and then developed around the content of its 'memory.' It is a community which lives by 'memory.'"[340] The CCCB has memories of successes and failures with which to celebrate its fifty years and from which to build its future. The story of these years is perhaps not dramatic. Comments made by John Paul II about Saints Cyril and Methodius seem also to describe the life and work of the Canadian bishops as a collegial assembly. The Pope emphasized "the peaceful way" in which these two missionaries built up the Church, "guided as they were by their vision of the Church as one, holy and universal." Their conviction, he added, "that each local Church is called to enrich with its own endowments the Catholic 'pleroma,' was in perfect harmony with their evangelical insight that the different conditions of life of the individual Christian Churches can never justify discord, disagreements and divisions in the profession of the one faith and in the exercise of charity."[341] Thus, through memory, the CCCB's past remains alive to help in the building of the future of the Church in this land.

Endnotes

[1] Bernard Lonergan, *Method in Theology*, London: Darton, Longman & Todd, 1971, p. 265.

[2] CCCB files show that the federal Department of Trade and Commerce handled the details for the bishops. At $1.65 a bushel, the Pethick Grain company was paid $123,750 for the wheat, plus $1,237.50 for "superintendence and outturn insurance." The ocean freight from Montreal to Castellamare was $33,750 and the marine and war risk insurance cost $1,275.75.

[3] Letter from Giovanni Battista Montini to Paul Bernier, December 11, 1945. Papal Charities file. CCCB Archives, Ottawa.

[4] For a detailed account of the establishment of the CCC, especially on Church law considerations and procedures, see *Episcopal Conferences and the Canadian Catholic Conference*, by Rev. Bernard A. Prince, doctoral thesis for the Canon Law Faculty, Pontificia Studiorum Universitas a S. Thoma Aquinate, Rome, 1966.

[5] The others today – Rimouski, Sherbrooke, Grouard-McLennan, Keewatin-Le Pas, Gatineau-Hull – have been created since the conference began.

[6] The content of this paragraph and subsequent accounts of early CCC meetings are drawn from official minutes in CCCB Archives, Ottawa.

[7] For details, see Minutes, Vol.1, No. 45, pp. 5-8, Quinquennial Plenary Meeting of the Canadian Hierarchy, Quebec, October 12-13, 1943. CCCB Archives, Ottawa. Unless otherwise stated, plenary meetings were held in Ottawa.

[8] André Cellard and Gérald Pelletier, *Faithful to a Mission: Fifty Years with the Catholic Health Association of Canada*, English translation by David R. Miller; Catholic Health Association of Canada, Ottawa, 1990, p. 42. The pages of this book, especially its first two chapters, were used to supplement CCCB Archives for some other details in this section.

[9] Cellard and Pelletier, at indicated pages.

[10] I use "Plenary Meeting" throughout the text; it is also called "Annual Meeting", "Annual Assembly" and "Plenary Assembly." Quinquennial Plenary Meeting of the Canadian Hierarchy, Quebec, October 12-13, 1943. Minutes, Vol. 1, Item 45, p. 16. CCCB Archives, Ottawa.

[11] One account of this decision is sketched in "Notes of a meeting held in Montreal on June 13-14, 1956," in CCCB Immigration files. As the family reunification plan was conceived in Geneva, the International Catholic Migration Commission (ICMC) made available to the CCC subsidies to an amount of $100,000 for interest-free travel loans, repayable by instalments. These subsidies were available on the basis of $100 for each person moved, provided the CCC would contribute a counterpart amount. On the basis of an average of $200 for passage from Europe to Canada, the CCC agreed to contribute $50 to the fund, the other $50 to be paid by the family head in Canada. CCC Immigration files, June 13-14, 1956. CCCB Archives, Ottawa.

[12] The following details about the CIS operation come from a 1961 report to the CCC board by Bishops Alexander Carter and Paul-Émile Charbonneau. In February 1961 the CCC board had asked for a more complete financial report from the CIS, and in May 1961 asked the two bishops to report in detail and make recommendations concerning the structure and financial situation of the CIS. CCC Immigration files. CCCB Archives, Ottawa.

[13] Letter in CCC immigration files. CCCB Archives, Ottawa.

[14] Minutes, Vol. 2, No. 11, Item h, p. 223. CCC Annual Meeting, October 13-15, 1953.

[15] See "Mémoire: Collecte de l'Épiphanie, Délégation apostolique," undated. Collecte pour l'immigration, 1966-73 file. CCCB Archives, Ottawa.

[16] Letter from Archbishop Sergio Pignedoli, Apostolic Delegate, to Charles Mathieu, CCC general secretary, March 31, 1966. Collecte pour l'immigration, 1966-73 file. CCCB Archives, Ottawa.

[17] CCC *Internal Communication*, No. 165, June 17, 1966. CCCB Archives, Ottawa.

[18] When the male religious community Fraternité sacerdotale slipped into serious bankruptcy, other religious communities and the CCC agreed to underwrite the situation until it could be stabilized through property sales and other arrangements.

[19] For details, see *Internal Communication*, No. 246, December 29, 1966. Also see Minutes, Vol. 1, No. 46, Item 25, p. 11. Meeting of the CCC Administrative Board, January 19-20, 1967. Also see Minutes Vol. 1, No. 48. CCC Executive Committee, March 8-9, 1967.

[10] For the 1943 CCC statement, see Minutes, Vol. 1, pp. 8, 9. Quinquennial Plenary Meeting of the Canadian Hierarchy, Quebec, October 12-13, 1943, Item 15, citation, p. 9. CCCB Archives, Ottawa. For a discussion of the pastoral letters of the 1930s, see *L'Enseignement social des évêques canadiens*, by Jean Hulliger; Fides, Montreal, 1958, p. 189-201.

[21] The details of the following account are drawn from a report prepared by Jean-Charles Leclaire of St. Hyacinthe, Que., for his bishop, Arthur Douville, who by then was also French secretary for the new CCC Committee for Social Affairs. Four years after the study days, Leclaire, by then a monsignor, would be named the first francophone social affairs director of the CCC, following Douville's offer of his services. CCC Social Action Department files. CCCB Archives, Ottawa.

[22] Another glimpse of Quebec's social structures at that time can be had from the account of the second congress of the chaplains of associations of owners and workers (Associa-

tions patronales et ouvrières). The March 25-28, 1946, sessions at Ste. Anne de Beaupré brought together 48 priests who came from 13 dioceses. Three were chaplains to Catholic Action, five to owner associations, 24 to associations of workers, seven to joint owner-worker groups, and seven to other associations; there were also three professors and one student of the social sciences. The Church in Quebec was entering the post-war period well organized, with direct clergy contacts into many levels of society. One of the difficulties faced by the bishops when the staff of their new conference began to work was, therefore, how to avoid overlapped jurisdictions and duplicated efforts.

23 The asbestos strike was one of the social questions in which Archbishop Joseph Charbonneau of Montreal was involved at the time of his unexpected and controversial resignation. CCCB files show no evidence that the Conference had any role in his resignation, so this history does not discuss it.

24 See July 16, 1965, memo by Bishop André Ouellette of Mont Laurier on "Relations entre le Département d'Action Sociale de la CCC et le Conseil Sacerdotal d'études sociales de la Province de Québec," Social Action Department files. CCCB Archives, Ottawa.

25 Letter from Francis Marrocco, bishop of Peterborough, to Grant Maxwell, July 16, 1973. Social Action Department files. CCCB Archives, Ottawa.

26 The Quebec sessions had begun in 1920 as a project of the Jesuits under leadership of Joseph-Papin Archambault, who continued as president until he was replaced by Richard Arès in 1958-59. The decision to launch an English section led the Vatican to urge that the same topic be chosen for both French and English sessions each year. There would be strength in a united message for the whole country – and the Vatican's task of preparing a traditional opening message from the Pope would be simplified.

27 Other details about the first Social Life Conference can be found in the CCC Social Action Department's 1953 files. CCCB Archives, Ottawa.

28 Francis Marrocco directed the preparations for the 1954 Social Life Conference in London, Ont., on "Immigration and Land Settlement" and the 1955 Vancouver conference on "Christian Citizenship." By the time of that conference, however, he had been named bishop, and on June 27, 1955, Francis Smyth of Antigonish had succeeded him. Smyth served until late in 1959 and was succeeded early in 1960 by Peter Nearing. In mid-1963, Nearing was succeeded in turn by John Shea, who was joined by William Ryan in mid-1964.

29 Interview with Emmett Carter by Bernard M. Daly, Toronto, July 21, 1992. Audio tape in CCCB Archives, Ottawa. Unless otherwise indicated, all interviews by Bernard Daly were made in Ottawa.

30 "Evaluation – 1964," Vol. 3, Recommendation 84, p. 322. CCCB Archives, Ottawa

31 Priests present at the November 19-20, 1944, meeting in Brooklyn were Gerald Berry, Lucien Desmarais and André-Marie Guillemette of Montreal; Francis Gallagher and John Fullerton of Toronto; John MacDonald of Ottawa, and Joseph Cook of London. "Copie," Catholic Charities files, box 27. CCCB Archives, Ottawa.

32 "Notes historiques de Caritas-Canada," Catholic Charities file. CCCB Archives, Ottawa.

33 Minutes, Vol. 1, No. 2, Item 20, p. 30. CCC Annual Meeting, January 17-18, 1945. CCCB Archives, Ottawa.

34 Minutes, Vol. 2, No. 6, Item 7, p. 89. CCC Annual Meeting, December 5-6, 1950. CCCB Archives, Ottawa.

[35] Minutes, Vol. 2, No. 6, Item 3, p. 166. CCC Annual Meeting, October 10-11, 1951. CCCB Archives, Ottawa.

[36] See details in "Notes historiques de Caritas-Canada," Catholic Charities file. CCCB Archives, Ottawa.

[37] Minutes, Vol. 2, No. 10, Item 39, p. 209. CCC Annual Meeting, October 7-9, 1952. CCCB Archives, Ottawa.

[38] Minutes, Vol. 2, No. 16, Item 15, p. 336. Meeting of the Administrative Board of the CCC, January 25, 1956. CCCB Archives, Ottawa. The study was confided to the bishops' commission for hospitals and welfare.

[39] *Re. Caritas-Canada*, Rapport No. 2, by Charles Mathieu, September 28, 1959. Caritas-Canada file. CCCB Archives, Ottawa.

[40] Minutes of Catholic Charities Conference, Lord Nelson Hotel, Halifax, N.S., October 13, 1961. Caritas-Canada file. CCCB Archives, Ottawa.

[41] "Conference catholique canadienne, Commission des hôpitaux et oeuvres d'assistance," Caritas-Canada, Doc. III a, Rome, October 17, 1963, par Valérien Bélanger, secrétaire de la commission. Caritas-Canada file. CCCB Archives, Ottawa.

[42] "Règlement de la question 'Caritas-Canada,' secteur francais," CCC Communication interne, No. 105, January 17, 1966. CCCB Archives, Ottawa.

[43] The directors were Frank Hennessey in Ottawa and Robert Riendeau in Montreal. Their respective successors were Murray Tardiff in Ottawa, and Rémi Migneault and Robert Morin in Montreal.

[44] Letter from Murray Tardiff to Archbishop Jean-Marie Fortier, December 19, 1973; letter from Fortier to Tardiff, February 15, 1974. CCCB Archives, Ottawa.

[45] Interview with Archbishop Gilles Ouellet by Bernard Daly, August 28, 1992. Audio tape in CCCB Archives, Ottawa.

[46] Details found in hand-written note by Paul Bernier, December 15, 1943, after the first meeting of the CCC executive committee at the archbishop's residence in Quebec City. Bernier also recorded that the note was written after an interview with Cardinal Villeneuve, during which he was informed that he had been named that same day as the first French general secretary of the CCC.

[47] According to Meunier, in an interview with Bernard Daly in July 1992, Markle was the second choice as English general secretary. Philip Pocock would have had the job but was named bishop of Saskatoon before his CCC post was announced, Meunier recalls. No CCC documents about this have been found.

[48] The third employee was Isabel Knight Richardson, hired in 1950 by Markle as his secretary at 447 Sussex Drive. Marie Clusiau came as secretary for the French general secretariat in 1951 after Granger was promoted to bookkeeper for both sectors. By then the secretariat also housed Francis Marrocco's social action and immigration activities, and Georges-Édouard Brosseau's French sector immigration project.

[49] Minutes of CCC Executive Committee, April 27, 1944. CCCB Archives, Ottawa.

[50] Minutes, Vol. 1, No. 3. Annual Meeting of the Canadian Episcopate, Quebec, September 26-28, 1945. CCCB Archives, Ottawa.

[51] Minutes, Vol. 2, No. 1. CCC Annual Meeting, October 13 and 14, 1948. CCCB Archives, Ottawa.

[52] See letter from John Carley, general secretary, to Gerald Berry, CCC president, November 1, 1960. CCCB Archives, Ottawa.

[53] Minutes, Vol. 2, No. 73. Meeting of the CCC Administrative Board, November 6-8, 1968. CCCB Archives, Ottawa.

[54] Minutes, Vol. 4, No. 94. Meeting of the CCC Administrative Board, September 3-4, 1970. CCCB Archives, Ottawa.

[55] Minutes, Vol. 4, No. 88. Meeting of the CCC Administrative Board, March 5-6, 1970. CCCB Archives, Ottawa.

[56] Minutes, Vol. 4, No. 89. CCC Annual Meeting, April 6-10, 1970. CCCB Archives, Ottawa.

[57] Minutes, Vol. 4, No. 94. Meeting of the CCC Administrative Board, September 3-4, 1970. CCCB Archives, Ottawa.

[58] Minutes, Vol. 4, No. 97. Meeting of the CCC Administrative Board, December 3-4, 1970. CCCB Archives, Ottawa.

[59] Minutes, Vol. 5, No. 100. Meeting of the CCC Administrative Board, March 25-26, 1971. CCCB Archives, Ottawa.

[60] *Evaluation-1972*, Vol. 3, p. 87-88. CCCB Archives, Ottawa.

[61] Minutes, Vol. 9, No. 150. CCC Annual Meeting, April 14-18, 1975. CCCB Archives, Ottawa.

[62] Minutes, Special meeting of the CCC Administrative Board, October 25, 1976. CCCB Archives, Ottawa.

[63] Pope John XXIII, *Motu proprio "Superno Dei Nutu,"* June 5, 1960, *Documentation catholique*, No. 1330, June 19, 1960, col. 705. Cited without reference in the English text of the Introduction of "Statement of the Canadian Hierarchy, April 25, 1960, The Second Vatican Council." See Minutes, Vol. 3, No. 31, annex, p. 195. Meeting of the CCC Administrative Board. CCCB Archives, Ottawa.

[64] See *Acta et documenta Concilio oecumenico Vaticano II apparando, Series I, Volumen II, Pars VI*. Typis polyglottis vaticanis, 1960.

[65] See Archbishop Antoine Hacault's reply to Communication interne, No. 1974. Reply Sheet 564, June 23, 1992. CCCB Archives, Ottawa.

[66] Bishop Albert Sanschagrin recalls that at the September 1962 plenary in Ottawa, he persuaded an anglophone bishop to second his motion proposing that a CCC secretariat be organized at the Canadian College in Rome. It was then customary for the ranking prelates to sit with the conference officers, facing the assembly. As Sanschagrin made his proposal, Cardinal Léger so frowned and shook his head to signal vigorous opposition that the would-be seconder did not rise and the idea was dropped. Bishop Albert Sanschagrin's personal papers. Vatican II file. CCCB Archives, Ottawa.

[67] Strictly speaking, there were no interventions in the name of the Canadian conference as such, although individual speakers sometimes announced that their remarks had the support of others. In his personal notes kept during the Council, Bishop Sanschagrin records his recollection of Cardinal Léger's request that the other Canadian bishops should accord him the privilege to say each time he spoke that he had their support. They refused to give him *carte blanche* and instead supported specific interventions as he made them. See Bishop Albert Sanschagrin's personal papers. Vatican Council files. CCCB Archives, Ottawa.

[68] For example, the minutes of the October 12-13, 1943, meeting at which the Conference was launched lists seven items under the heading "Propagation of the Faith." One item relates to an increase in annual fees for membership in the Society for the Propagation of the Faith; another to how those fees would be assigned to grants to poor Canadian dioceses, including at that time Gravelbourg, Prince Albert and Hearst. Other items show that the meeting briefly discussed how to protect the faith of Catholic Indians in new state-run hospitals, what to do to aid new Chinese, Japanese and Hindu immigrants, and how to win more converts from Protestantism. See Minutes, Vol. 1, No. 1, Items 40-46. Quinquennial Plenary Meeting of the Canadian Hierarchy, Quebec. CCCB Archives, Ottawa. In turn, the items on "Home Missions" in the minutes of the Conference's October 13-15, 1953, annual meeting referred to Catholic schools in the Yukon and Northwest Territories, and uniform regulations for foreign missionaries collecting funds in Canadian dioceses. See Minutes, Vol. 2, No. 11, Items 33-35. CCCB Archives, Ottawa.

[69] All above details about the CCC's Latin American project in response to Pope John XXIII are from the files of the CCC Commission for Latin America and Bishop Albert Sanschagrin's personal papers. CCCB Archives, Ottawa.

[70] The first directors of the CCC's Office for Latin America, set up in March 1960, were priests from two Canadian foreign mission societies, Marcel Gérin of Pont-Viau and Francis O'Grady of Scarboro. After Gérin was named bishop in Honduras and O'Grady died suddenly, Pierre Goyette of Pont-Viau served both French and English offices, as did Gérard Dionne who succeeded him. With a broadening of its mandate after 1972, the Office for Latin America became the Missions Office, again headed by English and French directors, William Smith of Scarboro and Louis-de-Gonzague Langevin, a White Father. Then, after Hubert Laurin of Pont-Viau had served as sole director for a time, the direction was confided to Claude Pagé of the White Fathers and Oblate Lorne MacDonald who, in turn, was succeeded by Jesuit Michael Murray. After the mandate had again been rewritten in the 1989 CCCB restructuring, the office reverted to a sole director, Oblate Lucien Casterman.

[71] The English sector groups four bodies: The Society of St. Peter Apostle, Propagation of the Faith, Holy Childhood, and the Pontifical Missionary Union. The French sector regroups these somewhat differently: Propagation of the Faith, Society of St. Peter Apostle, and Pontifical Missionary Union, as the adult sector; Service Mond'Ami, for children; and Jeunesse du Monde, youth sector.

[72] Details of the historic Quebec privilege, the more recent developments stemming from it, Cardinal Tomko's request and the January 1990 agreement can be found in "The CCCB and The Propagation of the Faith," *CCCB Internal Communication*, No. 1939, August 13, 1990. CCCB Archives, Ottawa.

[73] In Montreal, Clément Farly succeeded Gaston Fontaine as director of the CCC French liturgy office when the latter was named to the Consilium in Rome in 1966. Fontaine returned to direct the office from the early 1970s and has been succeeded, in turn, by Jean-Bernard Allard and Paul Boily. The first director of the English office was Bernard Mahoney who, from April 1966, filled the role on a part-time basis from St. Augustine's Seminary in Toronto, where he continued teaching duties as well. The English office was transferred to the CCC's Ottawa secretariat in 1969, with Leonard Sullivan as first full-time director. His successors have been Patrick Byrne (editorial assistant and acting director in 1976), David Walsh, Regis Halloran, Murray Kroetsch, John Hibbard and Donna Kelly.

[74] Named to the first ecumenical committee were Auxiliary Bishops Francis Allen of Toronto and Paul Grégoire of Montreal. During the 1965 plenary meeting, also in Rome, this committee was made a full commission, with six members in two sections. For the English, Allen was joined by Archbishop Martin Johnson of Vancouver and Auxiliary Bishop Joseph Raymond Windle of Ottawa; for the French, Auxiliary Bishops Antoine Hacault of St. Boniface and Adolphe Proulx of Sault Ste. Marie joined Grégoire. Before the end of 1965, John Keating was named director of a Toronto office to serve the commission's English sector. A similar office in Montreal for the French sector was placed under the direction of Irénée Beaubien.

[75] CCC *Information Service*, Vol. 9, No. 149, December 22, 1964. CCCB Archives, Ottawa.

[76] Sister of Charity Donna Geernaert, director of the CCCB's ecumenical office during the period of negotiations regarding associate membership, was a major architect of new bylaws and related structural changes of the Canadian Council of Churches. The CCCB offices established to assist the bishops in these initiatives have evolved over the years since 1965. When the CCCB was restructured in 1973-74, the Toronto office for ecumenism was closed. Since then, one member of the staff of the Ottawa secretariat has been responsible full-time for this work. Succeeding Keating have been, in turn, Michael O'Connell, Josephine McCarthy, Veronica O'Reilly, and Donna Geernaert. The Montreal office evolved differently. After 1973-74, it was restructured under an interdenominational board as The Canadian Centre for Ecumenism. With Stéphane Valiquette as assistant, Beaubien continued to head the centre until succeeded by Thomas Ryan.

[77] The description of events from the beginning of the Joint Working Group in 1968 to the entry of the CCCB into associate membership in the Canadian Council of Churches (CCC) in 1986 is drawn from the files of the CCCB Office for Ecumenism in the CCCB Archives. A CCCB leaflet, *Why Associate Membership?*, explained that associate membership was "seen by the CCCB and the CCC as a means of growing towards an ecumenical association which responds to the needs of the Christian churches in Canada. In the CCC, as it is currently organized, church representation and financial contributions are based on membership totals. Since statistics place about one half of the Christian population of Canada in the Catholic Church, full membership would present numerous difficulties for the CCCB as well as for the CCC and its member churches. Associate membership will provide a structured relationship which is flexible enough to respond to our present situation and to support further development."

[78] "Le Département d'Action sociale," by Louis Chabot, *L'Église canadienne*, Vol. 1, No. 6, June 1968, p. 196-97.

[79] John Paul II, *Encyclical letter "Laborem Exercens."* CCCB edition [1981], p. 10-11.

[80] "La pensée sociale des évêques canadiens de 1956 à nos jours," Arthé Guimond, *L'Église canadienne*, Vol. 15, No. 1, September 3, 1981, p. 11-13.

[81] The Conference on Health Services in Canada, November 29-December 1, 1965, was organized by representatives of the Anglican Church in Canada, Canadian Catholic Conference, Chamber of Commerce, Canadian Citizenship Council, Canadian Federation of Agriculture, Canadian Jewish Congress, Canadian Labour Congress, Canadian Lutheran Council, Confédération des syndicats nationaux, Conseil canadien de la coopération, Cooperative Union of Canada, Federated Women's Institutes of Canada, National Council

of Women of Canada, National Farmers Union, Presbyterian Church in Canada, and United Church of Canada.

[82] All details about the February 2, 1966, meeting in Edmonton are from the minutes for that meeting. CCCB Archives, Ottawa.

[83] William Ryan described this shift to an American audience in August 1967. See *Social Thought*, October 1, 1967. Ryan, an economics graduate from Harvard University, brought new research methods and skills to the CCC that were influential in changing the CCC social action program while he was co-director of the anglophone office from 1964 to 1971. Later, Tony Clarke's social ethics background from the University of Chicago was also influential for change in social action program directions.

[84] Conseil national d'action social (CNAS). Constitution and bylaws. Minutes of December 9, 1966. CCCB Archives, Ottawa. Members over the period of CNAS work from December 1966 to June 1972, included Marcel Pépin, Philippe Garigue, Jean-Réal Cardin, Madeleine Joubert, Anne-Marie Frenette, Irénée Desrochers, Jean Brunelle, Louis Deniset, Gilbert Finn, Lionel Sorel, Louis Bérubé, Henri Pichette, Yvon Daneau, Roger Fraser, Louis Laberge, Jean-Marie Lafontaine, Marielle Asselin, Lise Blanchette. All were from Quebec, except Finn, a Moncton businessman, and Deniset, a Winnipeg judge. CCC staff members of the CNAS were Jean-Guy Hamelin, Charles Saint-Onge and Suzanne Blais-Mauviel.

Besides the CNAS, the social affairs bishops and staff had various ad hoc consultative arrangements with a number of individuals and groups, including priest and lay social action activists across the country who were organized and animated by the CCC staff. Many of these consultants were heads of diocesan social action offices. Social action office staff during the post-Council period were Jean-Guy Hamelin, Jack Shea, William Ryan, Charles Saint-Onge, Grant Maxwell, Patrick Kerans, Suzanne Blais-Mauviel, Tony Clarke, Rémi Côté, Normand Paquin, Bernard Dufresne, and, most recently, Joseph Gunn.

[85] These "other statements by the Canadian bishops on social issues" are among the wide range of "releases, statements, pastoral letters, briefs, messages and ordinances" listed by the CCCB General Secretariat and reserved in CCCB archives. They include briefs to parliamentary committees on contraception, divorce, abortion, national energy plans, and immigration; pastoral letters on Development and Peace, abortion, immigration, housing, and the elderly; letters to Canadian government leaders on United Nations issues, native rights, capital punishment, deportation, immigration, refugees, and numerous specific human rights incidents and issues; and statements on specific topical issues, such as the anniversary of the UN Declaration on Human Rights, social justice in the Church, sharing national income, International Women's Year, International Year of the Child, Archbishop Romero's murder in El Salvador, the neutron bomb, and the imposition of martial law in Poland.

[86] "Poverty in Canada," CCC Labour Day Message, 1966. CCCB Archives, Ottawa. A collection of the bishops' statements can be found in E.F. Sheridan, ed., *Do Justice: The Social Teaching of the Canadian Catholic Bishops (1945-1986)*, Sherbrooke, Qué.: Éditions paulines; Toronto: Jesuit Centre, 1987.

[87] "The Economic Conditions under which the Canadian Family Lives," CCC 1967 Labour Day Statement, art. 7, 14, 15. CCCB Archives, Ottawa.

[88] Participating Church bodies were: Churches of Christ (Disciples), Greek Orthodox, Lutheran Council in Canada, Mennonite Central Committee (Canada), Roman Catholic,

Anglican, Baptist Federation, Pentecostal Assemblies, Presbyterians, Religious Society of Friends (Quakers), Salvation Army, United Church. See *Towards a Coalition for Development*, Strategy Committee Report, May 1969. CCCB Archives, Ottawa.

[89] "The Struggle against Poverty and Social Injustice," CCC 1968 Labour Day statement; CCC Official Document No. 151; September 2, 1968. CCCB Archives, Ottawa. At the Winnipeg plenary meeting soon after Labour Day, although the *Humanae Vitae* discussion grabbed all the headlines, the CCC also issued important statements decrying human rights violations in Vietnam, Biafra and Czechoslovakia. A year-end statement for the Universal Year of Human Rights noted concerns about constitutional guarantees of rights for a number of groups in Canada, including native peoples.

[90] Committee members directing the report were George Davy, Anglican Church, Toronto; Charles Forsyth, United Church, Toronto; Arthur Gowland, Presbyterian Church, Toronto; Romeo Maione, Development and Peace, Montreal; Clifton Monk, Lutheran Council of Canada, Winnipeg; Robert Riendeau, CCC health and welfare office, Montreal; Louis Roy, Société financière pour le commerce et l'industrie, Montreal; William Ryan, CCC social action office, Ottawa.

[91] *Towards a Coalition for Development*, Strategy Committee Report, May 1969, No. 24, p 9-10.

[92] At an October meeting in Ottawa, three priority goals were selected for the proposed "Coalition for Development." They were: "Tax reform that gives a fair deal to low-income Canadians; effective cooperation with new citizens' groups at local levels; and a greater Canadian role in world development." At a December meeting, "united support of native peoples" was added as a fourth priority. These are listed on p. 11 in the June 11, 1970 brief to the Special Senate Committee on Poverty by the executive committees of the Canadian Council of Churches and the Canadian Catholic Conference. CCCB Archives, Ottawa.

[93] Besides the bishops' conference and the Canadian Council of Churches (including most of its 11 member denominations), the partners in the coalition included the Canadian Chamber of Commerce, Canadian Council for International Co-operation, Canadian Labour Congress, Canadian Welfare Council, Canadian Catholic Organization for Development and Peace, Confédération des syndicats nationaux, Co-operative Union of Canada, Fédération des Caisses Populaires Desjardins and National Indian Brotherhood. See CCC-CCC Brief to Special Senate Committee on Poverty, June 11, 1970, p. 12. Launched with high hopes, the coalition had a short life at the national level.

[94] Brief to the Special Senate Committee on Poverty, by the executive committees of the Canadian Catholic Conference and the Canadian Council of Churches, June 11, 1970. Citation, p. 5. CCCB Archives, Ottawa.

[95] "New Power," CCC 1969 Labour Day Statement, Episcopal Commission for Social Action, CCC *Official Document*, No. 187, para. 1, 8, 10, 14. CCCB Archives, Ottawa.

[96] CCC *Official Document*, No. 204, p. 1, November 28, 1969. CCCB Archives, Ottawa.

[97] "Liberation in a Christian Perspective," CCC Labour Day Statement. Social Action Office, September 1970. CCC *Official Document*, No. 223, p. 1. CCCB Archives, Ottawa.

[98] Statement by Cardinal Maurice Roy, October 17, 1970. Assemblée des évêques du Québec Archives, Montreal.

[99] "A Christian Stance in the Face of Violence," CCC Labour Day Statement. September, 1971. CCC *Official Document*, No. 268. CCCB Archives, Ottawa.

[100] Members of the Canadian delegation to the May 18-21, 1971, Mexico City meeting with bishops from the U.S. and Central and South America were George Flahiff; Jean-Marie Fortier, Philip Pocock and Joseph-Aurèle Plourde, CCC president, with Everett MacNeil, general secretary. The Canada-U.S. text, "The Liberation of Men and Nations: Role of the Church in America," was written by William Ryan with substantial help from Grant Maxwell and Patrick Kerans of the CCC staff and U.S. theologian Joseph Komonchak. It was published with this note: "It was the consensus of the Interamerican Bishops' meeting that this working paper, after some revisions, should be circulated, in as much as it had proved useful in their deliberations at Mexico City. The revised text is being circulated in North America under the auspices of the U.S. and Canadian Justice and Peace Commissions." The citations here are from the version published in *Social Thought*, CCC Social Action Office, July 1, 1971. CCCB Archives, Ottawa.

[101] CCC *Official Document* No. 297. Emphasis in original. CCCB Archives, Ottawa.

[102] "Sharing National Income," April 21, 1972. CCC *Official Document* No. 299. CCCB Archives, Ottawa.

[103] "The Canadian Bishops and Political Life in Quebec," April 21, 1972. CCC *Official Document* No. 298. CCCB Archives, Ottawa.

[104] "Simplicity and Sharing," CCC Labour Day Statement, September 1972. CCC *Official Document*, No. 307. CCCB Archives, Ottawa.

[105] The views of the CCC's Administrative Board on capital punishment were published on January 26, 1973, in a message to members of the Senate and House of Commons. CCC *Official Document*, No. 315. CCCB Archives, Ottawa.

[106] With William Power were Bruce McLeod, United Church moderator; two Presbyterians: Max Putman, moderator, and Donald MacDonald, administrative secretary; Edward (Ted) Scott, Anglican primate; and John Zimmerman, president of the Lutheran Council in Canada.

[107] The Inter-Church Project on Population (ICPOP) ceased to be active after 1978 and GATT-Fly has been reorganized as the Ecumenical Coalition on Economic Justice. Project North is now the Aboriginal Rights Coalition (ARC). Other coalitions include the Inter-Church Committee on Human Rights in Latin America; Task Force on Churches and Corporate Responsibility; Project Ploughshares; Inter-Church Fund for International Development; Canada-Asia Working Group; Canada-China Programme; Inter-Church Committee on Refugees; Inter-Church Coalition on Africa; Task Force on the Feminine Face of Poverty; Inter-Church Committee for World Development; Church Council on Justice and Corrections.

[108] "Development Demands Justice: An Appraisal of Canada's Relations with the Third World." March 1973 brief to government by leaders of five Churches. Also presented to the Canadian people during "Ten Days for World Development" tour across Canada by Church leaders, March 9-19, 1973. CCCB Archives, Ottawa.

[109] "Inequality Divides: Justice Reconciles," CCC 1973 Labour Day Statement, CCC *Official Document* No. 328. CCCB Archives, Ottawa. The idea of linking global survival and moral necessity, the text noted, was taken from the work of economist Barbara Ward. The reference is one of many indications of her close involvement in the social messages of the Canadian bishops. She had become a friend of many of them during the Second Vatican Council, where she was a special resource person for the Council's *Constitution on*

the Church in the Modern World. She had extensive knowledge of Canada through her studies and numerous speaking engagements. With Brazilian Bishop Helder Camara, she had been a main speaker at the 1968 Montreal poverty conference co-sponsored by the Canadian Churches. She also worked closely with the CCC delegation during the "justice in the world" discussion at the 1971 Synod of Bishops. Ward worked closely with two of the CCC's social affairs staff. She and William Ryan took part in the April 1968 conference in Beirut on world development, organized by SODEPAX, the peace and development agency then co-sponsored by the Vatican and the World Council of Churches. With Grant Maxwell, she later collaborated in projects of the Pontifical Commission for Justice and Peace, of which she was a member and he a consultant.

[110] The Inter-Church Project on Population (ICPOP) sent observers, including Tony Clarke and Bernard Daly from the CCC, to the August 1974 UN Population Conference in Bucharest. They were also involved in GATT-Fly's monitoring of the Rome World Food Conference in November 1974.

[111] "Sharing Daily Bread," CCC Labour Day Statement, September 1974. CCC *Official Document*, No. 369. CCCB Archives, Ottawa.

[112] "On the Occasion of International Women's Year in 1975," CCC Annual Meeting, September 16-20, 1974. CCC *Official Document*, No. 370. CCCB Archives, Ottawa.

[113] CCC *Official Document*, No. 371. CCCB Archives, Ottawa.

[114] "Sharing National Income", June 11, 1975, CCC *Official Document*, No. 389. CCCB Archives, Ottawa.

[115] "Pastoral Letter on Immigration and Population Policies," July 11, 1975. CCC *Official Document*, No. 391. Brief to Special Joint Committee of the Senate and House of Commons, September 1975. CCC *Official Document*, No. 395. CCCB Archives, Ottawa.

[116] "Northern Development: At What Cost?" CCC 1975 Labour Day Statement, CCC *Official Document*, No. 393. CCCB Archives, Ottawa.

[117] "Justice Demands Action," Interchurch brief to the federal cabinet, March 2, 1976. CCCB Archives, Ottawa. Besides Emmett Carter, CCC president, the Church leaders included Norman Berner, president of the Canadian Council of Churches; Edward (Ted) Scott, Anglican primate; Donald MacDonald, Presbyterian general secretary; Wilbur Howard, United Church moderator; and Roger Nostbakken, president of the Lutheran Council in Canada. In addition to Prime Minister Pierre E. Trudeau, federal cabinet members included Judd Buchanan, Allister Gillespie, Marc Lalonde, Allan MacEachen, Bryce Mackasey, John Munro and Mitchell Sharp.

[118] "A Habitation Fit for Man." CCC *Official Document*, No. 408, May 21, 1976. CCCB Archives, Ottawa.

[119] "From Words to Action," CCC 1976 Labour Day Statement, September 1976. CCC *Official Document*, No. 413. CCCB Archives, Ottawa.

[120] "A Society to be Transformed," CCCB Annual Meeting, December 1, 1977. CCCB *Official Document*, No. 436. CCCB Archives, Ottawa.

[121] "Unemployment: The Human Cost," CCCB *Official Document*, No. 453. CCCB Archives, Ottawa.

[122] "The Neutron Bomb – Enough is Enough," CCCB Annual Meeting, October 26-30, 1981. CCCB *Official Document*, No. 473. CCCB Archives, Ottawa.

[123] The brief was presented by the CCCB general secretaries, Dennis Murphy and André Vallée, and by Tony Clarke, co-director of the social affairs office.

[124] Joining Henri Légaré, CCCB president, in presenting the brief were Robert Binhammer, president, Lutheran Church in America (Canada section); Russell Legge, president, Canadian Council of Churches; Clarke MacDonald, moderator, United Church of Canada; Edward (Ted) Scott, Anglican primate; Wayne Smith, moderator, Presbyterian Church in Canada.

[125] Interview with Archbishop Henri Légaré by Bernard Daly, August 31, 1992. Audio tape in CCCB Archives, Ottawa.

[126] "Defending Workers' Rights: A New Frontier," May 1, 1985; "Supporting Labour Unions: A Christian Responsibility," May 1, 1986. CCCB Archives, Ottawa.

[127] See "Bishop imputes wrong motives to Conrad Black," letter by Conrad Black in the *Toronto Star*, October 31, 1987; and "Conrad Black wrong about De Roo," reply by Bernard M. Daly, CCCB assistant general secretary, *Toronto Star*, November 24, 1987.

[128] "Fortress North America? Ethical Reflections on the Global Implications of the U.S.-Canada Free Trade Accord," Canadian Catholic Organization for Development and Peace, Toronto, July 1988.

[129] Minutes, Vol. 4, No. 43, Item 22. Meeting of the CCC Administrative Board, January 21, 1966. Members of the episcopal committee who made the recommendation to the board were Archbishops Michael O'Neill of Regina, George Flahiff of Winnipeg, Norbert Robichaud of Moncton and Maurice Baudoux of St. Boniface; Bishops James M. Hayes of Halifax, Gérard-Marie Coderre of St. Jean and Paul Émile Charbonneau of Hull; and Auxiliary Bishop Lionel Audet of Quebec. See also Minutes of the Bishops' Commission for Christian Education in NORE files. CCCB Archives, Ottawa.

[130] Minutes of Third Plenary Assembly of the Canadian Episcopate at the Cardinal's Palace, Quebec, Vol. 1, June 21-22, 1938. CCCB Archives, Ottawa.

[131] Minutes, Vol. 2, No. 13. CCC Annual Meeting, October 12-14, 1954. CCCB Archives, Ottawa.

[132] These details are from the Minutes, Vol. 1, No. 21, CCC Annual Meeting, November 11-15, 1958; the CCC Administrative Board Meeting, February 4, 1959, and the CCC Annual Meeting, October 6-8, 1959. The latter minutes extensively paraphrase the Carroll-MacEachern report.

[133] CCC *Information Service*, Vol. 6, No. 58. April 7, 1961. CCCB Archives, Ottawa.

[134] Minutes of meeting of the diocesan directors of the Confraternity of Christian Doctrine (CCD), Winnipeg, February 22, 1962. CCD files. CCCB Archives, Ottawa.

[135] CCC *Information Service*, Vol. 7, No. 110. June 25, 1962. CCCB Archives, Ottawa.

[136] Minutes of a meeting held on August 18, 1963, at the National Office of the CCD, Ottawa. CCD Files. CCCB Archives, Ottawa.

[137] See September 23, 1965, "To whom it may concern" letter from L'Office catéchistique provincial, signed by Suzanne Caron. CCD files. CCCB Archives, Ottawa.

[138] NORE Annual Report, May 1966. NORE files. CCCB Archives, Ottawa.

[139] For details of the 1970 reorganization of NORE, see Agenda No. 14, Meeting of the CCC Board, March 5-6, 1970. CCCB Archives, Ottawa. Other NORE files give details of these and later personnel changes. Jeffery succeeded Murphy and served as co-director

with May O'Hanlon and Robert Kennedy. Wilfrid Murchland served as assistant director in 1973. Peter Sanders succeeded Jeffery as director in May 1974, and was himself succeeded by Colleen Mahoney. Other NORE directors, in turn, have been Lawrence DeMong, Stephen Miletic, and Bernadette Tourangeau.

[140] Letter to Emmett Doyle from Dennis Murphy, November 25, 1968. NORE files. CCCB Archives, Ottawa.

[141] See correspondence in NORE files: Everett MacNeil, CCC general secretary, to Paul Tremblay, OCQ director, November 8, 1971; Martin Jeffery, NORE, to Alphonse Ruel, OCQ, September 19, 1972; Ruel to Jeffery, October 6, 1972.

[142] Letter from Sanders to Claire Dubé, director, CCCB Publications Service, November 9, 1978. NORE files. CCCB Archives, Ottawa.

[143] Second Vatican Council, *Dogmatic Constitution on the Church*, November 21, 1964, Art. 29.

[144] Other committee members were Joseph Wilhelm, archbishop of Kingston, and James Hayes, archbishop of Halifax; Lionel Audet, bishop of Quebec, and Gérard Couturier, bishop of Hauterive.

[145] Restauration du diaconat permanent. Personal notes by Bishop Albert Sanschagrin. Permanent Diaconate file. CCCB Archives, Ottawa.

[146] Minutes, Vol. 2, No. 72, Item 12, p. 13. CCCB Annual Meeting, September 23-27, 1968. CCCB Archives, Ottawa.

[147] Letter to Alexander Carter, CCC president, from Emanuele Clarizio, apostolic delegate, February 6, 1969. CCCB Archives, Ottawa.

[148] CCC *Information Service*, Vol. 9, No. 131, p. 7, November 3, 1964. CCCB Archives, Ottawa.

[149] See CCCB files, "Famille, femmes, Humanae Vitae," box 112. CCCB Archives, Ottawa.

[150] Minutes, Vol. 5, No. 105. CCCB Annual Meeting, September, 20-24, 1971. CCCB Archives, Ottawa.

[151] "Ministries of Women in the Church," by Cardinal George Flahiff. CCC Document, *For Your Information, No. 117*, October 11, 1971. CCCB Archives, Ottawa.

[152] Minutes, Vol. 6, No. 112. Meeting of the CCC Administrative Board, March 9-10, 1972. CCCB Archives, Ottawa.

[153] Minutes, Vol. 8, No. 140, Item 18, p. 9-10. Meeting of the CCC Executive Committee, May 23-24, 1974. CCCB Archives, Ottawa.

[154] CCC *Official Document*, No. 370, September 1974. CCCB Archives, Ottawa.

[155] Letter from Emmett Carter to Jean Villot, February 23, 1976. CCCB Archives, Ottawa.

[156] "Report of the Meeting of the CCC Officials and the Holy Father on the Day of March 18th at 10:45 a.m." Letters of the President file. CCCB Archives, Ottawa.

[157] Letter from Emmett Carter to Angelo Palmas, April 14, 1976. CCCB Archives, Ottawa.

[158] "Statement concerning the Declaration on Ordaining Women to the Ministerial Priesthood," CCCB Administrative Board, Ottawa, January 26, 1977. During the January 25-26 meeting prior to publication of Carter's statement, the CCCB board requested "that the Secretariat begin work immediately to study in depth the role of women in the Church and their possible ministerial and other roles in the believing community." Minutes, Vol. 11,

No. 177, Item 146, p. 8. Meeting of the CCCB Administrative Board, January 25-26, 1977. CCCB Archives, Ottawa.

159 CCCB Archives, Ottawa.

160 "Survey on the Participation of Women in the Official Pastoral Work of the Catholic Church in Canada, 1979." CCCB Archives, Ottawa.

161 CCCB Document *For Your Information*, No. 833, October 14, 1980. CCCB Archives, Ottawa.

162 "Male-Female Reconciliation in the Church," by Cardinal Louis-Albert Vachon, Synod of Bishops, October 3, 1983. CCCB Archives, Ottawa.

163 CCCB Document *For Your Information*, No. 1205, July 3, 1986. CCCB Archives, Ottawa.

164 "And No One Shall Make Them Afraid," CCCB Document *For Your Information*, No. 1524, March 6, 1992. CCCB Archives, Ottawa.

165 Minutes, Vol. 3, No. 24, Item 7, p. 60. Meeting of the CCC Administrative Board, January 13, 1960; and Minutes, Vol. 3, No. 26, art. 40, p. 92. CCC Annual Meeting, October 11-13, 1960. CCCB Archives, Ottawa.

166 Second Vatican Council, *Pastoral Constitution on the Church in the Modern World*, December 7, 1965, Art. 1.

167 Interview with Gordon George, by Bernard Daly at Pickering, Ont., July 21, 1992. Audio tape in CCCB Archives, Ottawa.

168 Letter from Philip Pocock to Gordon George, May 6, 1966. CCODP files. CCCB Archives, Ottawa.

169 Letter from Paul-Émile Léger to Charles Mathieu, May 5, 1966. CCODP files. CCCB Archives, Ottawa.

170 Present at the meeting were Robert Riendeau, director of welfare work from the Archdiocese of Montreal; Bernard Benoît, chargé d'affaires for Cardinal Léger; André Tremblay, president of the Saint-Jean-Valparaiso Fraternity, Montreal; Roger Tessier, Missions Commission secretary, Canadian Religious Conference; Pierre Goyette, director of the CCC's Latin America office; Jean-Guy Hamelin, French director of the CCC's social action office, and Jack Shea, his English counterpart; Francis Smyth, director of the Coady International Institute in Antigonish, and George Wicks, registrar of the Institute; Bernard Daly, editor of the CCC Information Service; John O'Mara, vice-chancellor of the archdiocese of Toronto; and Claude Mulvihill, director of Catholic Charities for the Archdiocese of Toronto. Special guests for the afternoon session were Philip Land from the Social Science Institute of the Gregorian University in Rome and James Norris, assistant to the executive director of the U.S. bishops' Catholic Relief Services in New York.

171 Philip Land and James Norris had been recruited by William Ryan who, as co-director of CCC social action office, was researching the directions the proposed Canadian initiative might take. Land and Norris had served as consultants for the Second Vatican Council discussion of poverty, and Norris had been active in promoting a special Vatican secretariat for world justice and development.

172 Minutes of a consultation on the establishment of a Canadian bishops' overseas aid organization, undated. CCODP File. CCCB Archives, Ottawa.

[173] Memo from John Shea, September 12, 1966, concerning the September 19, 1966, meeting of the ad hoc committee for the establishment of a Canadian Catholic overseas relief-development organization. CCODP file. CCCB Archives, Ottawa.

[174] Minutes, Vol. 4, No. 44. CCC Plenary Meeting October 12-14, 1966. CCCB Archives, Ottawa. Norms approved for selecting the first directors for the relief fund called for two from the ecclesiastical province of Montreal; one each from Quebec City, Sherbrooke, Rimouski and western Quebec (Hull, Amos, Mont Laurier); four from Ontario (three anglophones and one francophone – two from the north and two from the south); two from New Brunswick (anglophone and francophone); and one from each other province. Two would be named directly by the CCC to complete the twenty-five-member panel.

[175] Minutes Vol. 1, No. 51. CCC Annual Meeting, April 6-7, 1967. CCCB Archives, Ottawa.

[176] Minutes, Vol. 1, No. 54. Meeting of the CCC Administrative Board, June 9, 1967. CCCB Archives, Ottawa.

[177] From Archbishop Plourde's introduction on November 22, 1969, at the opening of the consultation for a Canadian Pastoral Council. Document 7-C. Pastoral Council files. CCCB Archives, Ottawa.

[178] Minutes, Vol. 1, No. 50. Meeting of CCC Administrative Board, March 10, 1967. CCCB Archives, Ottawa. The meeting named Pocock (Toronto), Plourde (Ottawa), Charbonneau (Hull) and Power (Antigonish) to be an ad hoc committee, chaired by Plourde, to study the nature and role of the CCC.

[179] Minutes, Vol. 2, No. 72. CCC Annual Meeting, September 23-27, 1968. CCCB Archives, Ottawa.

[180] Minutes, Vol. 3, No. 79. CCC Annual Meeting, April 14-18, 1969. CCCB Archives, Ottawa.

[181] "Canada's National Pastoral Council," by Bernard Daly, *Today's Parish*, May-June, 1970, p. 10.

[182] "Resume Report of the Steering Committee Meeting, Canadian Pastoral Council, November 21-23, 1969, Ottawa, Ontario." Canadian Pastoral Council files. CCCB Archives, Ottawa.

[183] Minutes, Vol. 4, No. 88. Meeting of CCC Administrative Board, March 5-6, 1970. CCCB Archives, Ottawa.

[184] Letter from Emmett Carter to Joseph-Aurèle Plourde, October 27, 1970. Canadian Pastoral Council file. CCCB Archives, Ottawa.

[185] Letter from Emmett Carter to Joseph-Aurèle Plourde.

[186] The English text of the proposal by André Desmartis carries the indication "'rough' translation – B.A.P." Bernard Prince, CCC staff, acted as interim secretary for the CPC. Canadian Pastoral Council file. CCCB Archives, Ottawa.

[187] "Pastorale canadienne et conseil pastoral canadien," by Bernard Lambert, mimeographed, October 11, 1970. Canadian Pastoral Council file. CCCB Archives, Ottawa.

[188] "Canadian Pastoral Council Study Committee Final Session, October 9-12, 1970," Canadian Pastoral Council file. CCCB Archives, Ottawa.

[189] Letter from Emmett Carter to Plourde.

[190] "Report on the Second Meeting of the Steering Committee for the Establishment of a Canadian Pastoral Council, Held in Scarborough, Ontario from October 9th to October 12th, 1970," by Shirley Scaletta of St. Boniface, Man., with a December 2, 1970, letter to Bernard Prince. Canadian Pastoral Council file. CCCB Archives, Ottawa.

[191] "Controverses autour d'un conseil pastoral canadien," by Georges Milot of St. Jean-Longueuil diocese. Canadian Pastoral Council files. CCCB Archives, Ottawa.

[192] The Dumont Commission was set up to study the situation of Catholic Action in francophone dioceses in Canada.

[193] Letter from William Power to Joseph-Aurèle Plourde, November 23, 1970. CCCB Archives, Ottawa.

[194] Minutes, Vol. 4, No. 97. Meeting of the CCC Administrative Board, December 3-4, 1970. CCCB Archives, Ottawa.

[195] Letter from Bernard Prince, CCC assistant general secretary, to CPC members, December 18, 1970. Canadian Pastoral Council file. CCCB Archives, Ottawa.

[196] Minutes, Vol. 1, No. 1, Item G, p. 10-11. CCC Annual Meeting, October 13-14. CCCB Archives, Ottawa.

[197] Marc-Henri Côté was the first full-time editor of the French service, from 1957 to 1962, when he was succeeded by Réjean Plamondon. Bernard Daly was full-time editor of the English service from 1958 until it was suspended in 1966. During the first few years of each service, several Ottawa journalists edited the bulletins on a part-time basis, including Germain Brière and Jean-Marc Poliquin in French, and Frank Williams in English. A public relations/information office was organized after 1967. Its English directors have been Ella Zink, Bonnie Brennan and Dennis Gruending; its French directors, Louis Chabot, Guy Poisson, Jacques Barnard, Jacques Binet and Gérald Baril.

[198] Minutes, Vol. 2, No. 6, Item 9, p. 95. CCC Annual Meeting, December 5-6, 1950. CCCB Archives, Ottawa.

[199] For details of the history of the Office de communications sociales (OCS), see Alain Gagnon, *Médias, culture et religion au Québec*, June, 1989, Office des communications sociales, Montreal. From its beginning until 1991, the OCS was directed by Lucien Labelle, now succeeded by Jacques Paquette.

[200] For the French Information Service, Claude Ryan attended the first session and Réjean Plamondon the other three, while for the English Service Bernard Daly covered all four sessions of the Second Vatican Council. For the OCNTD, Jean-Paul Belleville, Léo Beaudoin, Yvon Desrosiers and Pierre Forest worked at Vatican II; for the NCCC, Bonnie Brennan and Edward Bader.

[201] Minutes, Vol. 3, No. 26. CCC Annual Meeting, October 11-13, 1960. CCCB Archives, Ottawa.

[202] According to the Plenary mandate (English Sector Minutes, Vol. 4, No. 44, Item 3, p. 583, October 12-14, 1966), the Family Life Bureau (FLB) was to engage in research on family matters, especially those raised by civil law changes; collaborate with the Vanier Institute of the Family; share research findings with every level of the Church; serve family movements and organizations; and co-operate with other Churches and agencies on family questions. Bernard Daly served as director during its six years of activity. The limited resources and kind of questions facing the CCC inclined the FLB to adopt a participant-observer research method, rather than research by large-scale collection of data.

[203] The booklet contained the CCC statements on these topics and the interchurch brief about divorce, with suggested questions for use by study groups. It was presented as "an experiment: How can CCC statements be given more meaningful exposure than the usual initial press release and pulpit reading?" Eventually more than 3,500 copies were sold.

[204] "Activities 1971-1972," Family Life Bureau annual report, June 1972. CCCB Archives, Ottawa.

[205] The Paulist Fathers joined the CCC as co-sponsor of the seminar, particularly to explore it as a model for Paulist work in the U.S. Toronto Paulist William Dewan joined in designing the program with Robert Morin, co-director of the CCC's Montreal Office national du bien-être et de la santé, and Bernard Daly, Family Life Bureau director.

[206] The eight CCC participants were Cardinals Maurice Roy and George Flahiff; Archbishops Philip Pocock and James Hayes; and Bishops Paul O'Byrne, Guy Bélanger, Henri Légaré and Austin E. Burke. Edward (Ted) Scott and United Church general secretary Ernest Long were the other Church participants. Demography, sociology, economics, zoology, medicine, theology and ethics were the university disciplines represented. Government officials came from urban affairs, immigration, environment, science and technology, Indian affairs, citizenship and the Privy Council office.

[207] "Activities Report 1971-1972, pp. 4-5, June 1972." Family Life Bureau. CCCB Archives, Ottawa.

[208] "Activities Report 1968," July 1968. Family Life Bureau. CCCB Archives, Ottawa.

[209] "Activities Report 1970," p. 2. Family Life Bureau. CCCB Archives, Ottawa.

[210] On a motion by Paul O'Byrne, Bishop of Calgary, and Maurice Baudoux, Archbishop of St. Boniface, the CCC's April 1973 Plenary unanimously agreed: "a) that it is a priority for pastoral leaders to involve all the people of God in a learning and reflecting process regarding family life; b) that this pastoral leadership be given not so much by statements of principle as by dialogue with the faithful and specialists to arrive at the real questions (social, experimental, doctrinal, etc.) upon which pastors and people will reflect in the light of the Gospel; c) that this process of dialogue with the people concerning family life be a special part of the CCC preparation for participation in the Synod theme: The Evangelization of the Modern World; d) that CCC Offices should prepare materials to facilitate this process in close collaboration with people in each region who are interested and involved in family movements, as well as with specialized family services, movements, etc., at every level." Minutes, Vol. 7, No. 127, Item 8, p. 9. CCC Annual Meeting, April 2-6, 1973. CCCB Archives, Ottawa.

[211] The original staff team anglophone members were Hans Daigeler, theology; Michael O'Connell, ecumenism, and Bernard Daly, social affairs. The francophone members were Demetrius Michailides, theology; Léonard Rochon, religious education, clergy and laity, and Aubert April, social affairs. Later, Josephine McCarthy, Veronica O'Reilly and Donna Geernaert, in turn, succeeded O'Connell, and Jennifer Leddy succeeded Daly. Arthé Guimond and then Marcel Lefebvre succeeded Michailides; and Jean-Noël Gagné succeeded Rochon.

[212] Minutes, Vol. 3, No. 35. CCC Administrative Board Meeting, April 16, 1964. CCCB Archives, Ottawa.

[213] Minutes, Vol. 1, No. 51. CCC Annual Meeting, April 6-7, 1967. Document No. 1. Financial Situation of the CCC, p. 37. CCCB Archives, Ottawa.

[214] *Evaluation-1972*, Vol. 3, p. 76. CCCB Archives, Ottawa.

[215] *Evaluation-1972*, Vol. 3, p. 79. CCCB Archives, Ottawa.

[216] "From Winnipeg to *Fully Alive*," by Msgr. Vincent Foy, *Challenge*, April, 1992, p. 21. See also Alphonse de Valk, *Morality and Law in Canadian Politics: The Abortion Controversy*, Palm Publishers, Montreal, 1974; and "Understandable but Mistaken: Law, Morality and the Catholic Church in Canada, 1966-1969," *Canadian Catholic Historical Association, Study Sessions*, 49, 1982, pp. 87-109. Similar accusations can also be found in the writings of Anne Roche Muggeridge, *The Gates of Hell: The Struggle for the Catholic Church*, McClelland and Stewart, Toronto, 1975; and *The Desolate City: The Catholic Church in Ruins*, McClelland and Stewart, Toronto, 1985. For an overview of the development of the reactions of pro-life groups to the positions taken by the CCCB, see Michael W. Cuneo, *Catholics against the Church: Anti-abortion Protest in Toronto 1969-1985*, University of Toronto Press, 1989.

[217] "The Church and Family Life in Canada Today," Canadian Catholic Conference, September 9, 1966. CCCB Archives, Ottawa.

[218] "To the House of Commons' Standing Committee on Health and Welfare: On Change in the Law on Contraceptives," Canadian Catholic Conference, September 9, 1966. CCCB Archives, Ottawa.

[219] For details of the points summarized here, see "On Proposed Change of the Law on Divorce: To the Special Joint Committee of the Senate and House of Commons." Canadian Catholic Conference, April 6, 1967. CCCB Archives, Ottawa.

[220] Letter from Louis Lévesque, CCC president, "To the Most Reverend Members of the CCC re: Proposed Divorce Legislation," August 23, 1967. CCCB Archives, Ottawa.

[221] "A Statement to the Minister of Justice about the Proposals to Reform the Divorce Laws," November 8, 1967, prepared by the Christian Social Service of the Anglican Church of Canada, CCC Family Life Bureau, Division of Social Services of the Lutheran Council in Canada, Peace and Service Office of the Mennonite Central Committee (Canada), Board of Evangelism and Social Action of the Presbyterian Church in Canada, Marriage Guidance Council of the United Church of Canada. Box 111. CCCB Archives, Ottawa.

[222] "Brief to the Minister of Justice on the *Family Law Report* of the Law Reform Commission of Canada," CCCB Administrative Board, January 26, 1977. CCCB Archives, Ottawa.

[223] "Brief to the House of Commons Committee on Justice on Bill C-47: *An Act Respecting Divorce*," Canadian Conference of Catholic Bishops, June 18, 1985. CCCB Archives, Ottawa.

[224] See endnote 218.

[225] The CCC decision-making process on this question was described in detail by Remi De Roo when the CCC delegation met with the Commons Standing Committee on Health and Welfare. See *Minutes of Proceedings, Standing Committee on Health and Welfare*, March 5, 1968, p. 820 ff. House of Commons, Ottawa.

[226] "Pastoral Statement on Proposed Change of Canadian Law on Abortion," Canadian Catholic Conference, February 7, 1968. CCCB Archives, Ottawa.

[227] "For a Society Hospitable to Life," CCC Plenary Assembly Statement on Abortion, April 6, 1973. CCC *Official Document*, No. 320. CCCB Archives, Ottawa.

[228] "To Love and Serve Life," Canadian Conference of Catholic Bishops, April 7, 1986. CCCB *Official Document*, No. 547. CCCB Archives, Ottawa.

[229] "Why Can't the Bishops Get Across Their Message on the Abortion Issue?" by Mary Jo Leddy, *Compass*, Toronto, May/June, 1992, p. 22.

[230] "On the Supreme Court Decision Striking Down the Abortion Law," by Archbishop James Hayes, CCCB President, January 28, 1988. CCCB *Official Document*, No. 586. CCCB Archives, Ottawa.

[231] "Faithful to the Future: A Statement on Abortion," by Archbishop James Hayes, April 7, 1988. CCCB *Official Document*, No. 594. CCCB Archives, Ottawa.

[232] "Submission made on Behalf of the Permanent Council of the Canadian Conference of Catholic Bishops to the Parliamentary Committee on Abortion," by Bishop Robert Lebel, president. Permanent Council members were Aloysius Ambrozic, Bertrand Blanchet, Emmett Carter, Noël Delaquis, Gérard Drainville, Roger Ébacher, Adam Exner, Thomas Fulton, Paul Grégoire, Charles Halpin, Jean-Guy Hamelin, Maxim Hermaniuk, Robert Lebel, James MacDonald, John O'Mara, Louis-Albert Vachon. CCCB Document "*For Your Information*," No. 1430, January 31, 1990. CCCB Archives, Ottawa.

[233] Some signs used in the February 21, 1990, demonstration outside CCCB offices included the following: Bishops turn backs on Catholic teaching; Is 30 pieces of silver still the going rate for betrayal?; Bishops condemn not condone; Bishops support immoral Bill C-43; Wanted Pro-life bishops; The 5th commandment is 'Thou shalt not kill'; CCCB: Wolves in sheep's clothing; CCFB – Canadian Conference of Feminist Bishops; Real Catholics are pro-life; Protect the unborn; No Catholic may obey a law approving abortion in principle nor may he vote for such a law; 'Pluralistic Society' no excuse for cowardice; Adoption not abortion; Catholic bishops – the blood of unborn Canadians is on your hands; Bishops shirk obligation; Catholic bishops: we want peace and development in the womb; Abortion is uncivilized; Let the children come to me: do not hinder them; CCCB: Is there a John Fisher or Athanasius among you? CCCB: Quo vadis? CCCB statement smacks of heresy and schism; CCCB, lead us to Peter, perfection and heaven with Jesus; Forward ho! Loyal Catholics; Bishops mislead Catholics; Pope's barge saves all: CCCB boat leaks and loses most of its cargo; Bishops abandon unborn children; Herod loves the CCCB; Bishops sell out $$$$$; 5 betrayals in 30 years – 1969: Omnibus Bill; 1980: Charter; 1987: Mitges; 1988: Amendment A; 1990: Bill C-43.

[234] "Pro-vie proteste contre la position des évêques vis-à-vis l'avortement," *Le Devoir*, February 22, 1990; "Des catholiques pro-vie accusent la Conférence des évêques du Canada de favoriser l'avortement," *La Presse*, February 22, 1990; "Pro-vie veut plus de fermeté de la part des évêques," *Le Droit*, February 22, 1990; "Area Catholics to protest bishops' abortion bill stand," *Ottawa Citizen*, February 20, 1990.

[235] A detailed account and analysis of the criticisms of the Canadian bishops by members of various pro-life groups is provided by Cuneo in *Catholics against the Church*. However, his analysis of the bishops' stand and strategy lacks precision on a number of points.

[236] "Statement of the CCCB President on the Defeat of Bill C-43 in the Senate," CCCB *Official Document*, No. 631, February 1, 1991. CCCB Archives, Ottawa. The workshop on abortion is in the CCCB publication *The Gift of Life – The Right to Life*. The workshops on aging, death and dying, disabilities, immigrants and refugees, pornography,

prostitution, technology, unemployment and violence are in the CCCB publication *In the Name of Life*.

[237] Interview with James M. Hayes by Bernard Daly, August 30, 1992. Audio tape in CCCB Archives, Ottawa.

[238] Cuneo, *Catholics against the Church*, pp. 168-178.

[239] Interview with Alexander Carter by Bernard Daly, North Bay, Ont., August 7, 1992. Audio tape in CCCB Archives, Ottawa.

[240] Sean MacReamoinn, "Laylines," *Doctrine and Life*, No. 5, May-June, 1992, p. 321.

[241] CCC *Internal Communication*, No. 451, August 28, 1968. CCCB Archives, Ottawa. Members of the theology commission thus responsible for guiding the production of a statement were: English sector – Bishops Remi De Roo of Victoria, chairman; Paul Reding of Hamilton, secretary; Thomas McCarthy of St. Catharines, John O'Neil of Grand Falls, and Archbishop Philip Pocock of Toronto; French sector – Bishops André Ouellette of Mont Laurier, chairman; Laurent Noël of Trois-Rivières, secretary; and Paul-Émile Charbonneau of Gatineau-Hull, Bruno Desrochers of St. Anne de la Pocatière, and Laurent Morin of Prince Albert. All were present during the Plenary, though some did not attend every commission meeting. As chairman of the religious education commission, Bishop Emmett Doyle of Nelson also attended the commission meetings. Later in the week, Bishop Emmett Carter was asked to assist in the drafting.

[242] Many published accounts of the Winnipeg meeting correctly identify only Sheridan among the four invited theologians. See, for example, "Prelates and the Pill," by Douglas J. Roche, *Commonweal*, October 15, 1968, p. 84; also, Michael W. Higgins and Douglas R. Letson, *My Father's Business: A Biography of His Eminence G. Emmett Carter*, MacMillan of Canada, Toronto, 1990, p. 105. Other priests who had some roles in the process as the week went along are usually listed in error as having been invited for the beginning of the week. From the CCC's staff, Bernard Daly, director of the Family Life Bureau, and Charles Saint-Onge, assistant director of the French social affairs office, were authorized to work with the commission and experts as coordinators of the drafting and translating process.

[243] The bishops present were Remi De Roo and André Ouellette, co-chairmen, Paul-Émile Charbonneau, Bruno Desrochers, Emmett Doyle and Laurent Morin. Joseph Bisztyo, Édouard Gagnon, Édouard Hamel and Edward Sheridan were there, as were Bernard Daly and Charles Saint-Onge, as well as the English general secretary Gordon George, and his assistant, Everett MacNeil.

[244] The documents referred to in this paragraph are in the *Humanae Vitae* file. CCCB Archives, Ottawa.

[245] De Roo's paper outlined a series of points, including the following: Because the encyclical was for the whole world, the CCC had to apply it to the Canadian scene. A ministry of reconciliation of extremists for and against it was needed. A pastoral statement seemed indicated. The anguish of sincere people should be described in sympathetic terms. It should point out the need for openness towards the magisterium of the Church and reverence for the Pope's teaching office. It should be an invitation to continuing dialogue, serious discussion and study.

[246] Regarding the distribution of documents, the commission agreed that all the bishops should receive copies of a statement prepared by CCC office directors and of all reactions from various groups as they were received.

[247] Minutes, Vol. 2, No. 72, Item 4, pp. 10-11. CCC Annual Meeting, September 23-27, 1968. CCCB Archives, Ottawa.

[248] This account of the process is taken from "Confidential Memorandum on the Evolution of the CCC Statement on 'Humanae Vitae', September 21-27, 1968," by Everett MacNeil, assistant general secretary. *Humanae Vitae* file. CCCB Archives, Ottawa.

[249] Both Alexander Carter and Joseph-Aurèle Plourde, president and vice-president in 1968, stressed in 1992 interviews with the author that the Pope did not ask the bishops to support him, but that the people were asking for guidance. Audio tapes in CCCB Archives, Ottawa.

[250] Letter from Alexander Carter to Romeo Blanchette, Bishop of Joliet, Illinois, October 18, 1968. *Humanae Vitae* file. CCCB Archives, Ottawa.

[251] Letter from Emmett Carter to Alexander Carter, October 28, 1968. *Addendum* No. 32-B of Minutes, CCC Administrative Board Meeting, November 6-8, 1968. CCCB Archives, Ottawa.

[252] "Statement of the Canadian Bishops on 'Humanae Vitae': Collaboration with the Communication Media and Plenary Assembly Deliberations," approved by the CCC Administrative Board meeting in Ottawa, November 6-8, 1968. CCC *Official Document*, No. 160. CCCB Archives, Ottawa.

[253] Letter from Amleto Cicognani to Maurice Roy, October 18, 1968. *Humanae Vitae* file. CCCB Archives, Ottawa.

[254] Letter from Maurice Roy to Alexander Carter, November 1, 1968. *Humanae Vitae* file. CCCB Archives, Ottawa.

[255] Letter from Emanuele Clarizio to Alexander Carter, English and French texts, October 21, 1968. The French text said: "J'ai maintenant le plaisir à communiquer que le Saint-Père, d'après ce que m'écrit son Éminence le cardinal Amleto Cicognani, secrétaire d'État de Sa Sainteté, a pris connaissance avec satisfaction du document." CCCB Archives, Ottawa.

[256] Minutes. Vol. 2, No. 73. Meeting of the CCC Administrative Board, November 6-8, 1968. CCCB Archives, Ottawa.

[257] Minutes, Vol. 2, No. 74. Meeting of the CCC Executive Committee, December 5-6, 1968. CCCB Archives, Ottawa.

[258] Letter from André Ouellette to Alexander Carter, December 16, 1968. *Humanae Vitae* file. CCCB Archives, Ottawa.

[259] "Follow-up to Statement of Canadian Bishops on the Encyclical Humanae Vitae," CCC *Internal Communication*, No. 496, January 21, 1969. CCCB Archives, Ottawa.

[260] The committee members were Bishops Ouellette and Reding, André and Micheline Desmartis of Quebec City, Norma McCoy of Peterborough, Barry McGrory of Ottawa, Jean-Louis Gravel of Chicoutimi (replaced by Marcel Trudeau of Longueuil), Roland Dorris of Montreal, Julien Mercure of Ottawa, Joseph Cooney of Toronto, with Bernard Daly and Claude Michaud of the CCC staff as co-animators.

[261] A new member of the French theology commission at this meeting was the new bishop of St. Paul, Alberta, Édouard Gagnon, one of the four theologians invited to assist the bishops in Winnipeg.

[262] Minutes, Vol. 3, No. 79. CCC Annual Meeting, April 14-18, 1969. CCCB Archives, Ottawa.

[263] Minutes. Meeting of English social action commission, Edmonton, February 2, 1966. Social Action files. CCCB Archives, Ottawa.

[264] Minutes, Vol. 3, No. 38, Item 8, p. 441. Meeting of the CCC Administrative Board, April 21, 1965. Minutes, Vol. 4, No. 43, Item 7, p. 548. Meeting of the Board, January 27, 1966. CCCB Archives, Ottawa.

[265] Agenda No. 24, CCC Annual Meeting, October 12-13, 1966. CCCB Archives, Ottawa.

[266] "On the Occasion of the Hundredth Year of Confederation." Minutes, Vol. 1, No. 51. CCC Annual Meeting, April 6-7, 1967. CCCB Archives, Ottawa.

[267] Minutes, Vol. 3, No. 228, Item 12, pp. 5-6. Meeting of the CCC Administrative Board, November 19-20. 1980. CCCB Archives, Ottawa.

[268] Addendum No. 6-B, CCCB Executive Committee meeting, January 28-29, 1981. CCCB Archives, Ottawa.

[269] See Agenda No. 6, CCCB Executive Committee, January 28-29, 1981. CCCB Archives, Ottawa.

[270] Assemblée des évêques du Québec, "Observations des évêques du Québec sur la question constitutionnelle," January 29, 1981; Le Devoir, February 4, 1981.

[271] Interview with Bernard Hubert, *The Catholic Register*, Toronto, November 13, 1982.

[272] In February 1987, a second abortion-constitution dilemma arose over a private member's bill by Dr. Gus Mitges. It asked the government to "consider the advisability of amending the Constitution Act, 1982, to include unborn human persons." To the extent that the Mitges bill was opposed to abortion, the CCCB wanted to encourage it. To the extent that it touched upon a constitutional situation that excluded Quebec, they wanted to take no position either for or against it. Cf. "Note concerning Debate on Dr. Mitges' Private Motion," by Denis Robitaille and William F. Ryan, CCCB general secretaries, September 16, 1987. CCCB Archives, Ottawa.

[273] It was chaired by the Archbishop of Gatineau-Hull, Roger Ébacher. Adam Exner, Archbishop of Winnipeg, and James MacDonald, Bishop of Charlottetown (later Archbishop of St. John's) were joined as members by Gerard Copeman, Sault Ste. Marie priest; Nuala Kenny, Halifax doctor; Rita Cadieux of Ottawa; and André Boyer, Montreal area social worker. Four specialized work groups aided the committee. A group to revise the 1987 guidelines was headed by canonist Rev. Francis Morrisey. Social worker Paul McAuliffe headed the group on policies for pastoral care of victims and their families. Theologian and counsellor Jacques Gagné chaired a work group on long-term care and the future of priest abusers. Jeannine Guindon, a Montreal counselling specialist, chaired the group on guidelines and policies for selection and formation of future priests.

[274] *Breach of Trust, Breach of Faith: Child Sexual Abuse in the Church and Society; Materials for Discussion Groups*, Canadian Conference of Catholic Bishops, Ottawa, 1992 (published also in French).

[275] Members of the Steering Committee on Residential Schools were Stan Dixon, past chief, Sechelt Native Community, B.C.; Norma-Jean Dubray-Byrd, director, Circle Project, Regina; Patricia Laliberté, regional superior of the Sisters of St. Joseph, St. Hyacinthe, Que.; Achiel Peelman, Oblate theologian, Saint Paul University, Ottawa; Jacqueline Saint-Yves, Manitoba provincial superior Grey Nuns of Montréal; Archbishop Peter Sutton of Keewatin-Le Pas, Manitoba, and Lorne MacDonald, committee co-ordinator.

[276] *From Pain to Hope: Report from the CCCB Ad Hoc Committee on Child Sexual Abuse*, Ottawa, June 1992 (published also in French). The recommendations to the CCCB are on pp. 61-62.

[277] "Report of the President to the Plenary Meeting, Canadian Conference of Catholic Bishops," July 27 – August 1, 1992, Agenda Addendum No. 4, p. 2. CCCB Archives, Ottawa.

[278] Letter from Alexander Carter to Emanuele Clarizio, April 25, 1969. CCCB Archives, Ottawa.

[279] Letter from Alexander Carter, CCC president, to Pope Paul VI, April 25, 1969. CCCB Archives, Ottawa.

[280] Letter from A. Carter to Clarizio, April 25, 1969. CCCB Archives, Ottawa.

[281] Cited in letter from A. Carter to Clarizio, April 25, 1969. CCCB Archives, Ottawa.

[282] Letter from Clarizio to A. Carter, May 6, 1969. CCCB Archives, Ottawa.

[283] Minutes, Vol. 3, No. 81. Meeting of CCC Administrative Board, June 5-6, 1969. CCCB Archives, Ottawa.

[284] The seven first-instance courts were located in Quebec City, Montreal, Halifax, Ottawa, Toronto, Regina and Vancouver.

[285] See Official Minutes, "Convention of the Canadian Regional Tribunals, May 19-20, 1953." CCCB Archives, Ottawa.

[286] The appeal tribunals were in Toronto (for Vancouver, Edmonton and Regina first-instance cases), Montreal (for Toronto and Quebec cases), Ottawa (for Montreal cases), and Quebec (for Ottawa and Halifax cases).

[287] Report of the Canonical Affairs Committee, Addendum No. 10. CCC Annual Meeting, April 2-6, 1973. CCCB Archives, Ottawa.

[288] Minutes, Vol. 6, No. 118. CCC Annual Meeting, October 9-13, 1972. CCCB Archives, Ottawa.

[289] Minutes, Vol. 8, No. 145. Meeting of the CCC Administrative Board, November 20-21, 1974. CCCB Archives, Ottawa.

[290] Minutes, Vol. 9, No. 147. CCC Administrative Board, January 22-23, 1975. CCCB Archives, Ottawa.

[291] Interview with Guy Poisson by Bernard Daly, August 31, 1992. Tape in CCCB Archives, Ottawa.

[292] Minutes, Vol. 15, No. 260, Item 16, p. 12-13. CCCB Annual Meeting, September 12-16, 1983. CCCB Archives, Ottawa.

[293] Tribunal of the Apostolic Signatura, Prot. N. 15737/83 V.T.

[294] The 1984-85 data come from the Canadian Appeal Tribunal, "Report on Activities – October 1984 to October 1985." The 1992 figures are from the Tribunal's July 1992 report. CCCB Archives, Ottawa.

[295] Letter from James M. Hayes to Agostino Casaroli, September 18, 1987. CCCB Archives, Ottawa.

[296] Letter from Angelo Palmas to James M. Hayes, March 4, 1988. CCCB Archives, Ottawa.

[297] Letter from Angelo Palmas to James M. Hayes, October 24, 1988. Enclosed with it was the October 6, 1988, letter from the Apostolic Signatura setting out the questions.

[298] For details of the discussion at the 1991 CCCB Annual Meeting about the reply to the Vatican and the unanimous vote for definitive establishment of the Canadian Appeal Tribunal, see the September 16, 1991, letter from Marcel Gervais to Zenon Grocholewski, secretary, Vatican Apostolic Signatura, September 16, 1991. CCCB Archives, Ottawa.

[299] See letter from Jean-Marie Fortier to Jean Villot, October 14, 1975. CCCB Archives, Ottawa.

[300] Memo from Gilles Ouellet to the metropolitan archbishops of Canada, August 5, 1978. CCCB Archives, Ottawa.

[301] Conversation between Jean-Marie Fortier and Bernard Daly, August 27, 1992. Fortier told the story again during the CCCB's 50th anniversary banquet in Ottawa, August 28, 1993.

[302] Interview with William Power by Bernard Daly, August 27, 1992. Audio tape at CCCB Archives, Ottawa.

[303] Statement by the CCCB president, Bishop Robert Lebel, January 31, 1990. CCCB *Official Document*, No. 622, February 2, 1990. CCCB Archives, Ottawa.

[304] "Report of the Meeting of the CCC Officials and the Holy Father on the Day of March 18th, at 10:45 a.m." Letters of the President file. CCCB Archives, Ottawa.

[305] Addendum No. 17. Meeting of the CCCB Administrative Board, June 18-19, 1980. CCCB Archives, Ottawa.

[306] Minutes, No. 240, *Agenda*, Item 4. CCCB Executive Committee Meeting, December 2-3, 1981. CCCB Archives, Ottawa.

[307] CCCB *Internal Communication*, No. 1611, March 3, 1983. CCCB Archives. Ottawa.

[308] CCCB *Internal Communication*, No. 1616, April 27, 1983. CCCB Archives. Ottawa.

[309] The original suggestion for Toronto was "Technology and Communications." John Paul II preferred "Technology and the Human Person." The diocesan themes, in the order of the actual visit, were Faith and Culture, Quebec City; Mary, Cap-de-la-Madeleine; Mystery of God, Montreal; Family, St. John's; Community, Moncton; Missionary Activity, Halifax; Technology and the Human Person, Toronto; Faith and Culture in a Multicultural Society, Winnipeg; Canada and the Third World (at home and abroad), Edmonton; Native Rights, Fort Simpson; Mystery of God in the Person of Jesus Christ, Vancouver; Peace, Ottawa-Hull. CCCB Papal Visit documentation, Pastoral Planning Desk files. National Archives of Canada, Ottawa.

[310] Minutes, Vol. 15, No. 260, Item 17, p. 14. CCCB Annual Meeting, September 12-21, 1983. CCCB Archives, Ottawa.

[311] Letter from John Sherlock to Omer Robidoux, July 9, 1984. CCCB Papal Visit documentation. National Archives of Canada, Ottawa.

[312] Details of the drafting work by the Pope and his staff and of the last-minute translations in Ottawa, come from personal interviews by Bernard Daly with John Sherlock, Jean-Guy Hamelin, William Ryan and Guy Poisson.

[313] See Gallup Poll report to CCCB of reactions to the papal visit. CCCB Archives, Ottawa. Visit planners for the CCCB and federal government made two "dry runs" across the country, checking every site – once in late June 1984 with Jesuit Roberto Tucci, the Pope's visit co-ordinator, and again in late August, without him. David Knapp and Donald Dixon, director and associate director of the CBC's visit operations, participated in these tours to locate every camera site and plan every camera angle.

[314] Letter from André Vallée, CCCB general secretary, to Roberto Tucci, papal visit co-ordinator, August 13, 1984. CCCB Papal Visit documentation. National Archives of Canada, Ottawa.

[315] Texts of Pope John Paul II's visit to Canada, 1984. CCCB Archives, Ottawa. Also, CCCB Papal Visit documentation. National Archives of Canada, Ottawa.

[316] CCCB *Internal Communication*, No. 1611, March 29, 1983. CCCB Archives, Ottawa.

[317] CCCB *Internal Communication*, No. 1659, February 2, 1984. CCCB Archives, Ottawa.

[318] CCCB *Internal Communication*, No. 1696, December 12, 1984. CCCB Archives, Ottawa.

[319] CCCB Financial Statement for the year ending December 31, 1986. CCCB Archives, Ottawa.

[320] CCCB *Information*, May 8, 1987. CCCB Archives, Ottawa.

[321] CCCB Press Release for June 18, 1987. CCCB Archives, Ottawa.

[322] Some English translations of what he said in French contained an error. Referring to the earlier missionaries, the erroneous version had the Pope saying, "They taught you to love and appreciate the spiritual and cultural treasures of your way of life." *Osservatore Romano*, October 5, 1987, had the correct English: "They learned to love you and the spiritual and cultural treasures of your way of life."

[323] The main change was to insert a reiteration of two phrases from the Pope's 1984 talk, to have him say: "Once again I affirm the right to a just and equitable measure of self-government, along with a land base and adequate resources necessary for developing a viable economy for present and future generations." Also, at the end of a sentence noting that the Canadian Churches had called for "a 'new covenant' to ensure your basic Aboriginal rights," the phrase was added, "including the right to self-government." The third proposed change was not made. After noting his awareness that native leaders were talking with the Prime Minister and provincial premiers about constitutional protection of native rights, the Pope's text said: "I pray with you that a new round of conferences will be beneficial." Clarke had proposed that the text say, "I pray with you that a new round of talks will be undertaken," to reflect more precisely the doubt that surrounded the point. See author's personal notes, including the page on which Tony Clarke wrote his proposed amendments. Fort Simpson visit files. CCCB Archives, Ottawa.

[324] The CCCB has had a team of specialists and staff at each Synod since 1969. The following people have been involved: 1969 – Charles Mathieu, general secretary; Bonnie Brennan and Jean-Paul Belleville, media; 1971 – Yvan Desrochers, Edmund Roche, William Ryan and Julien Harvey, specialists; Bonnie Brennan and Guy Poisson, media; 1974 – Everett MacNeil, general secretary; Jacques Grand'Maison and William Marrevee, specialists; Guy Poisson, media; 1977 – Guy Poisson, general secretary; Gilles Langevin and Thomas Francoeur, specialists; 1980 – Dennis Murphy, general secretary; Bernard Daly and Claude Michaud, specialists; 1983 – André Vallée, general secretary; Charlotte Poulin, Martin Moser and Raymond Vaillancourt, specialists; 1985 – William Ryan, general secretary; Jacques Binet, media; 1987 – William Ryan, general secretary; Annine Parent-Fortin, Janet Somerville and Paul Tremblay, specialists; Romeo Maione, invited observer; 1990 – Alexandre Taché, general secretary; Margaret Ferris, Marc Pelchat, Terrence Prendergast, specialists; Jeannine Guindon, invited observer.

[325] Letter from Alexander Carter to Paul VI, September 7, 1967; letter from Alexander Carter to Ladislaus Rubin, September 7, 1967; letter from Ladislaus Rubin to Alexander Carter, September 16, 1967; letter from Cardinal Cigognani to Alexander Carter, September 25, 1967. CCCB Archives, Ottawa.

[326] Minutes, Vol. 1, No. 51, Item 24, p. 19. CCC Annual Meeting, April 6-7, 1967. CCCB Archives, Ottawa.

[327] The CCC vice-president, Joseph-Aurèle Plourde, went to Rome for the Synod period, October 11-29, 1969, to be available as a consultant and to provide English and French media comments. Two staff members from the Toronto and Montreal national Catholic media offices, Bonnie Brennan and Jean-Paul Belleville, also went to Rome.

[328] Letter from Ladislaus Rubin to Alexander Carter, March 1, 1969. Letter from Ladislaus Rubin to Charles Mathieu, July 18, 1969. Letter from Ladislaus Rubin to Charles Mathieu, September 8, 1969. The September 8 letter indicated that six other general secretaries had been invited, from the United States, Germany, Spain, Brazil, England and Italy.

[329] "Report of the Canadian Catholic Conference on the Draft Schema for the Extraordinary Synod of Bishops to be held in Rome from October 11 to 29, 1969." CCCB Archives, Ottawa.

[330] "On the Future of the Synod," note of the Synod secretariat submitted by Joseph-Aurèle Plourde, Rome, 1971. Synod files, box 104. CCCB Archives, Ottawa.

[331] Interview with Gilles Ouellet by Bernard Daly, August 28, 1992. Audio tape in CCCB Archives, Ottawa.

[332] In the following discussion of Canadian Synod interventions, the footnoting of each individual text has been omitted. All these short texts are available from CCCB Archives, Ottawa, by referring to the appropriate Synod, delegate and topic.

[333] All the quotations in these paragraphs are taken from taped interviews with former CCCB presidents and from responses by other members to the questionnaire sent to them. The decision not to identify individuals was the author's. Audio tapes and questionnaire returns are in the CCCB Archives, Ottawa.

[334] The bishops gave their conference an orientation to research and action through the 1964 board resolution that restructured its general secretariat. Major re-evaluations were undertaken in 1968 and 1972. Further adjustments were made before and after promulgation of the 1983 Code of Canon Law. The conference accepted in 1990 the far-ranging organizational and procedural changes proposed by the Task Force on CCCB Future Directions. The Task Force itself adopted as the guiding principle for its work the idea that the CCCB should be shaped and directed not according to an abstract a priori theory but by active responses to the contemporary demands of the Gospel, Church tradition, pastoral needs and world conditions.

[335] Hervé Legrand, "Reflections on Conferences and Diocesan Bishops," *The Nature and Future of Episcopal Conferences*; Legrand, Manzanares and Garcia, editors; Catholic University of America Press, 1988, p. 133.

[336] CCC *Information Service*, Vol. 9, No. 129, October 21, 1964, p. 8. CCCB Archives, Ottawa.

[337] Minutes, Vol. 3, No. 35, p. 296. Meeting of the CCC Administrative Board, February 14, 1964. CCCB Archives, Ottawa.

[338] The CCCB has had eleven French and seven English general secretaries since its beginning (see Table 4). Three of the French general secretaries – Paul Bernier, Valérien Bélanger and André Vallée – were named bishop, as were four French office directors: Marcel Gérin, Gérard Dionne and Louis-de-Gonzague Langevin from the missions office, and Jean-Guy Hamelin from social affairs. The only bishop from among the English staff was Francis Marrocco, the first social action director.

In 1966, the position of assistant general secretary was established with the appointment of Everett MacNeil (later general secretary) in the English Sector, and Roland Dufour in the French Sector. Subsequent English assistant general secretaries were Drake Will, Patrick Kennedy, Bernard Prince, Bernard Daly and Bede Hubbard. In the French sector, Dufour was succeeded by Marguerite Cloutier, Denis Robitaille (later general secretary), Roland Denis, and Fernand Tanguay.

The 1986-90 CCCB Task Force recommended that much of the administrative work of the general and assistant general secretaries be done by the business manager, who would be on the same level as the assistant general secretaries. The redefined position of business manager was first held by Claude Lortie, who in turn has been succeeded by Hervé De Jordy.

[339] Minutes, Vol. 3, No. 35, p. 296. Meeting of the CCC Administrative Board, February 14, 1964. CCCB Archives, Ottawa.

[340] Jean-Marie Tillard, "Mémoire et fête," *Bulletin national de liturgie*, No. 130, Summer 1992, p. 31.

[341] John Paul II, *Encyclical letter "Slavorum Apostoli,"* June 2, 1985, Nos. 12-13 (emphasis in original).

Map, Tables and Appendices

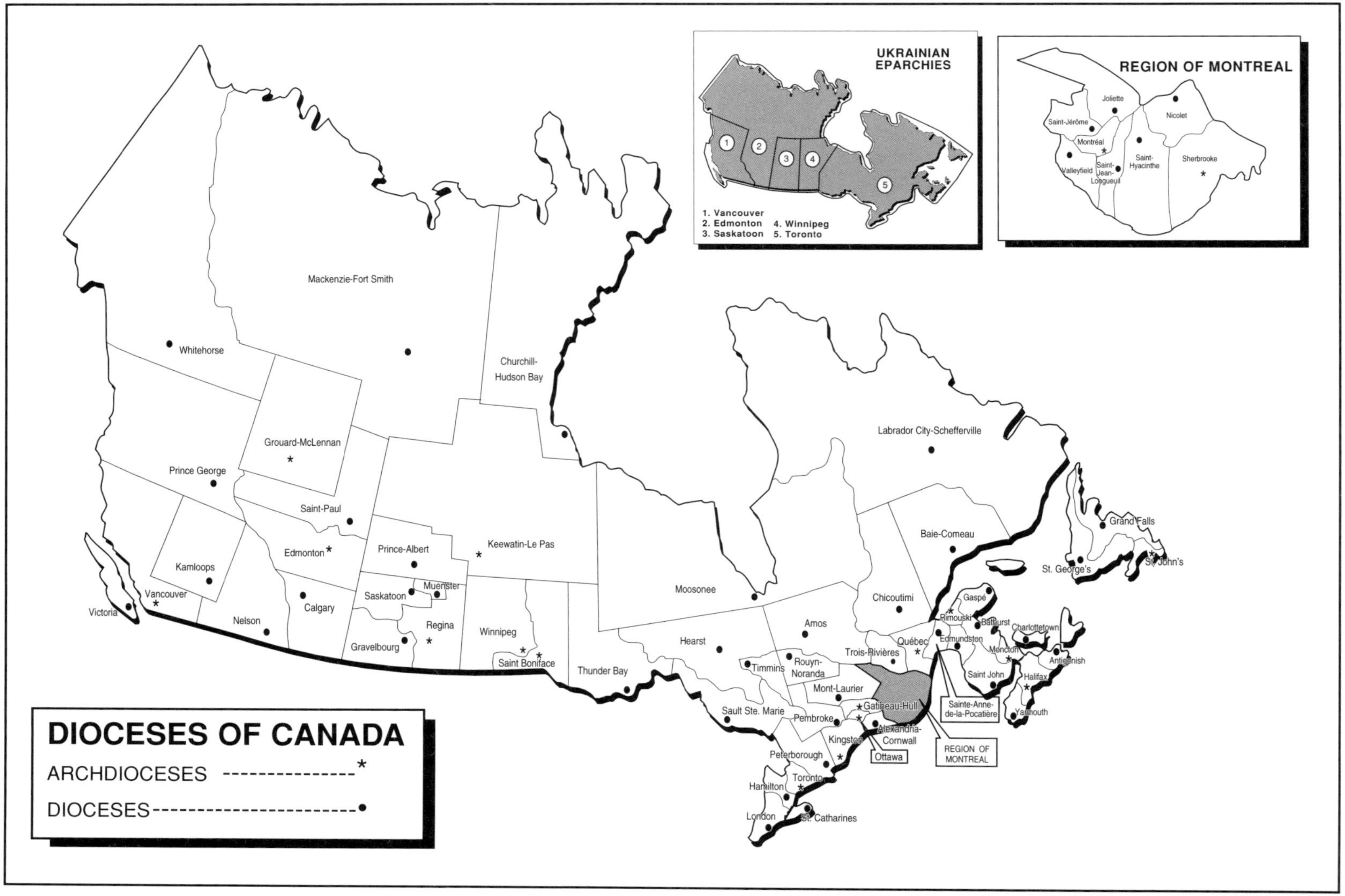
DIOCESES OF CANADA
ARCHDIOCESES ---------------*
DIOCESES-----------------------●
UKRAINIAN EPARCHIES
1. Vancouver
2. Edmonton
3. Saskatoon
4. Winnipeg
5. Toronto
REGION OF MONTREAL
Joliette
Saint-Jérôme
Nicolet
Montréal
Valleyfield
Saint-Jean-Longueuil
Saint-Hyacinthe
Sherbrooke
Mackenzie-Fort Smith
Whitehorse
Churchill-Hudson Bay
Grouard-McLennan
Prince George
Saint-Paul
Edmonton
Prince-Albert
Keewatin-Le Pas
Kamloops
Muenster
Saskatoon
Vancouver
Victoria
Nelson
Calgary
Regina
Winnipeg
Gravelbourg
Saint Boniface
Thunder Bay
Moosonee
Hearst
Timmins
Rouyn-Noranda
Amos
Labrador City-Schefferville
Baie-Comeau
Chicoutimi
Québec
Trois-Rivières
Mont-Laurier
Gatineau-Hull
Sault Ste. Marie
Pembroke
Kingston
Alexandria-Cornwall
Ottawa
REGION OF MONTREAL
Peterborough
Toronto
Hamilton
London
St. Catharines
Grand Falls
St. George's
St. John's
Gaspé
Rimouski
Bathurst
Charlottetown
Edmundston
Moncton
Antigonish
Saint John
Halifax
Sainte-Anne-de-la-Pocatière
Yarmouth

TABLE 1:

Presidents of the Canadian Conference of Catholic Bishops

Cardinal Jean-Marie **VILLENEUVE**, O.M.I., Archbishop of Quebec and Primate of Canada	1943-47
Alexandre **VACHON**, Archbishop of Ottawa	1948-51
Cardinal Paul-Émile **LÉGER**, Archbishop of Montreal	1951-53
John C. **CODY**, Bishop of London	1953-55
Maurice **ROY**, Archbishop of Quebec and Primate of Canada	1955-56
Philip F. **POCOCK**, Co-adjutor Archbishop of Winnipeg	1956-58
Paul **BERNIER**, Bishop of Gaspé (First francophone general secretary of the Conference; named archbishop as Apostolic Nuncio to Costa Rica and Panama, 1952-57)	1958-60
J. Gerald **BERRY**, Archbishop of Halifax	1960-62
Maurice **BAUDOUX**, Archbishop of Saint Boniface	1962-63
George B. **FLAHIFF**, C.S.B., Archbishop of Winnipeg	1963-65
Louis **LÉVESQUE**, Co-adjutor Archbishop of Rimouski	1965-67
Alexander **CARTER**, Bishop of Sault Ste. Marie	1967-69
Joseph-Aurèle **PLOURDE**, Archbishop of Ottawa	1969-71
William E. **POWER**, Bishop of Antigonish	1971-73
Jean-Marie **FORTIER**, Archbishop of Sherbrooke	1973-75
G. Emmett **CARTER**, Bishop of London	1975-77
Gilles **OUELLET**, Archbishop of Rimouski	1977-79
Joseph N. **MacNEIL**, Archbishop of Edmonton	1979-81
Henri **LÉGARÉ**, O.M.I., Archbishop of Grouard-McLennan	1981-83
John **SHERLOCK**, Bishop of London	1983-85
Bernard **HUBERT**, Bishop of Saint-Jean-Longueuil	1985-87
James M. **HAYES**, Archbishop of Halifax	1987-89
Robert **LEBEL**, Bishop of Valleyfield	1989-91
Marcel A.J. **GERVAIS**, Archbishop of Ottawa	1991-93
Jean-Guy **HAMELIN**, Bishop of Rouyn-Noranda	1993-95

TABLE 2:

Members of the Canadian Episcopate attending the Fourth Quinquennial Plenary Meeting, Quebec City, October 12-13, 1943*

Cardinal Jean-Marie-Rodrigue **VILLENEUVE**, O.M.I., Archbishop of Quebec and Primate of Canada
William Mark **DUKE**, Archbishop of Vancouver
James Charles **McGUIGAN**, Archbishop of Toronto
Peter J. **MONAHAN**, Archbishop of Regina
John Hugh **MacDONALD**, Archbishop of Edmonton
John T. **McNALLY**, Archbishop of Halifax
Alexandre **VACHON**, Archbishop of Ottawa
Joseph **CHARBONNEAU**, Archbishop of Montreal
Georges **CABANA**, Archbishop Coadjutor of Saint Boniface
Norbert **ROBICHAUD**, Archbishop of Moncton
James **MORRISON**, Bishop of Antigonish
Joseph-Eugène **LIMOGES**, Bishop of Mont-Laurier
François-Xavier **ROSS**, Bishop of Gaspé
Louis **RHÉAUME**, O.M.I., Bishop of Timmins
Joseph-Alfred **LANGLOIS**, Bishop of Valleyfield
John Thomas **KIDD**, Bishop of London
Alfred-Odilon **COMTOIS**, Bishop of Trois-Rivières
Georges **COURCHESNE**, Bishop of Rimouski
J.-Arthur **PAPINEAU**, Bishop of Joliette
Gerald C. **MURRAY**, C.Ss.R., Bishop of Saskatoon
Joseph-Aldée **DESMARAIS**, Bishop of Amos
Joseph Anthony **O'SULLIVAN**, Bishop of Charlottetown
Martin **LAJEUNESSE**, O.M.I., Vicar Apostolic of Keewatin
Anastase **FORGET**, Bishop of Saint-Jean-de-Québec
Ralph Hubert **DIGNAN**, Bishop of Sault-Sainte-Marie
Francis P. **CARROLL**, Bishop of Calgary
Jean Louis **COUDERT**, O.M.I., Coadjutor Vicar Apostolic of the Yukon and Prince Rupert
Patrick Albert **BRAY**, C.J.M., Bishop of Saint John, N.B.
Martin M. **JOHNSON**, Bishop of Nelson
John C. **CODY**, Bishop of Victoria
Charles Leo **NELLIGAN**, Bishop of Pembroke
Joseph F. **RYAN**, Bishop of Hamilton
Philippe **DESRANLEAU,** Bishop of Sherbrooke
Réginald **DUPRAT**, O.P., Bishop of Prince Albert

Napoléon-A. **LaBRIE**, C.J.M., Vicar Apostolic of the Gulf of Saint Lawrence
Albini **LAFORTUNE**, Bishop of Nicolet
Arthur **DOUVILLE**, Bishop of Saint Hyacinthe
Henri **BELLEAU**, O.M.I., Vicar Apostolic of James Bay
Georges **MELANÇON**, Bishop of Chicoutimi
Joseph-M. **TROCELLIER**, O.M.I., Vicar Apostolic of Mackenzie
Albini **LeBLANC**, Bishop of Hearst
Rosaire **BRODEUR**, Bishop of Alexandria
Camille-André **LeBLANC**, Bishop of Bathurst
John Roderick **MacDONALD**, Bishop of Peterborough
Severin **GERTKEN**, O.S.B., Abbot-Ordinary of Saint Peter (Muenster)

Also present:

Marie-Joseph **LEMIEUX**, O.P., Apostolic Administrator of Gravelbourg

Absent:

Alfred Arthur **SINNOTT**, Archbishop of Winnipeg
Basil Vladimir **LADYKA**, O.S.B.M., Apostolic Exarch of the Ukrainian Ordinariate of Canada (Winnipeg)
Ubald **LANGLOIS**, O.M.I., Vicar Apostolic of Grouard
Marc **LACROIX**, O.M.I., Vicar Apostolic of Hudson Bay

Vacant:

Archdiocese of Kingston

* Listed in order of liturgical precedence. (*Sources:* Minutes, Vol. 1, No. 1, pp. 5-6, Quinquennial Plenary Meeting of the Canadian Hierarchy, Quebec, October 12-13, 1943; and caption for 1943 photograph of bishops in attendance. CCCB Archives, Ottawa)

TABLE 3:

Members of the Canadian Conference of Catholic Bishops, 1993

Georges **ABI SABER**, Archeparch of Montreal for the Maronite Catholics of Canada
Aloysius M. **AMBROZIC**, Archbishop of Toronto
René **AUDET**, Bishop Emeritus of Joliette
Gilles **BÉLISLE**, Auxiliary Bishop of Ottawa
Jacques **BERTHELET**, C.S.V., Auxiliary Bishop of Saint-Jean-Longueuil
Bertrand **BLANCHET**, Archbishop of Rimouski
Isidore **BORECKY**, Eparch of Toronto
Austin E. **BURKE**, Archbishop of Halifax
Michael **BZDEL**, Archeparch of Winnipeg, Metropolitan for the Ukrainian Catholics of Canada
Vincent **CADIEUX**, O.M.I., Bishop of Moosonee
Colin **CAMPBELL**, Bishop of Antigonish
Alexander **CARTER**, Bishop Emeritus of Sault Ste. Marie
Cardinal G. Emmett **CARTER**, Archbishop Emeritus of Toronto
Gilles **CAZABON**, O.M.I., Bishop of Timmins
Paul-Émile **CHARBONNEAU**, Bishop Emeritus of Gatineau-Hull
Donat **CHIASSON**, Archbishop of Moncton
André **CIMICHELLA**, O.S.M., Auxiliary Bishop of Montreal
Robert B. **CLUNE**, Auxiliary Bishop of Toronto
Gérard-Marie **CODERRE**, Bishop Emeritus of Saint-Jean-Longueuil
Jean-Guy **COUTURE**, Bishop of Chicoutimi
Maurice **COUTURE**, S.V., Archbishop of Quebec and Primate of Canada
Gérard **COUTURIER**, Bishop Emeritus of Baie-Comeau
Denis **CROTEAU**, O.M.I., Bishop of MacKenzie-Fort Smith
Leonard **CROWLEY**, Auxiliary Bishop of Montreal
Myron **DACIUK**, O.S.B.M., Eparch of Edmonton
Roman **DANYLAK**, Apostolic Administrator, Ukrainian Catholic Eparchy of Toronto
Nicola **De ANGELIS**, C.F.I.C., Auxiliary Bishop of Toronto
Noël **DELAQUIS**, Bishop of Gravelbourg
Remi **De ROO**, Bishop of Victoria

Roger **DESPATIE**, Bishop of Hearst
Gérard **DIONNE**, Bishop Emeritus of Edmundston
James **DOYLE**, Bishop of Peterborough
W. Emmett **DOYLE**, Bishop Emeritus of Nelson
Gérard **DRAINVILLE**, Bishop of Amos
Paul **DUMOUCHEL**, O.M.I., Archbishop Emeritus of Keewatin-Le Pas
Roger **ÉBACHER**, Archbishop of Gatineau-Hull
Adam **EXNER**, O.M.I., Archbishop of Vancouver
Clément **FECTEAU**, Auxiliary Bishop of Quebec
Basil **FILEVICH**, Eparch of Saskatoon
Jean-Marie **FORTIER**, Archbishop of Sherbrooke
Vernon J. **FOUGERE**, Bishop of Charlottetown
Thomas B. **FULTON**, Bishop of St. Catharines
Cardinal Edouard **GAGNON**, Bishop Emeritus of Saint Paul
André **GAUMOND**, Bishop of Ste-Anne-de-la-Pocatière
Marcel A.J. **GERVAIS**, Archbishop of Ottawa
Arthur J. **GILBERT**, Bishop Emeritus of Saint John
Henri **GOUDREAULT**, O.M.I., Bishop of Labrador City-Schefferville
Jean **GRATTON**, Bishop of Mont-Laurier
Cardinal Paul **GRÉGOIRE**, Archbishop Emeritus of Montreal
Antoine **HACAULT**, Archbishop of Saint Boniface
Michel **HAKIM**, Archeparch for the Greek Melkite Catholics of Canada
Charles A. **HALPIN**, Archbishop of Regina
Jean-Guy **HAMELIN**, Bishop of Rouyn-Noranda
James M. **HAYES**, Archbishop Emeritus of Halifax
Frederick B. **HENRY**, Auxiliary Bishop of London
Maxim **HERMANIUK**, Archeparch Emeritus of Winnipeg
Bernard **HUBERT**, Bishop of Saint-Jean-Longueuil
John Stephen **KNIGHT**, Auxiliary Bishop of Toronto
Jean-Paul **LABRIE**, Auxiliary Bishop of Quebec
Michael Pearse **LACEY**, Auxiliary Bishop Emeritus of Toronto
Fernand **LACROIX**, C.J.M., Bishop Emeritus of Edmundston
Raymond J. **LAHEY**, Bishop of St. George's
Jacques **LANDRIAULT**, Bishop Emeritus of Timmins
Louis-de-Gonzague **LANGEVIN**, Bishop of Saint-Hyacinthe
Eugène-P. **LaROCQUE**, Bishop of Alexandria-Cornwall
Robert **LEBEL**, Bishop of Valleyfield
Camille-André **LeBLANC**, Bishop Emeritus of Bathurst
Marc **LECLERC**, Auxiliary Bishop of Quebec

Henri **LÉGARÉ**, O.M.I., Archbishop of Grouard-McLennan
Jules **LEGUERRIER**, O.M.I., Bishop Emeritus of Moosonee
Marie-Joseph **LEMIEUX**, O.P., Archbishop Emeritus of Ottawa
Louis **LÉVESQUE**, Archbishop Emeritus of Rimouski
Thomas J. **LOBSINGER**, O.M.I., Bishop of Whitehorse
Gilles **LUSSIER**, Bishop of Joliette
James H. **MacDONALD**, Archbishop of St. John's
Joseph F. **MacDONALD**, Bishop of Grand Falls
Joseph N. **MacNEIL**, Archbishop of Edmonton
James P. **MAHONEY**, Bishop of Saskatoon
Peter J. **MALLON**, Bishop of Nelson
Paul **MARCHAND**, S.M.M., Auxiliary Bishop of Ottawa
Attila **MIKLOSHAZY**, S.J., Bishop for Hungarian Emigrants
Blaise **MORAND**, Bishop of Prince Albert
Laurent **MORIN**, Bishop Emeritus of Prince Albert
Pierre **MORISSETTE**, Bishop of Baie-Comeau
Laurent **NOËL**, Bishop of Trois-Rivières
Peter **NOVECOSKY**, O.S.B., Abbot Ordinary of St. Peter's, Muenster
Brendan **O'BRIEN**, Bishop of Pembroke
Paul J. **O'BYRNE**, Bishop of Calgary
Hubert P. **O'CONNOR**, O.M.I., Bishop Emeritus of Prince George
Fergus J. **O'GRADY**, O.M.I., Bishop Emeritus of Prince George
John A. **O'MARA**, Bishop of Thunder Bay
Gilles **OUELLET**, P.M.É, Archbishop Emeritus of Rimouski
André **OUELLETTE**, Bishop Emeritus of Mont-Laurier
Bernard F. **PAPPIN**, Auxiliary Bishop of Sault Ste. Marie
Marius **PARÉ**, Bishop Emeritus of Chicoutimi
Roch **PEDNEAULT**, Auxiliary Bishop of Chicoutimi
Alphonsus L. **PENNEY**, Archbishop Emeritus of St. John's
Jean-Louis **PLOUFFE**, Bishop of Sault Ste. Marie
Joseph-Aurèle **PLOURDE**, Archbishop Emeritus of Ottawa
William E. **POWER**, Bishop Emeritus of Antigonish
André **RICHARD**, Bishop of Bathurst
Reynald **ROULEAU**, O.M.I., Bishop of Churchill-Hudson Bay
Raymond **ROY**, Bishop of Saint Paul
Michael **RUSNAK**, C.Ss.R., Eparch for the Slovaks of the Byzantine Rite in Canada
Lawrence **SABATINI**, C.S., Bishop of Kamloops
Jude **SAINT-ANTOINE**, Auxiliary Bishop of Montreal
Raymond **SAINT-GELAIS**, Bishop of Nicolet

Albert **SANSCHAGRIN**, O.M.I., Bishop Emeritus of Saint-Hyacinthe
Nersès Mikaël **SETIAN**, Apostolic Exarch for Catholic Armenians in Canada and the United States
John M. **SHERLOCK**, Bishop of London
Francis J. **SPENCE**, Archbishop of Kingston
Peter A. **SUTTON**, O.M.I., Archbishop of Keewatin-The Pas
Anthony F. **TONNOS**, Bishop of Hamilton
Gérard **TREMBLAY**, P.S.S., Auxiliary Bishop Emeritus of Montreal
J. Edward **TROY**, Bishop of Saint John
Jean-Claude **TURCOTTE**, Archbishop of Montreal
Matthew **USTRZYCKI**, Auxiliary Bishop of Hamilton
Cardinal Louis-Albert **VACHON**, Archbishop Emeritus of Quebec
André **VALLÉE**, P.M.É., Bishop for the Military Ordinariate of Canada
Charles **VALOIS**, Bishop of Saint-Jérôme
Martin **VEILLETTE**, Auxiliary Bishop of Trois-Rivières
Leonard J. **WALL**, Archbishop of Winnipeg
Jerome **WEBER**, O.S.B., Abbot Ordinary Emeritus of St. Peter's, Muenster
Gerald **WIESNER**, O.M.I., Bishop of Prince George
Joseph L. **WILHELM**, Archbishop Emeritus of Kingston
Joseph R. **WINDLE**, Bishop Emeritus of Pembroke
James M. **WINGLE**, Bishop of Yarmouth

* Listed according to alphabetical order. (*Source*: Canadian Conference of Catholic Bishops, *1992-1993 Directory*, Ottawa)

TABLE 4:

General Secretaries of the Canadian Conference of Catholic Bishops

Anglophone

1944-51	Rev. Basil Markle, C.S.
1951-65	Msgr. John A. Carley
1966-68	Rev. Gordon F. George, S.J.
1968-77	Rev. Everett MacNeil
1977-84	Msgr. Dennis Murphy
1984-90	Rev. William F. Ryan, S.J.
1990-	Msgr. V. James Weisgerber

Francophone

1943-47	Rev. Paul Bernier, C.S.
1947-51	Rev. J.-Lucien Beaudoin
1951-55	Rev. Jean-Denis Cadieux
1955-56	Msgr. Valérien Bélanger
1956-63	Msgr. Raymond Limoges
1964-75	Msgr. Charles E. Mathieu
1975-79	Rev. Guy Poisson, P.S.S.
1979-85	Rev. André Vallée, P.M.É.
1985-88	Rev. Denis Robitaille
1988-94	Rev. Alexandre Taché, O.M.I.
1995-	Rev. Émilius Goulet, P.S.S.

TABLE 5:

Staff of the Canadian Conference of Catholic Bishops 1993

Jonas **ABROMAITIS**	National Office of Religious Education – youth project specialist
Aubert **APRIL**	Professional pastoral group – sociology, statistics, and relations with associations of clergy, religious and laity
Annette **ARBIQUE**	Office of the General Secretary (English-language) – executive secretary
Gérald **BARIL**	Public Relations (French-language) – director
Luc **BEAUCHAMP**	Administrative Services – mail clerk
Lise **BERGERON**	General Secretariat – agenda secretary
Anita **BISSONNETTE**	Pastoral Offices – secretary
Paul **BOILY**	National Office of Liturgy (French-language) – director
Lise **BOUDREAULT**	Canadian Appeal Tribunal – administrative secretary
Claire **BOULT**	Administrative Services – accounting clerk
Claire **BOUVIER**	Publications Service – typesetter
Simonne **CARR**	National Office of Religious Education – administrative assistant
Lucien **CASTERMAN**, OMI	Missions Office – director
Monique **CHABOT**	National Office of Religious Education – secretary
Joanne **CHAFE**	National Office of Religious Education – adult project specialist
Tony **CLARKE**	Social Affairs Office – English-language director
Danielle **D'ALESSIO**	National Office of Liturgy (French-language) – secretary

Hervé **De JORDY**	Business Manager
Colette **DESFORGES**	Publications Service – production manager
Maurice **DIONNE**, CSsR	Canadian Appeal Tribunal – judicial vicar
Claire **DUBÉ**	Publications Service – director
Bernard **DUFRESNE**	Social Affairs Office – French-language director
Yvonne **DUFRESNE**	Administrative Services – human resources officer
Thérèse **DUPUIS**	Office of the Assistant General Secretaries – secretary
Jean–Claude **ÉTHIER**, SC	Religious education (French Sector) – national coordinator
Gilles **FAUVELLE**	Administrative Services – press operator
Jeannette **FILTHAUT**, SP	National Office of Religious Education – in-service manager
Adèle **GAUVREAU**	Social Affairs Office – secretary
Donna **GEERNAERT**, SC	Professional pastoral group – ecumenical and interfaith relations
Johanne **GNASSI**	Publications Service – administration coordinator
Monique **GODARD**	Administrative Services – accounting clerk
Sylvia **GRAVEL**	Public Information Office (English-language) – secretary
Dennis **GRUENDING**	Public Information Office (English-language) – director
Gaëtan **GUÉNETTE**	Administrative Services – superintendent
Joyce **HARPELL**	National Office of Religious Education – project coordinator
John **HIBBARD**	National Office of Liturgy (English-language) – director
Bede **HUBBARD**	Assistant General Secretary (English-language)

Monique **HUDON**	Archives and Library – documentation technician
Roger **LADOUCEUR**	Administrative Services – accounting director
Marie **LAFORTUNE**	Publications Service – sales clerk
Madeleine **LALONDE**	Canadian Appeal Tribunal – office coordinator
Robert **LARIVIÈRE**	Canadian Appeal Tribunal – defender of the bond
Nicole B. **LAUZIER**	Publications Service – sales supervisor
Denise **LAUZON**	Publications Service – typesetter
Yves **LECLAIR**	Publications Service – sales manager
Jennifer **LEDDY**	Professional pastoral group – ethical and legal affairs, and relations with associations of priests, religious and clergy
Marcel **LEFEBVRE**	Professional pastoral group – theology
Huguette **LÉPINE**	Office of the General Secretary (French-language) – executive secretary
Anne L. **MAHONEY**	National Office of the Religious Education – writing and editing specialist
Benoit **MAINVILLE**	Publications Service – warehouse supervisor
Louise **MAINVILLE**	Public Relations Office (French-language) – secretary
Denis **MALETTE**	Publications Service – warehouse clerk
Lyne **MALETTE**	Administrative Services – clerk
Danièle **MANOR**	Canadian Appeal Tribunal – secretary
Nancy **MARCOUX**	Canadian Appeal Tribunal – communications secretary
Thérèse **MARTIN**	Administrative Services – secretary

Patricia **McKALE**	General Secretariat – documentation secretary (English-language)
Claire **PAQUETTE**	Administrative Services – receptionist
Myrtle **POWER**	National Office of Religious Education – child project specialist
Dorothy **RIOPELLE**	National Office of Liturgy (English-language) – secretary
Micheline **ROUSSEL**	General Secretariat – documentation secretary (French-language)
Kevin **RYALL**	National Office of Religious Education – child project specialist
Christine **SABOURIN**	Canadian Appeal Tribunal – secretary
Nicole **ST-PIERRE**	Canadian Appeal Tribunal – secretary
Nira **SANGAL**	Canadian Appeal Tribunal – judge
Alexandre **TACHÉ**, OMI	General Secretary (French-language)
J. Fernand **TANGUAY**	Assistant General Secretary (French-language)
Jacqueline **TANGUAY**	National Office of Liturgy (French-language) – secretary
François **THÉRIAULT**	Production and Technical Services – director
Bernadette **TOURANGEAU**	National Office of Religious Education – executive director
Ron **TOURANGEAU**	Publications Service – art and design manager
Marjolaine **TREMBLAY**	Publications Service – secretary
Céline **VERMETTE**	Missions Office – secretary
Pierrette **WARWICK**	Social Affairs Office – secretary
V. James **WEISGERBER**	General Secretary (English-language)

APPENDIX 1:

Canadian Conference of Catholic Bishops: Nature and Role

- The Canadian Conference of Catholic Bishops (CCCB) is the collegial assembly of the Canadian hierarchy. Its purpose is to enable the bishops, united with the Pope, to discharge their collective pastoral office with and for other members of the People of God in the mission confided to the whole Church. This involves working with all men and women to evangelize contemporary culture and to build a society of justice and love called for by Jesus Christ. It also involves the promotion of unity among Christian churches and of understanding with other religions.
- To accomplish its purpose, the Conference has established certain goals, together with the means to achieve them. It works through its Plenary Assembly, Permanent Council, Executive Committee and various commissions. These bodies are supported by a staff of lay persons, religious, and priests who form the Conference Secretariat.

Goals

1. To make actual and visible the collegial solidarity of Canada's bishops.
2. To help bishops discharge their obligation to serve the Catholic community, locally and universally, in collaboration with laity, religious, and priests.
3. To foster good relations between the bishops and the Canadian people.
4. To strengthen the union of the bishops of Canada with the bishop of Rome and with all other Catholic bishops.
5. To cooperate with the Holy Father, his immediate collaborators, other episcopal conferences, and international bodies with which the Conference may establish relations.

Means

1. By providing opportunities for bishops to work together.
2. By offering those services which are best provided at the national level.
3. By collaborating with national lay and religious organizations in fulfilling their mission in the Church and in the world according to the human and evangelical values affirmed by Vatican II.

4. By ensuring frequent communication with the Holy Father and his immediate collaborators on behalf of the Canadian bishops as a group.
5. By establishing links with other episcopal conferences, especially neighbouring ones.
6. By participating in discussion of national and international issues to help build the society of justice and love that Christ has enjoined us to create.
7. By engaging in dialogue and collaboration with representatives of other Christian churches and other religions.
8. By applying universal Church legislation in the Canadian context and in accordance with the Code of Canon Law.
9. By seeking to ensure in Canada full understanding of the Apostolic See's teachings and directives and regularly communicating to the Apostolic See the Canadian viewpoint on important matters.
10. By providing national guidelines for pastoral direction in response to the needs of the Church in Canada.
11. By ensuring research, planning, and leadership for Conference programmes in such areas as social communications, religious education, social justice, liturgy, ministries and the apostolate, missions, ecumenism, faith and culture, and theology.

– Approved by the 1988 Plenary Assembly

APPENDIX 2:

Message of Pope John Paul II on the Occasion of the 50th Anniversary of the Canadian Conference of Catholic Bishops

To the Most Reverend Marcel Gervais,
President of the Canadian Conference of Catholic Bishops

On the occasion of the Fiftieth Anniversary of the establishment of the Canadian Episcopal Conference, I share the joy and gratitude of you and your Brother Bishops, and in my thoughts and prayers I am united with all the Christian faithful entrusted to you as Successors of the Apostles.

For some years now you have chosen to have frequent contacts with the Holy See, and I am very gratified by this. It is a means for you to express the bonds uniting the local Churches with Peter's Successor and with those who assist him in his mission of presiding over the communion and of comforting his brethren in the faith. You have made it your care to preach the Gospel of Christ the Saviour in season and out and thereby to stir up the sense of communion and mission which is so much a part of the great tradition of the Church in your country. I encourage you to continue to build up the Body of Christ within the portion of the People of God entrusted to you, so that the faith of all believers will increase. As leaders of the flock, Bishops must untiringly and in fidelity to the tradition of the Church teach the Christian Mystery received for the Apostles, and see to it that the faithful do not lack the help of the sacraments so that their hearts may be filled with grace. To this end you are striving to communicate the Lord's call and to put into place the structures necessary so that young men, instructed in the truths of the faith and formed in the spiritual life, will gladly give themselves completely to Christ in the ministerial priesthood for the service of others.

The Christians of your Dioceses have devoted themselves to pursuing dialogue with their brothers and helping them to discover the Lord who is the truth of man. Along this path, as Pope Paul VI reminded Cardinal Maurice Roy, "the Christian can draw from the sources of his faith and the Church's teaching the necessary principles and suitable criteria to avoid permitting himself to be first attracted by, then imprisoned" within any sort of system, for his life is Christ (*Octogesima Adveniens*, 36).

In the current national and international situation, the Church has a duty to come with the strength of the Gospel to the aid of society so that it will not lose hope, but find the urgent means for a solidarity encompassing the nation, the continent, and the world, in order that each individual may live in dignity and achieve his rightful status. The Christian community cannot remain silent and inactive in the face of the sufferings and difficulties of our contemporaries, while men and women living in inhuman conditions are scorned, treated as objects or persecuted for their faith. Quite the contrary, charity toward the dispossessed is a source for its mission and is the criterion for that mission (cf. *Redemptoris Missio*, 60). Christian communities are called to contribute with all the nation's strength to overcoming the challenges to development and peace (cf. *Sollicitudo Rei Socialis*, 47).

Trusting that this celebration will renew God's gift in the hearts of all the faithful, and invoking upon them the grace of the Spirit through the intercession of the Virgin Mary, Mother of the Church, and through the prayers of the Saints of your country, I cordially impart my Apostolic Blessing to all the Bishops of the Episcopal Conference as well as to the priests, deacons, men and women Religious, the laity working with you, and all the faithful belonging to your Dioceses.

From the Vatican, July 31, 1993

Bibliography

Abbott, Walter M. (ed). *The Documents of Vatican II, with Introductions, Commentaries and Responses*. New York: Guild Press, 1966.

Alberigo, Giuseppe. *Decrees of the Ecumenical Councils*. 2 vols. Edited by Norman P. Tanner. London: Sheed & Ward; Washington, D.C.: Georgetown University Press, 1990.

______, Jean-Pierre Jossua and Joseph A. Komonchak (eds.). *The Reception of Vatican II*. Washington, D.C.: University of America Press, 1987.

Anderson, Floyd (ed.). *Council Daybook: Vatican II*, 3 vols. Vol. 1: Sessions 1 and 2. Vol. 2: Session 3. Vol. 3: Session 4. Washington: National Catholic Welfare Conference News Service, 1965-1966.

Assemblée des évêques du Québec. Comité de recherche sur les communautés chrétiennes. *L'avenir des communautés chrétiennes*. Report of the provincial congress held in Montreal, October 1991. Collection "L'Église aux quatre vents". Montreal: Fides, 1993.

Baum, Gregory. *Catholics and Canadian Socialism: Political Thought in the Thirties and Forties*. Toronto: J. Lorimer, 1980.

______. *The Church in Quebec*. Saint Paul University, Ottawa: Novalis, 1991.

Berkouwer, Gerrit C. *The Second Vatican Council and the New Catholicism*. Grand Rapids, Mich.: Eerdmans, 1965.

Brown, Robert McAfee. *Observer in Rome: A Protestant Report on the Vatican Council*. Garden City, N.Y.: Doubleday, 1964.

Butler, Basil C. *The Theology of Vatican II*. London: Darton, Longman & Todd, 1967.

Canadian Catholic Conference. *Messages des évêques canadiens à l'occasion de la Fête du Travail, 1956-1974*. Montreal: Éditions Beauchemin, 1974.

Caporale, Rock. *Vatican II: Last of the Councils*. Baltimore: Helicon, 1964.

Cartus, F.E. *Vatican II and the Jews*. New York: Commentary Magazine, 1965.

Cullmann, Oscar. *Vatican Council II: The New Direction. Essays selected and arranged by James D. Hester*. Religious Perspectives, 19. New York: Harper & Row, 1967.

Daniel-Rops, Henry. *The Second Vatican Council: The Story Behind the Ecumenical Council of Pope John XXIII*. New York: Hawthorn Books, 1962.

Dulles, Avery. *The Reshaping of Catholicism: Current Challenges in the Theology of Church*. San Francisco: Harper & Row, 1988.

Dushnyck, Walter. *The Ukrainian-Rite Catholic Church at the Ecumenical Council, 1962-1965: A Collection of Articles, Book Reviews, Editorials, Reports, and Commentaries with Special Emphasis on Ukrainian-Rite and Other Eastern Churches*. Shevchenko Scientific Society, Ukrainian studies, English section, v. 5 (23). New York: Shevchenko Scientific Society, 1967.

Falconi, Carlo. *Pope John and his Council: A Diary of the Second Vatican Council, September-December 1962*. London: Weindenfeld and Nicholson, 1964.

Fesquet, Henri. *The Drama of Vatican II: The Ecumenical Council, June 1962 - December 1965*. New York: Random House, 1967.

Flannery, Austin. *Vatican Council II: The Conciliar and Post Conciliar Documents*, rev. ed. Vatican Collection, vol. 1. Grand Rapids, Mich.: Eerdmans, 1988.

Gilbert, Arthur. *The Vatican Council and the Jews*. Cleveland: World Publishing Co., 1968.

Guimond, Arthé. "La pensée sociale des évêques canadiens de 1956 à nos jours". *L'Église canadienne*, vol. 15, no. 1, Septembre 3, 1981, pp. 11-13.

Hastings, Adrian (ed.). *A Concise Guide to the Documents of the Second Vatican Council.* London: Darton, Longman & Todd, 1968-1969.

______, (ed.). *Modern Catholicism: Vatican II and After.* London: SPCK; New York: Oxford University Press, 1991.

Heston, Edward L. *The Press and Vatican II.* Notre Dame, Ind.: University of Notre Dame Press, 1967.

Hollis, Christopher. *The Achievements of Vatican II.* The Twentieth Century Encyclopedia of Catholicism, 1. New York: Hawthorn Books, 1967.

Horgan, Thaddeus D. (ed.). *Walking Together: Roman Catholics and Ecumenism Twenty-Five Years after Vatican II.* Grand Rapids, Mich.: W.B. Eerdmans, 1990.

Horton, Douglas. *Towards an Undivided Church.* New York: Association Press, 1967.

Hughes, Kathleen. *The Monk's Tale: A Biography of Godfrey Diekmann, O.S.B.* Collegeville, Minn.: Liturgical Press, 1991.

Hulliger, Jean. *L'enseignement social des évêques canadiens de 1891 à 1950.* Montreal: Fides, 1958.

John Paul II (Wojtyla, Karol, Cardinal). *Sources of Renewal: The Implementation of the Second Vatican Council.* London: Fount Paperbacks; San Francisco: Harper and Row, 1980.

Küng, Hans. *The Council, Reform and Reunion.* New York: Sheed and Ward, 1961.

Latourelle, René (ed.). *Vatican II: Assessment and Perspectives: Twenty-five Years After (1962-1987)*, 3 vols. New York: Paulist Press, 1988-1989.

Leeming, Bernard. *The Vatican Council and Christian Unity: A Commentary on the Decree on Ecumenism of the Second Vatican Council, together with a Translation of the Text.* London: Darton, Longman & Todd, 1966.

Legrand, Hervé-Marie, Julio Manzanares and Antonio García y García (eds). *The Nature and Future of Episcopal Conferences.* Washington, D.C.: Catholic University of America Press, 1988.

MacEoin, Gary. *What Happened at Rome? The Council and its Implications for the Modern World.* New York: Holt, Rinehart and Winston, 1966.

McNamara, Kevin (ed.). *Vatican II: The Constitution on the Church; A Theological and Pastoral Commentary.* Chicago: Franciscan World Press, 1968.

Miller, John H. (ed.). *Vatican II: An Interfaith Appraisal.* International Theological Conference, University of Notre Dame. Notre Dame, Ind.: University of Notre Dame Press, 1966.

Moorman, John R.H. *Vatican Observer: An Anglican Impression of Vatican II.* London: Darton, Longman & Todd, 1967.

O'Dea, Thomas F. *The Catholic Crisis.* Boston: Beacon Press, 1968.

Perin, Roberto. *Rome in Canada: The Vatican and Canadian Affairs in the Late Victorian Age.* Toronto: University of Toronto Press, 1990.

Prince, Bernard A. *Episcopal Conferences and the Canadian Catholic Conference.* Doctoral Thesis for the Faculty of Canon Law. Rome, Pontificia Studiorum Universitas a S. Thoma Aquinate, 1966.

Rahner, Karl. *The Church after the Council.* New York: Herder and Herder, 1966.

Ramsey, Michael and Léon-Joseph Cardinal Suenens. *The Future of the Christian Church.* New York: Morehouse-Barlow, 1970.

Richard, Lucien, Daniel T. Harrington and John W. O'Malley (eds). *Vatican II, the Unfinished Agenda: A Look to the Future.* New York: Paulist Press, 1987.

Ruokanen, Miikka, *The Catholic Doctrine of Non-Christian Religions, according to the Second Vatican Council.* Leiden, New York: E. J. Brill, 1992.

Rynne, Xavier. *Letters from Vatican City: Vatican Council II. First Session, Background and Debates.* New York: Farrar, Straus & Co., 1963.

_______. *The Second Session: The Debates and Decrees of Vatican Council II, September 29 to December 4, 1963.* New York: Farrar, Straus & Co., 1964.

_______. *The Third Session: The Debates and Decrees of Vatican Council II, September 14 to November 21, 1964.* New York: Farrar, Straus & Giroux, 1965.

_______. *The Fourth Session: The Debates and Decrees of Vatican Council II, September 14 to December 8, 1965*. New York: Farrar, Straus & Giroux, 1966.

Schillebeeckx, Eduard. *The Real Achievement of Vatican II*. New York: Herder and Herder, 1967.

Schner, Georges P. (ed). *The Church Renewed: The Documents of Vatican II Reconsidered*. Lanham, Md.: University Press of America, 1986.

Sheridan, Edward F. (ed). *Do Justice! The Social Teaching of the Canadian Catholic Bishops (1945-1986)*. Sherbrooke, Que.: Éditions Paulines; Toronto: The Jesuit Centre for Social Faith and Justice, 1987.

_______. *Love Kindness! The Social Teaching of the Canadian Catholic Bishops (1958-1989)*. Sherbrooke, Que.: Éditions Paulines; Toronto: The Jesuit Centre for Social Faith and Justice, 1991.

Stacpoole, Alberic (ed). *Vatican II by Those Who Were There*. London: G. Chapman, 1986.

Stogre, Michael. *That the World May Believe: The Development of Papal Social Thought on Aboriginal Rights*. Sherbrooke, Que.: Éditions Paulines, 1992.

Suenens, Léon-Joseph Cardinal. *Coresponsibility in the Church*. New York: Herder and Herder, 1968.

______. *Essays on Renewal*. Ann Arbor, Mich.: Servant Books, 1977.

Tavard, George H. *The Church, Community of Salvation: An Ecumenical Ecclesiology*. New Theology Studies, 1. Collegeville, Minn.: Liturgical Press, Michael Glazier Books, 1992.

_______. *Meditation on the Word: Perspectives for a Renewed Theology*. Glen Rock, N.J.: Paulist Press, 1968.

_______. *Two Centuries of Ecumenism*. Westport, Conn.: Greenwood Press, 1978.

Voisine, Nive, André Beaulieu and Jean Hamelin. *Histoire de l'Église catholique au Quebec, 1608-1970*. Montreal: Éditions Fides, 1971.

Vorgrimler, Herbert (ed.). *Commentary on the Documents of Vatican II*, 5 vols. New York: Herder and Herder, 1967-1969.

Wycislo, Aloysius J. *Vatican II Revisited: Reflections by One Who Was There*. Staten Island, N.Y.: Alba House, 1987.

Index